1·50.

Language and education

Derek Grant.

Oxford studies in education

Language and education

Andrew Wilkinson

Professor of Education
University of Exeter

Oxford University Press 1975

Oxford University Press, Ely House, London W1

Glasgow New York Toronto Melbourne Wellington
Cape Town Ibadan Nairobi Dar es Salaam Lusaka Addis Ababa
Delhi Bombay Calcutta Madras Karachi Lahore Dacca
Kuala Lumpur Singapore Hong Kong Tokyo

Set by Hope Services, Wantage, and
printed in Great Britain by
T. H. Brickell & Son Ltd, The Blackmore Press
Gillingham, Dorset

For Elizabeth

Contents

Introduction: the study of language

Part 1 Communication

1 Aspects of communication 2
2 Means of communication 7
3 What is communicated? 15
4 Paralinguistic communication 20
5 Animal communication 26

Language

6 Aspects of language 34
7 Universals of language 39
8 Basic language 44

Language functions

9 Functions of language 49
10 Descriptions of language function 54

Language and thought

11 Relationships of language and thought 58
12 Influence of language on thought 62

Language and learning

13 Non-verbal communication in the classroom 67
14 Language in the classroom 75
15 Language in education 85

Acquisition of language

16   Communication in early childhood   95
17   How is language acquired?   103
18   Theories of language acquisition   107
19   The creation of language   112

Development of language

20   The development of language   117
21   'Good at English'?   123
22   'Good at English': some criteria   128
23   'I's in difficults miss'   134

Part 2   **Further work**   139
            Bibliography   228
            Acknowledgements   236
            Index   239

Note
Speech transcriptions in this book are normally printed according to the accepted convention with a minimum of capitalization, and with pauses indicated by diagonal strokes. However, particularly in transcriptions kindly provided by others, it has not always been possible to check the original recordings, and in these cases the transcriptions have been printed in the form supplied, using the conventions of written punctuation.

Introduction:
the study of language

This is a book about children, and people, cannibals, chimpanzees, Granny; in Chapter 1, for those interested, the Greater European Bustard and Romping Molly are both mentioned. It is also about language.

The reason for expressing the matter thus is to obtain a perspective. 'Language' has become an OK term in education. It seems as if in some magic way a study of language will provide a solution for our present discontents. The sad history of educational fashions gives no encouragement to this belief. (What *was* programmed learning?) People are complex, and no one innovation is likely to have a major or immediate effect. In the case of language it is often talked of as though separated from 'communication' in general, the total means by which the human personality presents itself. To mention 'communication', of course, is to introduce another OK word. When they told Emerson that Maine could now talk to Florida by electric telegraph, he said 'Yes, but has Maine anything to *say* to Florida?'

Nevertheless, if we do not set our expectations absurdly high, the study of language and communication would seem to have value in education, not to give the teacher a body of information to teach, but to heighten his awareness of the nature of relationships between human beings, and between language, learning, and thought. It can also dissipate the many misconceptions about language, which are often derived from folk myth. The fact that many people are unaware of their own often false linguistic assumptions make these more not less effective in influencing behaviour. A study of language should be essentially exploratory, and for this reason we have attempted to set down here the possible form it should take by means of a series of questions.

1 What is language?

The answer often comes pat: 'words'. At a superficial level this is indisputable, and leads insidiously to the easy equation of language ability with vocabulary. Language, however, is also a system of rules governing relationships: what language we have is less important than what we do with what we have. Language is often thought of as standard, but in fact all language symbols are arbitrary, and their usage is a social and geographic matter. Thus a study of varieties and dialects of English is relevant. Again, an apparent commonplace, such as that we communicate by means of language, must be seen as not excluding other means of communication—paralinguistic and non-linguistic. One danger of a course in 'language' might be that it was about language alone.

2 What does language do?

Language, it may be said, communicates. But if the word 'communicate' implies only passing information from A to B then this is a superficial answer. Language is used for a wide range of purposes: to influence, to interact by means of, to explore, to celebrate, to explain oneself to oneself as well as to others, to establish, assert, and maintain identity, both group and individual. Through these means it is a fundamental instrument in the personal growth of the individual. It is possible to classify language from various viewpoints. For instance, the language we use as observers has a different function from that we use as participants. The important thing is that classifications should be attempted. To ask why a thing is said is to gain in understanding of what is said. A study of function is a valuable corrective to the notion that the teacher simply 'communicates', that is, conveys information to a passive class.

3 How does language relate to thought?

This topic is commonly studied in courses in education. Two elements may be mentioned specifically. One is the way in which language is said to structure reality, both in the young child's view of his universe, and in the adult's culturally determined view of phenomena. This can be considered together with possible evidence of it in action: 'how men use words, and how words use men'. The second is how far a child's ability to think internally is related to the external evidence of this thinking, by words.'Few words, few thoughts' is a common assumption, but our passive vocabulary is always greater than our active. A standard language use is often equated with good-standard thoughts; but this may not be the case.

4 How does language relate to learning?
This is in a sense the central problem. Language and other means of communication create an atmosphere, which has its effects on learning in the classroom: the way the children are grouped and the tasks they are given may encourage—or may discourage—an exploratory supportive language. Language offers and develops concepts; subjects traditionally have their technical vocabularies and characteristic ways of expressing things. The question to be asked here is whether the language of teacher and that of subject facilitate or interfere with learning. Thus it is important to examine the language of the classroom, in various subjects, and in such materials as text books. The study of 'language across the curriculum', as it is termed, is now receiving a good deal of attention. The language of the school is a wider aspect of the same topic.

5 How is language acquired?
The general stages of early language growth should be known. The nature of the child-adult dialogue in the acquisition of language in children needs to be emphasized. There are too many misunderstandings in this area, such as that children need not be talked to until they can talk back. A general idea of what use of language we may expect in children at, say, the age of 4 needs to be gained. With the needs of immigrants in mind, some knowledge of second and foreign language acquisition, particularly in relation to age and culture, would also be advantageous. Some students, of course, will need more than a background knowledge.

6 How does language develop?
'By acquiring more words' is one popular but mistaken answer. Other answers suggest teaching children abstract grammatical categories and expecting transfer, but they are equally erroneous. Nonetheless, 'good/ poor at English' is often thought of as a final description of a child.

But language performance varies from situation to situation. Those situations which best enable the solution of linguistic problems (the expression of meaning) are most favourable for development since they motivate the tackling of greater linguistic problems, and help provide the language for their solution. Under favourable circumstances the linguistic command displayed is often surprising. Linguistic performance in particular varies between written and spoken language; the reasons for this, partly because of the abstract context-free nature of much written language, need to be looked at.

7 How is reading learned?

The subject is riddled with folk myth, such as the belief that there is one best way of learning to read. It is important to know the general factors affecting reading acquisition; and particularly that reading should be seen in the context of other linguistic skills. Thus the language the child already has, and the skills he exercises in it, are very relevant. He is not learning a new language, but merely substituting graphic for phonic symbols. It would be impossible, and not very desirable, to acquaint the intending teacher with the variety of schemes available; but he should know the principles of the main approaches, and have some awareness of the nature of reading problems.

In the present book approach is made to all these questions except one—'How is reading learned?'—on which there is a huge literature. However, this book is conceived in many ways as complementary to the author's *The Foundations of Language* (O.U.P.) where three chapters are devoted to the topic.

The book is conceived as 'task oriented'. It is designed so that the reader may work at whichever of three levels he chooses. Part 1 provides an introduction to each topic. Part 2 presents papers and materials for further work, and certain items in this part, marked with an asterisk, are for the reader who wishes to explore more deeply. It is hoped that in this way the book will meet the needs both of students in initial training and those taking advanced courses, as well as the needs of the interested layman.

Part 1

1

Aspects of communication

1.1 Features of communication

If someone said 'Leave my hippopotamus alone', we should presumably regard this as a piece of communication. At least we should if it was in English. If it was said in Zulu, which we did not understand, we might still say it was a piece of communication which did not communicate. That is, of course, absurd. Communication can only be said to take place if meaning results.

It could be, of course, that we did get some meaning out of the utterance, perhaps from the threatening way in which it was said, or from the protective stance the speaker adopted towards his hippopotamus. Communication, then, may take place through words, tone of voice, and other devices, such as position of speaker, as long as we understand what these things mean.

If someone said 'Leave my hic 'opothamush alone' we should have a similar understanding with one addition: that the speaker was drunk. This is presumably information about himself he did not intend to convey. A good deal of what we communicate to others is not intentional or conscious. Much of this unintentional information may come in our tone of voice or our general behaviour. The speaker may, for instance, adopt a protective stance close to the hippopotamus without being aware he is doing it.

Words are not necessary to communication. A lady who ogles the tax inspector is consciously ingratiating herself with him. On the other hand, the tax inspector's look of consternation is not deliberate, and perhaps he is unaware of it, believing he is displaying that grave impassiveness which was encouraged in his training. People communicate about themselves by the way they dress, by their personal appearance and behaviour. When this is too conscious it is known as presenting an image, and ad.-men make money improving the images of politicians.

This depends to some extent on suitable stage props. A man with a blonde in a Jaguar is offering an image of (somewhat *passé*) virility.

Non-human creatures communicate without words. The call of the Greater European Bustard will be understood by other Greater European Bustards, presumably by many other creatures, and by ornithologists who have learned to distinguish, for instance, its mating from its alarm call. The Bustard's calls are certainly intentional. But what about the messages given us by Romping Molly and other plants? Romping Molly is a type of polygonum, a weed with thick, tall, hollow stems, pale green leaves, and white flowers. Man derives messages— 'Spring is here', 'The garden needs weeding'—from it. In no real sense can the plant be said to have sent these, but it does perhaps transmit scent messages to the bee about a source of pollen.

We do not derive messages from the world of nature only, but also from the work of man's hands. Until recent years banks were massive buildings, often fronted with stone and even with Corinthian pillars to emphasize the security offered and the dignity of money. In the nineteenth century schools were frequently built in a gothic, ecclesiastical style to emphasize that they too led to heaven. The message that we now receive from some of these schools, with their high windows and gloomy corridors, is somewhat different.

Some forms of communication between human beings don't appear to use words—the sign language of the deaf and dumb, or the morse code, for instance. But in fact both these are ways of spelling out letters. ···⁻⁻··· spells out the letters SOS. Even 'mathematical language' like $2 + 2 = 4$ is another way of writing an English sentence: 'Two plus two equals four'. There is, however, a difference: the former could be understood by, say, a Russian, who would supply his own words for it, and the latter could not.

That language only communicates as long as we know the meaning of the language might seem obvious: few of this book's present readers would understand it if it were written in Japanese, or even in Cornish, which no one has spoken since the eighteenth century. But to 'know the language' is by no means enough. Anyone who is greeted with 'Oh, do come in. Grandma won't mind waiting at the station', and thinks he is being welcomed, cannot really be said to know English. It is necessary to know the meaning behind the apparent meaning of the words.

1.1.1 Discussion

So far, then, we can say several things about communication. It can be verbal (the warning about the hippopotamus) or non-verbal (the wink). It can be conscious ('Two and two makes four') or unconscious (the taxman's concerned expression). It can come from people (their words, their image); or it can come from things (Romping Molly 'saying' it is spring; a bank building 'saying' ' Save with us'). In every case communication implies interpretation on somebody's part.

We can mention one more characteristic of communication. It is coded or uncoded. The tax inspector looking apprehensive is giving us a *sign* of his inner feelings. (People throughout the world look apprehensive in a similar way.) This is an uncoded message. The girl winking, however, is giving us a *symbol* of her feelings. This is a coded message. Not everyone in the world does a wink to give a confidential 'come hither' message. It might be a sign she has something in her eye. Language too is made up of symbols: a beast like a hippopotamus will be represented by a different word (or symbol) in different languages.

1.2 Communication models

If we want to discover at a glance the relative position and accessibility of certain towns, we consult a map. For this purpose a map without details other than main roads may be the best. Similarly, in thinking about a complex problem we may often find it helpful to strip away the inessentials and confine ourselves to a simple outline or diagram of the main points: this is fashionably called a 'model'.

In discussions of communication one of the most popular models is derived from engineering.

origin	message	transmitter	medium	receiver	destination
person A	message	radio	radio waves	radio	person B

This is too simple to represent the things we have discussed about communication. We would need to construct a model on the following lines:

origin	message	form	medium	receiver	interpretation
person A	deliberate/non-	coded/	verbal/	person B	communication
thing A	deliberate	uncoded	non-verbal		

It is only at the last stage that we can say communication takes place. Let us now exclude the non-deliberate transmission of messages from things (buildings, flowers, and so on), which widens the discussion unduly, and concern ourselves with people. In that case Person A is commonly called the addressor, and Person B the addressee.

addressor	message	form	medium	addressee	interpretation
	deliberate/	coded/	verbal/		
	non-deliberate	uncoded	non-verbal		

1.2.1 Their limitations

This model seems to contain the essential elements, but like all models it has limitations. It suggests that communication is only one way, from speaker to listener without feedback. It does not indicate that the speaker also receives his own message. Further, the idea of a 'message' is too restricted.

Let us enlarge briefly on these three. Most everyday communication is two-way, taking place in conversation and discussion, with continual interaction between the participants. It is only in the so-called 'communications media'—radio, television, the press—that the addressee cannot answer back immediately. Also, many uses of language are not for others so much as for ourselves. This is true not only when we speak our thoughts aloud ('Now where did I leave my hippopotamus?'), but when we write a letter which is apparently to a friend but which is really sorting out some problem for ourselves. We shall discuss this in more detail later in the book. And again 'message' is not a very satisfactory word. Its normal usage suggests that a brief piece of information ('The Sioux are attacking', for example) passes directly from one person to another, who is usually at a distance. This is not sufficient for all the various functions language and non-verbal signals serve. For the Elizabethans the word 'communication' meant a participating, a sharing together, and this would be a more useful connotation than the present one.

1.3 Summary

Communication can be deliberate or not, coded or uncoded, from animate or inanimate things, by words or by other means. It is only meaningful to speak of communication when there is interpretation on the part of the recipient.

It is common, but mistaken, to think of communication merely as the passing of information from A to B. Language and non-verbal signals serve a variety of functions in addition to this.

2

Means of communication

Not all communication is through words. The smile, the head turned away, the contemptuous gesture, the scent of a perfume, these and many more may be taken as conveying messages. Let us look at the various means of communication between human beings.

2.1.1 The linguistic means
In discussing the linguistic means we need to consider two aspects of language: first, the words and phrases themselves, and second, the noises we make uttering them. The reader of this book has before him at present only the first of these, the words on the page. If he reads the words aloud, he puts sounds to them. He doesn't have much choice about these sounds. The word 'about', for instance, is to be pronounced with its second syllable stressed, somewhat similar to 'a bowt': if it is pronounced 'a boot', as in lowland Scots, there is confusion with another word; if it is stressed on the first syllable it becomes almost indistinguishable from 'abbot'. We refer to the sound system which we use in pronouncing the words as *phonology*. These two aspects of the language—its words and phrases, and its phonology—we shall examine in more detail later.

2.1.2 The paralinguistic means
The rules of phonology are compulsory, in that if we do not obey them fairly closely we shall not be understood. But, when we are speaking, the listeners hear more than the phonology: they hear our tone of voice, the loudness or softness of our delivery, the quality of our voice, the speed at which we speak, the pauses and hesitations we make. We call these properties *paralinguistic*, as they run alongside (*para*) the language. They tell us a good deal about the person speaking. From one point of view it is appropriate to describe *accent* as paralinguistic, in

that, like the other phenomena, it is the person's individual contribution to what he is saying rather than something belonging to it as
'language'.

Animals use this channel in communicating, and the sounds they
make, whilst in general similar within each species, have some individuality, at least in the higher species close to man. For example, the
varied size and construction of the vocal organs, including mouth, in
different dogs of the same breed would lead to differences in sound
even if no temperamental differences were represented.

2.1.3 The visual means

The linguistic means may be used to give people information—'Two and
two make four', for instance. If someone writes that, nothing about him
as an individual emerges. But if he writes 'I detest the whole idea that
two and two make four', then we are beginning to get some impression
of him as a person, and these impressions by paralinguistic means are
increased if he speaks the words. The *visual* means normally gives the
latter type of information—about the person.

The appearance of people often provides the first information we
have about them. The most obvious indications lie in the things they can
alter more or less at will, such as their clothes or their hair. These may
indicate the group to which they feel they belong, and their image of
themselves. The business-man's suit is as much a badge of identity as
the soldier's uniform. A few years ago dress and length of hair gave
clear messages about a person's sex, and still do to a large extent,
though those sad tales one hears about the motorist picking up a
dazzling blonde in jeans, only to find he is giving a lift to the captain of
the rugby club, are a warning that superficial clues cannot necessarily be
trusted.

There are things about people which they cannot change so easily, if
at all, and from which we derive information, not necessarily correct,
about them. Large physical size may convey the message 'I am a person
to be reckoned with', though this may be misleading. People are
attracted by good looks, and tend to attribute other virtues to their
owners which they may not possess (ugly but able politicians may feel
themselves at a disadvantage in a television age). The attempt to relate
character to physical type goes back to the ancient Greeks, and we have
inherited something of their attitude. We tend to stereotype people
according to their physique: we may expect a fat person to be 'slow'

and 'affable', or 'amiable'. Shakespeare's Julius Caesar wanted men about him who were fat: 'Cassius has a lean and hungry look . . . such men are dangerous'. Caesar happened to be right on that occasion, but this insight should not therefore be taken as a universal truth.

People do, of course, tend to be influenced by what others expect them to be: the stupid-looking child may become 'stupid' because nobody thinks it worth while to teach him anything. It is said that people make their own faces, and it is true that over the years habitual moods and attitudes—worry, for instance—may be reflected in habitual expressions. Even so, we must be cautious in making judgements. A few years ago psychologists were fond of an experiment whereby the photographs of criminals were mixed up with photographs of virtuous citizens and people were asked to judge which was which. The results were nearly always the same: acid bath killers and necrophiliacs appeared to many people to be virtuous citizens, whilst clergy of blameless life in Tunbridge Wells would frequently be picked out as convicted murderers.

2.1.4 The proxemic means

The placing of people in relation to others is another means by which we make deductions about them. This can be observed in an apparently simple matter such as standing up and sitting down. Often the person of inferior status will stand while the superior sits. Courtiers traditionally stand while the king and queen sit; the soldier stands before his commanding officer, the employee before his boss. In formal social situations sex may confer superiority in that the woman remains seated while the man, standing, is introduced to her. However, in other situations a different rule applies and the person higher up is superior. For example, a lecturer or speaker stands, even on a platform, while addressing a seated audience; a teacher stands before a seated class; subjects may prostrate themselves before a monarch. The means through which this information is conveyed is called *proxemic*.

One set of rules for conveying information by these means, then, concerns 'highness' or 'lowness'. Another set concerns the distance of an individual from a group. Members of an interviewing panel will often arrange themselves along a long table while the candidate is placed some distance away in isolation: they are then in the superior position. On the other hand, a tutor seated behind his desk, with the students sitting round in a group beyond it, is in a superior position, even though he is

on the same level as they are. In both these situations a 'stage prop'—
the table or desk—is used to indicate status. The chairman of a committee, or the head of a family, may sit at the head of a table, where
there is probably greater distance between him and the rest than
between the individuals sitting side by side. Closeness often indicates
intimacy, at least temporarily, though not when one is pressed in a
crowd of strangers. A couple leaning forward towards each other with
their 'heads together' at a table may be getting on very well. From these
examples it is evident that different situations may impose quite
different rules—the grouping of the students has the opposite meaning
to the grouping of the interviewing panel.

It is important to remember also that not all positions have the same
meaning to different people, or in different cultures. In certain South
American countries it is the custom, in ordinary matters of business and
social life, to speak with one's face very close to the other person's face.
In Anglo-Saxon cultures, however, if we stand closer than about three
feet to another person, we begin to feel uncomfortable and back away.
The Anglo-Saxon puts his face nearer than that to someone else's only
in moments of amorousness or extreme aggression.

There is yet another set of conventions, which govern who goes first
and who follows. These are seen at their most formal on ceremonial
occasions and in processions. For example, in a state procession the
most important person—the monarch or president—may well come near
the end. On the other hand, a general traditionally leads his troops.
Going through a door, the superior precedes the inferior: the man
follows the woman, and children are often taught to hold the door open
for their elders.

2.1.5 The kinesic means

We receive messages from people's body movements, whether these are
of the whole person, as in walking, or of a small but significant part of
the person, like the eyes or the corners of the mouth. The means by
which these messages of movement are conveyed is becoming known as
kinesic.

Traditionally the soldier has a military bearing, and the sailor a
rolling gait supposed to come from trying to keep upright on a moving
deck. The Victorian young lady was taught to work consciously at her
'deportment'; African peoples attain a similar dignity of carriage, not
from conscious effort but as a result of being trained from early

childhood to carry baskets on their heads. The way the head is held—bowed shamefacedly, erect, or even tilted, 'nose in the air'—is often taken as a mark of character or of class.

The arrangement of the limbs is significant. Women sitting wearing short skirts keep their knees together in the presence of men—not to do so may be taken as provocative or slovenly—but they are not so careful in the presence of other women only, or when wearing slacks. Goffman (1971, p. 119) tells us that Shetland domestic workers of both sexes would use crofter 'postural patterns' when together in a hotel kitchen, the women sitting with their legs up, but they would not have done this in the presence of the British middle-class guests. The way people sit often indicates how much they feel at home. A guest who lies back in a chair in your house and spreads his legs wide has practically taken over. The expression 'sitting with one's feet up' suggests that he may formerly have gone even further, though this does not seem to be practised very much nowadays in civilized society, except of course in the House of Commons, where the front benchers may perhaps sit with their feet on the clerk's table.

Gestures of the hands and arms tend to have more formalized meanings. To scratch one's head indicates puzzlement; to circle one's finger quickly means 'I am trying to find the right word and can't'; a thumb pointed downwards has had a negative meaning for centuries. Authorities may deliberately design or encourage certain gestures: consider, for instance, the range of hand signals for use in motoring that the *Highway Code* advocates. Insulting gestures such as the V-sign are well known.

Some gestures seem to be in effect reflexes—finger tapping, for example, which indicates anxiety. However, a very high proportion of gestures which we think of as natural are in fact culturally determined, and mean different things in different countries. LaBarre (1964, p. 202) comments:

In a restaurant, an American raises a well-bred right fore-finger to summon a waiter. To express 'come here!', a Latin American makes a downward arch with the right hand, almost identical with an American jocular gesture of 'get away with you!' The Shans of Burma beckon by holding the palm down, moving the fingers as if playing an arpeggio chord.

Many facial gestures, which appear unambiguous and universal, are also culturally determined. To stick one's tongue out is, in Britain, a child's gesture of defiance: in southern China to put the tongue out and in quickly is a way of acknowledging that one has made a *faux pas*. Common gestures of the head among Anglo-Saxon people are nodding for 'yes', and shaking it for 'no': in Ceylon traditionally the same gestures have opposite meanings.

Gestures of the head and face are common. People tend to move their heads and bodies when talking, as though the energy they were producing was more than enough and needed to be dissipated. The most significant facial movements are those of the eyes. Most people do not think of them as gestures at all. The English language contains many expressions, such as 'Their eyes met', 'He couldn't take his eyes off her', 'He avoided my gaze', 'I caught his eye', which refer to what is now being studied under the term *eye-contact* (see, for instance, Argyle, 1967, Chapter 6). It appears that a speaker will focus on another's eyes to initiate what he wants to say, look intermittently as he begins his statement, and look at the end, saying in effect 'Over to you'. Looking at the other's eyes seems to happen more when the speaker feels friendly, though this act may have just the opposite meaning if his facial expression is hostile—it is then aggressive. Long eye-contact has special meaning: it is perhaps an attempt at dominance ('staring someone out'), or a sexual overture. A speaker who is saying something he thinks the other will not like keeps his eyes away, as will a listener who is about to disagree with the speaker. People whose eyes meet feel under some sort of obligation to each other, for instance, to say something. Two people at a party, who are aware of each other's presence, but who do not want to meet, avoid catching each other's eye. If their eyes do meet, they will appear to be snubbing each other if they do not speak.

2.1.6 The tactile means

We also communicate by touch. It seems that from birth the young human or animal needs the security which constant handling and body contact, particularly from the mother, bring. A large amount of touching occurs in families, particularly between parents and children. Jourard (1966) has investigated the whole matter, and shows that the amount and placing of touches on another's body varied between male and male, male and female, father and male or female child, mother and male or female child. The meaning varies from case to case, and depends on such factors as the relative ages of those concerned, the situation, and so on. Shaking hands is an obvious conventional way of touching;

to put one's arm round someone's shoulder for friendship or support is accepted between men; for a man to put his arm round a woman's shoulder, particularly a young woman, may have a different significance. A slap on the back is a conventional congratulation. Kissing is not accepted between men in Anglo-Saxon cultures, but is among certain Latin peoples; kissing of women by women is accepted, however, rather on the cheek than on the mouth. In Japan it is necessary to censor kissing scenes in films from America and other western countries because kissing is considered a private act of love-making, disgusting when performed in public.

2.1.7 The olfactory means

The sense of smell is very important with animals. Observing a dog, one infers that every lamp-post, corner, and blade of grass has its own particular message. In Anglo-Saxon countries, amongst others, human body smell is considered offensive and the manufacturers of soaps, scents, and deodorants have made large profits getting rid of it, substituting instead a variety of other smells, whose sexual value in particular is stressed. It may be, however, that body smell, perceived subliminally, is one of the unexplained factors in sexual attraction. In some experiments with rats, males deprived of their sense of smell ceased to be interested in mating. Doctors make use of the messages smells give. They must be able to recognize 'the stink of uremia, diabetes, alcoholism, lung abscesses, and other serious illness' (Otswall, 1964, p. 16). Schizophrenia is known to have its own distinctive smell.

2.1.8 The taste means

It seems that taste is closely related to smell. There appear to be only four basic flavours—sweet, sour, bitter, and salt—and what we call 'tastes' are degrees and combinations of these with different smells. Chemists who know what they are about may initially test a substance with the tip of their tongue, and we may say that the substance communicates to them. Young children too put objects in their mouths, but otherwise it seems that this means is not much used. Cooks, however, may send deliberate messages (as the saying goes, 'The way to a man's heart is through his stomach'). Lovers also communicate with each other by taste. In the *Song of Solomon* (4.11) the king says:

Thy lips, O my spouse, drop as the honey-comb:
Honey and milk are under thy tongue . . .

2.2 Combined operations

These means of communication sometimes operate separately. On the
telephone, for instance, we only use the linguistic and paralinguistic
means. But commonly there are several in use: our facial expression,
our eyes, our posture, our distance from others, our gestures, all are
sending messages. They are, however, messages of different sorts.
Posture cannot say the twelve times table: language is necessary for that.
On the other hand, what we know as a 'meaningful look' can indicate
things which could not really be put into words.

2.3 Summary

Communication is not only by language: there are other means of
communication, both paralinguistic and non-linguistic. They commonly,
but not necessarily, operate together, but have varied functions.

3

What is communicated?

3.1 Cognitive and affective information

'Never darken my doorstep again' is a command conveying information about someone's future conduct. But it also conveys an attitude of hostility. We may say for convenience that in communication between human beings there are broadly speaking two types of messages passed. Cognitive messages are those concerned with facts and ideas; affective messages are those concerned with attitudes and emotions. Thus 'Washington D.C. is the capital of the U.S.A.' is cognitive, as is 'The square on the hypotenuse equals the sum of the squares on the other two sides'. On the other hand, 'My love is like a red red rose' is much more affective, as is 'Come into the garden, Maud'. Of course, these last two contain certain information, but it is overlaid with considerable emotion. Scientific and scholarly treatises attempt to be cognitive. The compilers of dictionaries certainly do. The instances in Dr. Johnson's *Dictionary* where he allows his feelings to influence his definitions are famous. Thus he defines 'lexicographer' as 'A writer of dictionaries: a harmless drudge' and 'oats' as 'A grain, which in England is generally given to horses, but in Scotland supports the people'. On these occasions affective information occurs where one would expect, and indeed require, cognitive information.

Language communicates both cognitive and affective messages, but since the non-linguistic means are not well able to cope with cognitive messages, their province tends to be the affective. Through them our attitudes tend to be conveyed.

3.2 Psychological information

3.2.1 View of self by self
A person's self image is the way he conceives himself to be and normally

tries to present himself to others. Actors in particular are concerned with how they appear to others, but so are the rest of us, though this concern may not be completely or even largely conscious. Nor is the concern only with physical matters, a wish to appear smart or well-dressed. People present themselves as 'down-to-earth', 'non-joiners', 'anti-establishment', 'sex-kittens', or 'not the sort of person who would do such a thing'. One major element in self-presentation is group identity: we recognize which group a person conceives himself as belonging to.

3.2.2 View of self by others
This might not at all coincide with the previous view. The person may be completely unaware of the kind of impression he is giving (he may seem rude rather than witty, or forward rather than friendly). Sometimes the gap between inner aspiration and observed reality is great, often in matters of social class or age, as the phrases 'giving oneself airs', 'talking la-di-da', and 'mutton dressed as lamb' indicate.

3.2.3 View of others by self
In our human relations we constantly convey, often not consciously, attitudes towards those around us. We may regard them as superior, equal, inferior, close, even intimate, or distant, hostile, or friendly, and so on. This is seen most clearly in modes of address. Some people we address by their first names, others by a title (Mr., Mrs.), others again by their surnames only (in certain circles). People with whom our relationship is not clear we often avoid addressing by name, and get away with 'you'.

3.2.4 View of other things by self
We constantly convey attitudes towards ideas, objects, and situations, again often not consciously. We may dislike tripe and football matches, and distrust tinned food, and hill-climbing, but not TV commercials. A teacher might fail to teach effectively because, although the subject, say, an aspect of poetry, is one within his professional expertise, he may be lukewarm about it, and this attitude will carry over to his students.

All this is not to suggest that people have unchanging attitudes. They are constantly shifting, sometimes from second to second as they do in a conversation. The way a person suddenly smiles might cause us to revise what we have been thinking about him, and perhaps about what he has been saying.

3.3 Biological information

The cognitive and affective information described above may be called 'psychological', in that it concerns thinking and feeling. However, there is information we present about ourselves which can be called 'biological', in that it concerns our physical state. We do not usually set out to give this information: people deduce it from observing us.

Thus at a glance we take in a person's size and physique. It used to be easy to make immediate judgements about a person's sex just from their clothing, but now there are a number of styles used by both sexes. Perhaps as a reaction against such ambiguity some men grow a large amount of facial hair which (at least most) women cannot hope to emulate, and some women adopt traditional feminine clothes—long dresses reminiscent of regency styles—which (at least most) men would find it embarrassing to copy. But, regardless of clothing, the physical differences between the sexes are normally sufficient for an accurate judgement to be made.

A person's age can similarly be deduced from his appearance, but not necessarily very accurately. Such things as hair loss in men, type of skin (susceptibility to wrinkles), and body metabolism (susceptibility to fatness or scragginess) are genetically programmed, and may give a mis-leading indication of age. Anxiety, stress, overwork, all may cause premature aging, and conversely an absence of these maintains a youth-ful appearance. Many women in western cultures spend large amounts of money on makeup to disguise the effects of aging: whereas Granny used to go greyer as she got older, she may now go blonder. It is a constant source of amazement that women of 40 can turn into women of 30 for an evening party, after a visit to the hairdresser's and two hours in the bathroom.

We can often deduce age with reasonable accuracy, but would find it difficult to say how we do it. Thus the amateur stage stereotype of an old man as bent double with a drooping head is not well observed. With aging the shoulders and neck naturally fall forward a little, and the head

17

is often held well up to compensate for this. Thus many old men present a very erect appearance.

Medical state may be in general deduced from visual clues. Certain illnesses or disorders affect the condition of the skin and hair, or the light of the eyes; bags under the eyes may be a sympton of sleeplessness or over-indulgence. Doctors have necessarily to read such symptoms, in conjunction with others, much more intensively than we do, for they need to arrive at a much more accurate diagnosis than that someone is 'looking a bit rough' or is 'under the weather'.

3.4 Social information

There is another kind of information which we deduce about other people: information about their social class, occupation, education, and regional or national origin.

Sociologists find the idea of class difficult to define, and some would claim it is meaningless. That may be so, but it is nevertheless true that in Britain at the moment people classify others as being 'working class', 'middle class', and so on. (In America or Canada this would be much less true.) Paralinguistics, particularly accent, would provide the main clues for such judgements. A major clue to many occupations would be provided by clothing: men in professional occupations tend to wear dark suits; policemen and soldiers wear uniforms. Despite an increasing similarity in the leisure clothes of all classes (it is well known that duchesses shop at Marks and Spencers), working clothes have in some cases become more not less distinctive. Thus a construction worker on the job nowadays will wear a bright yellow or orange jacket with a protective helmet, whereas a few years ago he would have worn any clothes he wished.

A person's education is often judged by general confidence, by linguistic fluency, sometimes by accent. Most people would expect the standard forms of English in an educated speaker. Regional origin may be identified by a local accent, sometimes by dialect words or constructions. Native speakers of other languages carry over into their speaking of English pronunciations from their own languages. A German's English is quite distinguishable from a Frenchman's English.

What is communicated?

3.5 Summary

We communicate both cognitive and affective information, the former being concerned with facts and ideas, and the latter with feelings and attitudes.

We may classify information as psychological (thoughts, feelings, and attitudes), biological (concerned with physical state), and social (concerned with class, education, occupation, origins).

4

Paralinguistic communication

4.1 Explanation

Here is an extract from a novel that will never be written:

'No, no!' he said, in a rapid, high-pitched adenoidal, hesitant way, his Bootle tones modified by a long pre-adolescent stay in Shepherds Bush.

'Yes, yes,' she replied, in a slow, musical, fluent, low-toned, breathy, warm way, trying hard under stress of emotion, to prevent her carefully nurtured cockney slipping back to its native Roedean.

This novel will never be written because, though it obviously has the makings of greatness, it includes detail that will bog the reader, and the writer, down. Yet all the information given would be present in the voices of the speakers could we but hear them—not in what they say, but in the way they say it—and would tell us a good deal about them. This is paralinguistic communication (as we defined it in 2.1.2). We will now examine some aspects of it.

4.2 Aspects of paralinguistic communication

It is impossible to pronounce language without *accent*: 'Received Pronunciation' or RP (that used by BBC announcers on official occasions) is just as much an accent as that of Birmingham, or of Boston, U.S.A. There is also *speed*, the rate at which language is uttered; degree of *loudness*; relative *continuity* (some people punctuate their language more than others with pauses and hesitations); *voice quality* (a voice may be hoarse, gruff, sepulchral, adenoidal, piping); and *tone* in the popular sense, connected with the emotion and attitude conveyed (warm, distant, aggressive, superior, and so on). Of course, these elements are not necessarily separate. For instance, the aggressiveness of a voice would often be conveyed through both its speed and its loudness.

4.2.1 Accent

Accents are commonly thought of as regional and social. Many accents enable us to tell which country or region a speaker comes from, even if English is not the speaker's first language. British English speakers differ from American English speakers, or from Australian, or South African, and within these groups there are regional variations. In England 'Received Pronunciation' is the least local, though it is more common in London and the South-East than elsewhere and would be classified by the majority of English speakers as 'southern'. Most English speakers in the British Isles use English with at least some trace of its regional origins—lowland Scots, southern Welsh, Lancashire, and so on. It is easy enough to distinguish between these three, but although many people pride themselves on being able to recognize accents from parts of England they often seem to be less successful than they imagine. The easiest broad division to make is between northern and southern accents, the two most obvious differences being between the vowel sounds in, for instance, 'cut', 'some' (where southern English is nearer 'cat', 'sam'); and the vowel in 'grass', 'path' (short in northern, long in southern).

Accents also have class associations. Various studies in England have shown that people rate accents in terms of status, with Received Pronunciation at the top, various regional accents following, and industrial accents lowest (Wilkinson, 1965, p. 51, Giles, 1970). In New York Labov (1964) took five sounds, and showed that the pronunciation of these had a relation to social class. For instance, the pronunciation *th* (as in 'thing') is the high prestige form; whereas *t* ('ting') is the low prestige form. There is also a form combining the two, 't-thing'.

When we hear certain accents it seems that we attach personality traits to their owners. Strongman and Woozley (1967) asked students to rate London and Yorkshire accents on tape. Both northern and southern students (Staffordshire was the dividing line) rated Yorkshire speakers to be more honest and reliable than the London speakers and the London speakers to be more self-confident than the Yorkshire. Northerners judged the Yorkshire speakers to be more industrious, and southerners judged them to be more serious than the London speakers.

Northerners also judged the Yorkshire speakers to be more generous, good-natured, and kind-hearted than the London speakers, whom they rated as slightly more mean, irritable, and hard. In a study by Cheyne (1970), English voices were rated higher by English and Scottish men and women for wealth, prestige, and intelligence; and they were even rated taller! On the other hand, both English and Scots rated the Scots higher on friendliness, and the Scots men rated Scotsmen higher on generosity, goodheartedness, and likeability. Nobody rated them as mean. Here, of course, characteristics other than personality alone are being considered. It should be added that in neither study are we told what the term 'London' or 'English' accent implies. If it means RP, then Giles's study, in which southern Welsh and Somerset are compared with RP, points in the same direction: on the whole RP is respected for competence (intelligence, self-confidence, etc.), but the regional accent users are more respected for personal integrity (reliability, kindliness, etc.) and social attractiveness (sociability, sense of humour, etc.). Incidentally, southern Welsh speakers were judged more talkative than Somerset, and Somerset more good-natured than southern Welsh. It should be emphasized that these stereotyped judgements represent people's immediate responses.

4.2.2 Speech rate
The speed at which people speak varies from individual to individual. An individual also will vary his speech rate from situation to situation, perhaps influenced by his relationship with the listener, his knowledge of and interest in the topic, his mood at the time, and so on. Even so, there is only a relative degree to which any one person raises or lowers his speed of talking for any length of time. The fast speakers remain consistently fast and the slow speakers consistently slow: speech rate is more a facet of personality than of promptings of the situation (Goldman-Eisler, 1968).

4.2.3 Loudness
There seems to have been no separate investigation of the degree of loudness in which people talk. One would guess that extroverts speak more loudly than introverts, men more loudly than women. Loudness is often linked with anger: people quarrelling often raise their voices. Some deaf people talk loudly because they are unable to hear the

amount of noise they are making. People talking to foreigners who have the misfortune not to understand English raise their voices as though this were a way of penetrating their apparent stupidity. Quietness seems often linked to tenderness or secrecy; but it may be a device in the expression of an intense anger.

4.2.4 Continuity

Pauses in speaking obviously occur partly because the speaker is observing the normal grammatical pauses, represented in writing by commas, full-stops, and so on. However, there are often reasons for pausing that override these. Sometimes people pause for breath in the middle of a grammatical unit, sometimes they pause because they are seeking to express a particular idea, the words for which are eluding them. Sometimes they are nervous or tense, either on a particular occasion, or from predisposition, and their speech may be marked by pauses, hesitations, false-starts, repetitions, even stuttering.

In a series of experiments Goldman-Eisler examined the relationship of the pauses either 'unfilled' (silent) or 'filled' (containing a sound like *mm* or *er*) to the 'predictability' of the language following them. She used G. Hughlings Hackson's distinction between 'old organized' and 'new now organizing' speech. The former refers to speech we seem to have heard many times before. Thus in the greetings 'How are —', 'Very — to meet you', 'It's a — day, isn't it — ?, we have no real difficulty in filling each gap with some sensible word. Much conversation is of this kind. Even if we can guess the exact word the speaker will use next, we are not surprised when he uses it, nor does he need to search for it. This predictability in language is one reason for fluency in speech. The latter, 'new now organizing' speech, on the other hand refers to speech that the speaker is, as it were, coining as he goes along: he is newly organizing it for himself. It is likely to be more cognitive and less predictable. It carries more 'information' (in information theory 'high information' is defined as 'less predictable'). Goldman-Eisler shows that, in her experiments, there are more and longer pauses before less predictable words (Goldman-Eisler, 1958). She also finds that unfilled pauses are more common compared to filled pauses in dealing with abstract rather than concrete material. She also suggests that unfilled pauses are related to cognitive activity and tolerance of silence, and filled pauses related to emotional activity and less tolerance of silence (Goldman-Eisler, 1961).

4.2.5 Voice quality
'Voice quality' in this context has been defined as the 'quasi-permanent' quality of a voice. It derives fundamentally from the nature of a person's vocal equipment: the length of the vocal chords, for example, determines the range of the voice, in the same way that the shortening of a guitar string by the finger produces a higher note. It also derives from long-term muscular adjustments or 'settings' as they have been called (Honikman, 1964). Thus actors have been trained to use a much fuller range of voice than other people.

Laver (1968) uses popular, impressionistic labels for voice quality, such as 'ginny', 'husky', 'golden', 'piping', 'bleating', 'light-blue', 'hoarse', 'gruff', 'sepulchral', 'adenoidal'. In surveying the research Laver finds that a good deal of biological information can be detected from voice quality. Thus a person's size and physique seem generally related to the size of their larynx and vocal tract. Big tall men are more likely to have deep strong voices than are little weedy men. And we have little difficulty in detecting sex or age from the voice, though the latter cannot be detected so reliably. Medical state may also be detected from the voice (breathy voices might indicate poor health). Alcohol in excess over a period can affect the vocal organs, and this is the origin of the 'ginny', 'whisky', or 'beery' voice. Social and psychological information seems to be less clearly indicated by voice quality alone than it is by voice quality in combination with other aspects, such as accent. Thus a certain amount of nasalization is a feature of much British Received Pronunciation, whilst Liverpool, England, has an adenoidal tone in which the speaker prevents any sound coming through the nose.

4.2.6 Tone of voice
That the voice indicates a particular attitude or emotion—warmth, sincerity, hostility, and on—is traditionally recognized. It seems that the tone of voice used may have a greater power to communicate attitude than what we actually say. Thus Argyle and his associates (1970) found that the manner of presentation of a passage overrode its contents in terms of communication of attitude. Three similar passages were taken, displaying in *their language* a superior, an equal, and an inferior attitude. Thus the first might say there was little point in telling the listener about an experiment since he would not understand it, and so on. These passages were read in three different ways, the tone

conveying in turn superior, equal, and inferior attitudes. In each case the listeners were influenced by the tone rather than the meaning of the passage.

4.3 Interpretation of paralinguistic messages

As we have seen, paralinguistics provides a good deal of information about people, for between them the different aspects provide a variety of clues. Biological information such as sex and age can most obviously be determined. On psychological information about personality in general, people seem to judge more often right than wrong, but on more detailed traits like intelligence the reverse has been shown to be true (Fay and Middleton, 1940). Social information such as place of origin is quite well estimated, but other information such as class and occupation is not so well estimated. Mistakes about class and occupation often occur because stereotyped judgements are made. People have expectations that a doctor is likely to talk with Received Pronunciation, although most doctors probably do not. And once the stereotype is detected then people attribute other qualities to it. Thus in the investigation discussed earlier in this chapter, people doubtless recognized the English or Scottish accents, and this prompted them to record the qualities that are connected with the stereotype. The English were thought of as 'intelligent', though for all evidence there is to the contrary they might be much more stupid than the Scots; in any case all English cannot be more intelligent than all Scots.

4.4 Summary

Paralinguistic messages are carried by such non-verbal features of the voice as accent, speech rate, degree of loudness, continuity, quality, and tone. In many cases people interpret the messages correctly, except when there is some interference from preconceptions, such as national or occupational stereotypes.

5

Animal communication

5.1 Communication in non-human creatures

Literature is full of stories of talking animals, birds, and fishes, and such stories continue to be written despite the fact that, in the nature of things, they must be a pack of lies. No non-human creatures talk in the sense that we understand it (though there have been some interesting experiments that we shall discuss later). This does not mean to say that animals do not communicate: they do so continually by a wide variety of means. The cat fluffs out her fur to deter an aggressor; the peacock displays his fan as part of his courtship; robins sing to mark out their territory and presence; dogs, rabbits, and guinea pigs urinate to mark theirs; acquatic mammals have quite an elaborate system of sound signals; many creatures have mating and alarm calls.

These and similar means of animal communication differ from human language in a variety of ways. A speech message is sent through the air at a particular point in time: a scent left by an animal lingers, so that communication could take place over a period of time. In principle any message can be said by any speaker, whereas it is only the male cuckoo that can say 'cuckoo', Words can be used in different combinations to mean different things, but the robin cannot put his mating call next to his territorial call, so as to mean 'Get the hell out of here, even though I love you'. We can invent new words (astronaut, jet) or give new meanings to old (bikini, fairy), but the nightingale is stuck with his old repertoire which was 'heard in ancient days by emperor and clown', as Keats said (making a different point).

We need not go into further detail here about the differences between human and animal communication. Sufficient to say that animal communication seems to lack some characteristics of human communication. Nevertheless, there are amongst some creatures remarkably elaborate communication systems. This is particularly true of bees.

5.2 Bees

Thanks mainly to the work of Karl von Frisch and his associates, described in his monumental *The Dance Language and Orientation of Bees* (1967), we know a good deal about how bees communicate.

5.2.1 A bee indicates food sources nearby

Von Frisch found that particular groups of bees are devoted to specific types of flowers, and rest when these are not supplying food. He found he could substitute sugar water in a watch glass for nectar and interest a group of bees in it. The bees resting have scouts out searching. The scout finding the sugar water drinks and fills her honey stomach. She returns to the hive and distributes sugar water from her mouth to other bees with proboscis outstretched. She then begins a 'round dance', sometimes reversing and going round in the opposite direction. Food may be distributed again, and the dance resumed two or three times. During the dance she draws in her wake other bees who follow her changes in direction. Those belonging to her group (recognized in the experiments because they have been marked) immediately prepare to fly to the food source. The bees of the same group recognize one another by the flower fragrance which clings to the body. The round dance is a sign food is to be fetched. They already know where it is, seek it out and return to the hive, performing the dance when they return, so that things in the hive get more and more lively. This dance is

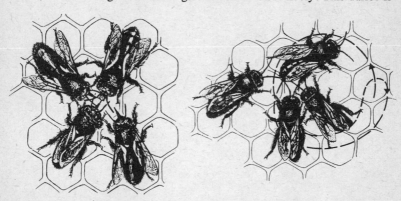

Figure 1 A scout (lower left) returns to the hive and gives nectar to three other bees

Figure 2 In the round dance the scout is followed by three bees, who receive information

used for food up to 100 metres away. New recruits know that it is only
a short distance, but they do not know where. They will fly out and
seek in various directions until they find it, guided by the scent.

5.2.2 A bee indicates food sources further away

A bee that finds food at a distance will, as before, return to the hive
and dance, pausing to distribute food. It seems, incidentally, that a
follower can, by a squeak, halt the dance until feeding takes place.
(Bees cannot hear but are sensitive to vibrations.) This dance, used for
distances over 100 m, is more complicated. It consists of a run in a
straight line with a half-circular return to the starting point, to the left
and to the right alternately. The longer the straight run and the slower
the circuits, the further is the distance (for example, for a distance up
to 300 m the bee will run over 1 or 2 cells, for a distance up to 4500 m,
4 or 5 cells). During the straight run the bee wags her tail. This is the
'tail wagging dance' and its duration indicates distance. The distance
indicated is not the actual distance over the ground: it is a statement of
the amount of effort involved in reaching the goal. Thus a bee will

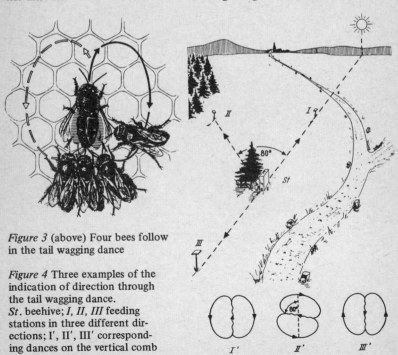

Figure 3 (above) Four bees follow
in the tail wagging dance

Figure 4 Three examples of the
indication of direction through
the tail wagging dance.
St. beehive; *I, II, III* feeding
stations in three different directions; I', II', III' corresponding dances on the vertical comb

signal a greater distance to a goal if there is a headwind than if it is calm.

The other bees will also need to know direction. If the dance is performed outside the hive on a horizontal surface the direction to be taken is that of the straight line of the dance. A prerequisite is that the bee must be able to see the sun or polarised lights. This is because the bee orients by the sun, and carries out the dance with the same orientation to the sun as in her outward flight. Inside the hive the dance normally takes place on the honey comb which hangs vertically. The hive is so dark that she cannot orient in relation to the sun. In this case she acts as if the sun is at the top of the comb, sensing the vertical by her perception of gravity, and making her tail wagging dance upwards at the same angle to the vertical as her outward flight was to the sun.

5.3 The higher apes

The absolute distinctions between human language and that of animals have been blurred of recent years by a number of experiments in teaching animals forms of human language. The various attempts to teach them to talk have concentrated on the chimpanzee and they have all been monumental failures. It may be that the gorilla or the orang-outang has a greater potentiality for speech than the chimpanzee, but these animals have not seemed to display that dedication to the cause of science which would have rendered the attempt worthwhile. The chimpanzee, on the other hand, has always done his best. For six years Dr. and Mrs. Hayes tried to teach a chimpanzee called Vicki to speak. She seems to have understood a fair number of words but only learned to mouth 'mama', 'papa', 'cup', and 'up' (Hayes and Hayes, 1955).

5.3.1 Washoe

The vocal organs of the chimpanzee are in fact different from those of human beings. They make many different sounds, but only in a state of excitement. In captivity they are rather silent. On the other hand the movement of their limbs is a means of expression, not only in leaping and swinging, but also in embracing and grooming each other. With this in mind, another husband and wife team, the Gardners (Gardner and Gardner, 1969), adopted a young female chimpanzee, Washoe, and proceeded to teach her a sign language, ASL—the American Sign Language used by deaf and dumb people. It differs from the British deaf and dumb language, which is a system of spelling by individual letters. The signs in ASL are equivalent to whole words, just as the flat open hand of the traffic policeman raised vertically means 'Halt'.

The system has three means of signalling. The first is the way the hand is arranged (pointing, fingers spread, etc.); the second is where it is placed (near nose, or shoulder, etc.); the third is the action carried out (moving up or down, for example). Washoe lived in a room similar to a human dwelling, and whilst awake always had one or more human companions with whom she took part in the routines of the day—feeding, bathing, dressing, playing games, looking at books and magazines. Only ASL was used for communication.

Washoe is reported to have mastered 87 signs or 'words' in three years. When she makes mistakes they can often be shown to be because she is classifying items in categories (for example, brush, clean, soap, comb, oil, lotion, toothbrush) and is offering one from the category. Sometimes the signs she uses originate as her inventions: it is claimed that she described a bib by drawing an outline of it on her chest. She has gone beyond the examples offered her: 'you' refers to any companion, not just to those with whom she was taught the word. She can use words of appeal ('gimme', 'more', 'please'), or location ('there' 'down'), of action ('hug', 'come', 'comb', 'look'), of object ('hat', 'cheese', 'pants', 'key'), of agent ('me', 'you', 'Washoe', 'Roger'), and attribute ('black', 'funny', 'sorry').

Further, she uses words in combination. She has twelve pivot[1] words (listed here in order of frequency): 'come gimme', 'please', 'you', 'go', 'me', 'hurry', 'more', 'up', 'open', 'out', 'in', 'food'. And she is able to combine these with various other words in such combinations as agent-action ('Roger tickle'), action-object ('tickle Washoe') object-attribute ('comb black'). This capacity strongly suggests the beginnings of grammar. It resembles the first language combinations of young children.

5.3.2 Sarah

Anne and David Premack (Premack and Premack, 1972) have been training another chimpanzee, Sarah, in language. Like the Gardners they argue that language consists of signs which are given meaning. It doesn't in the last resort matter whether 'stop' is spoken, is written, is indicated by a red light, or by someone with a hand raised: the essential

1 A 'pivot' word is one of a small number of the kind which are found at a certain stage in the vocabulary of young children, used with a larger number of 'open' words; thus in 'want dindin', 'want mum', 'want teddy', 'want' would be the pivot word. See Part 2, further work on Chapter 5.

meaning is still the same. So if a chimpanzee, when given a red plastic ring, understands stop, and gives it to you intending you to stop, she is using language.

As it happens 'stop' was not one of the verbs taught to Sarah, but she was taught verbs such as 'is', 'give', 'take', 'insert', 'wash'; nouns such as 'Sarah', 'pail', 'dish', 'chocolate', 'banana', 'Mary'; and adjectives such as 'red', 'yellow', 'brown', 'green'. Also she learned a class of words (called concepts/conditionals) to relate one word to another,

Figure 5 The symbols on the magnetic board read 'Sarah insert pail banana dish'. Sarah correctly put the apple in the pail and the banana in the dish, thus indicating that she understood sentence structure, not just word order (from *Scientific American*, October 1972, p.92)

such as 'same', 'different', 'colour of', 'no/not', 'if/then'. Each word was represented by a plastic symbol, varied in colour, shape and size, and backed with metal so that it would adhere to a magnetic board.

Sarah learned the word 'banana', for example, in the following way: she was given a slice of banana on numerous occasions; then one day the slice of banana was placed out of reach but a pink plastic square was placed close to her. She had to place the square on the magnetic board before receiving the banana. When she could do this, 'apple' was substituted and she had to place a blue plastic triangle on the board, and so on. Later on she was taught 'give'. Attention was paid to ensuring she could distinguish it from other words. When she put 'give apple' on the board she was given an apple; when she put up 'wash apple' the apple was placed in a bowl of water and washed. A significant step forward came when she learned the words 'name of' (a real apple and the plastic symbol were placed side by side and she was required to put the symbol 'name of' in between). When she has grasped this, she could learn new nouns by placing the symbol, 'name of', and the object side by side.

Sarah is reported to be able to form sentences of the order of 'Mary give raisin Sarah', 'Raisin different apple', 'Red colour of apple'. She can even read and carry out the instruction 'Sarah insert apple pail banana dish', getting the apple in the pail and the banana in the dish. However, unlike Washoe, who seems to initiate utterances, Sarah seldom does this, but principally responds to problems set by the experimenter. When plastic tokens are left at hand she almost never makes use of them to give a message.

5.4 Discussion

The communication of bees, fascinating and complex though it is, obviously does not resemble human language. Bees have an angry aggressive hum when they are disturbed, but a bee could not combine this hum with its round dance (meaning nectar is within 100 metres) to mean 'An enemy is within 100 metres and must be exterminated'. In contrast human beings can combine their symbols: we can say 'enemy at 100 metres' or 'nectar at 100 metres' without any difficulty. Obviously we do so according to certain rules—it would be meaningless to say '100 nectar metres at'—and these are the rules of grammar. There are obviously ways in which the communication of Washoe and Sarah is unlike human language (see Hockett's list in Part 2, further work on Chapter 5), but in one important way it does seem to be like language: the various symbols can be used in relation to each other, in something the same way that humans combine symbols to produce language.

Previously it had been thought that animals were able to understand individual words and even (as in the case of Vicki) to use a few of them, but not to be able to understand them (much less to use them) in combination. The case of Washoe, and much more of Sarah, casts doubt on this. They seem to be understanding words in combination, the combinations being those of a human language (English). One difference between apes and human beings certainly seems to be that while man evolved his own language with its rules, the chimpanzees have not done so, although they can at least learn something of these rules and their applications. It seems that, when given training, they are capable of using words in relation to one another, and this implies a capacity for thought beyond what we would expect. How far they would develop these thinking powers in the wild without training we do not know.

Two notes of warning have been sounded by Roger Brown (1973, p. 45). He refers to the 'clever Hans problem' and the 'ping-pong' problem. Before the First World War there was a horse called Hans. His trainer would pose him a problem in addition or multiplication, for instance, and the horse would give the correct number of taps with his forefoot. However, it was proved that his trainer's posture, held until the right answer was reached, gave the horse his clue. Blindfolded his arithmetic was non-existent. Again, the psychologist Skinner trained pigeons to play something that looked very like ping pong, but was not in essentials. The point of the first story is that we must be sure that the apparent successes of Sarah do not derive from clues other than language; the point of the second is that what seems similar to human language is not necessarily the same as human language. It is fair to say that the experimenters are very much aware of these difficulties.

5.5 Summary

Certain creatures such as bees seem to have quite a complex signalling system. It is fixed, however, and thus does not resemble human language. Recently certain chimpanzees have been taught a visual language which has apparently some features of human language (such as elementary grammar).

6

Aspects of language

6.1 Questions about language

There were two cannibals. One cannibal said, 'I don't like your mother-in-law'. The other replied, 'Never mind, just eat the chips'.

Let us suppose these cannibals spoke English as their native language. We would not consider their ability to make such remarks extraordinary: they would seem to constitute an everyday exchange on an everyday matter (without, of course, the humour they may have for us). Yet to produce comparatively simple sentences like these requires the knowledge of a variety of rules, which both use, but which neither could state.

We may uncover some of these rules if we take the first sentence, and ask about two of the words the following questions:

Why, is the word placed where it is?

Why does it have the form that it does?

Why is it pronounced as it is?

6.1.1 Why is it placed where it is?

I Why, for instance, is this sentence

(a) 'I don't like your mother-in-law' not

(b) 'Don't I like your mother-in-law'

(b) 'Don't like I your mother-in-law'

(c) 'Don't like your I mother-in-law'?

If we place the subject, 'I', after the auxiliary verb, the sentence becomes a question. In quaint Victorian poetry we might get 'don't like I' but it is surprising. The last example begins to be confusing. We place words in a particular order, in this case the subject before the verb and the auxiliary verb, because we understand them to have particular meaning in that order. There are some permissible variants to change meaning, as in (b), but others are quite meaningless, as in (d).

Like The only variant position for 'like' which would make any sense would be at the end—'I don't your mother-in-law like'—and this would sound like a comic foreigner in a TV commercial.

6.1.2 Why does it have the form it does?
I The first person singular need not be represented by 'I': it can be represented by 'me'. The reference is the same. But when we use it as a subject, the convention is that we use 'I'; when we use it as an object, or when it is governed by a preposition, the convention is that we use 'me'.
Like Two forms—'like' and 'likes'—are possible in the present tense. The convention is that only the third person singular (he/she/it) takes 'likes'. If 'like' is used there will be no confusion. 'Liked' indicates the past tense, and if used in the sentence would cause confusion about the time of the action.

6.1.3 Why is it pronounced as it is?
I If we pronounced 'I' to rhyme with 'me', it might be confused with 'he', for example. The same applies to 'like', which could be confused with 'lake' perhaps. We pronounce words in certain ways because that is how we understand them.

There are, however, two other matters connected with pronunciation we should mention. One is pitch. If the second cannibal had echoed the first—'You don't like my mother-in-law?' —the pitch would have risen at the end, and the statement become a question. The other is stress. In the sentence 'I don't like your mother-in-law', the natural stresses come on 'like' and 'moth-': to stress other words ('in', for example) would either create somewhat different meanings, or sound rather peculiar. 'I' is not heavily stressed: to stress it would imply a contrast between the speaker and those who adore the mother-in-law.

6.1.4 Discussion
Let us attempt to draw together the preceding ideas.

Language consists of words, that is, *lexis*, and of rules for using them. These rules are rules of *grammar* and rules of *phonology*. The first two questions we asked were about grammar, the third about phonology.

The first question we asked was about the arrangement of words in the sentence—its *syntax*. The cannibal saying 'I don't like your mother-in-law' is using English syntax. He knows in which order the words must be used in order to make the sense he intends, and we mentioned some of the rules he is unconsciously using. The rules are not the same in every language. If the comic foreigner says 'I don't your mother-in-law like', it is doubtless because in his own language the verb naturally (and uncomically) comes at the end of the sentence.

The second question concerned the form of words. This aspect of grammar is called *accidence*. We alter words for particular reasons. Sometimes the alteration is so great that there is no apparent connection between one form of the word and the other, as in the case of the present and past tense of some verbs—is/was, bring/brought. Sometimes there is a minor difference—like/likes, hurry/hurries. The main reasons for alterations are in changes of tense, and changes of number (singular to plural, or vice versa).

If the syntax is different from what we intend, the meaning goes wrong. A phrase such as 'Men like women' is not the same as 'Women like men'. But if our accidence is unconventional, as in 'Mens like womens', the sentence is, if strange, perfectly understandable. In general, accidence is less important than syntax in conveying meaning.

The third question concerned the pronunciation of words and sentences. This is called phonology—the pronunciation of individual sounds and groups of sounds; their pitch; the stresses upon them. These last two together make up the tune or intonation of a sentence. The intonation of 'Only here for the beer' is different, if it is a question, from the intonation if it is a statement. In the sentence 'What's his name' the phonology is different according to whether it is:

(a) a reply to 'Who's coming?' (when it is equivalent to 'thingummy')
(b) a question by someone who has forgotten the name
(c) a question by someone who does not know the name.

6.2 Levels of language

We thus have what are called three levels of language:

1 The words themselves (lexis)
2 The rules for arranging them and adjusting them (grammar)
3 The rules for using them in speech (phonology).

But words are sounds, and to arrange sounds by rules is useless unless some meaning results. Supposing we have three discs—red, green, yellow. In themselves, in whatever order they are arranged, they have no meaning. But they become meaningful in two ways. Firstly because we assign a meaning to each: red for danger, green for safety, yellow for caution. Secondly, because we arrange them in a particular order—red, yellow, green (the traffic signals)—in relation to one another. This, we might say, is their syntax. But they also have to be lit up, in the order red, red-and-yellow, green, yellow, red. This we could regard as being equivalent to a rule of phonology.

6.3 Meaning

We are now able to answer a further question about our original cannibal sentence.

6.3.1 Why does it mean what it does?

I We agree that the sound we represent on paper by 'I' shall refer to the speaker himself (the first person singular). But this is not sufficient to determine meaning if the sentence is spoken, because this sound is exactly the same as that for 'eye' and 'aye'. So we need to know about the word or words next to it, its context. That word is 'don't'. We have, therefore, a subject and a verb, which are very likely to occur together. Had the next word been 'lash', the probability of the first word being 'eye' would have been much higher. But against that we don't usually begin a sentence with 'eyelash'. It is unlikely to be 'aye' ('aye, lash' being perhaps only possible as a confirmation to the bosun to wield the cat o' nine tails).

Like This point about the relationship of one word to the next is brought out further in the word 'like'. We may consider we know the meaning of this word. But the humour of the story is dependent on the fact that the two sentences give us two possible meanings for it. We take the first cannibal to mean 'have affection for', whereas it is clear from the second cannibal's answer that he in fact meant 'enjoy the taste of'.

There is another clue to the meaning—the situation itself. The two cannibals are feasting, so it is quite natural they should talk about the food. But the listener perhaps does not quite realize this at first.

Clues to meaning, therefore, arise from words themselves, in the context of other words, and in the context of situation.

6.3.2 Words and meaning

There is, of course, no essential relationship between the words and their meanings. A man called Bert Smellie recently changed his name to Fred Smellie, but he was still the same man. If we all agreed that the names 'hippopotamus' amd 'headmaster' should be exchanged, so that the principal of the school was called a hippopotamus and the African beast a headmaster, this would be perfectly satisfactory. No one would be surprised when we spoke of the hippopotamus taking morning assembly, and the headmaster wallowing in the mud. Thus we say language is arbitrary: any word can have any meaning, *as long as we all agree to it.*

6.4 Summary

Language is thought of as having three aspects or levels—lexis, grammar, phonology—which together make up meaning. (Meaning is sometimes called the fourth level.) Language is arbitrary in that there seems no particular reason why one set of symbols or group of them should have one meaning rather than another.

7

Universals of language

7.1 Language families

Even a casual observer notices that there are similarities between
different languages. English schoolchildren learning their first French
lessons find words, like *table, crayon, balle,* and *ballon*, that resemble
English words. There are a variety of reasons for these similarities.
Sometimes one language has borrowed from another; sometimes one
language goes back to a common origin with another.

The Romans took Latin throughout Europe, and over centuries it
changed differently in different countries, becoming Italian, Spanish,
French, or Roumanian, and this accounts for the many resemblances
between these languages. It has long been held that we can go much
further with this 'family tree' idea, and that in fact very many European
and Indian languages can be traced back to a single language, Indo-
European, originally spoken in 3000 or 4000 B.C. by peoples living in
Northern or Central Europe. Similarly it has been argued that there are
twelve other language groups in other parts of the world. Latin is clearly
the common ancestor of several languages, but whether we can say that
a large number of Indian and European languages did develop from a
single original, like the branches of a family tree, and whether this
applies in other language groups, is now being questioned. Perhaps
instead a large number of languages grew up independently, but over-
lapped like rings made by throwing a number of stones into a pond, and
where this happened they shared or developed words in common.

7.2 Similarities in syntax

At any rate the similarity of languages in certain particulars is un-
questionable. But it goes much further than the borrowing of certain
words, such as 'piano', 'ravioli', or 'spaghetti' from Italian.

Let us take an English sentence: 'The little dog bites the big man'. In other languages this is

Le	petit	chien	mord	le	gros	monsieur	(French)
Der	kleine	Hund	beisst	den	grossen	Mann	(German)
	xiao	gou	yao		da	ren	(Chinese)
To	mikro	skilli	dagoni	ton	megalo	andra	(Greek)

It is interesting that in these sentences the order or syntax of the words is exactly the same. It is true that in French adjectives (other than short common adjectives like *petit* and *gros*) follow the noun, but the French order is still basically the same as the others. Where differences arise they are in the accidence: in French the adjectives agree with the nouns in gender and number; the same is true in German, which has the additional feature that a distinct form can be found for subject and object. In these languages, and a large number of others, the pattern is subject verb object (SVO). There are languages with other orders, such as SOV: in Amharic, spoken in Ethiopia, the sentence would be

| Tinishu | wusha | tilikun | sawun | yineksal |
| Little | dog | big | man | bites |

But even in this example the subject precedes the object.

7.2.1 Syntactic patterns
But the interesting question is not so much why there are differences between the grammars of some languages, as why there is such a lot of similarity. Why should Chinese have exactly the same pattern as English, though there can have been no possible connection between them at the time they were being evolved? Why should languages which do not necessarily have completely the same order, such as Amharic and English, nevertheless all contain subjects, verbs, and objects? These similarities we call 'linguistic universals'—what is universal, or common to a large number of languages.

7.3 Linguistic universals

7.3.1 Syntax
As far as syntax is concerned, in all the world's languages there seems to be a basic subject-verb-object relationship, though not necessarily in

that order. Greenberg (1961, Ch. 5) examined 30 languages and found that this relationship exists in all of them, and that there is a dominant order. In a simple declarative sentence, the dominant order is the one in which the subject precedes the object. The orders are given below, but with English words for convenience.

Boy eats cake	(SVO)
Boy cake eats	(SOV)
Eats boy cake	(VSO)

As far as is known, however, we do not find

Eats cake boy	(VOS)
Cake boy eats	(OSV)
Cake eats boy	(OVS)

7.3.2 Accidence

The samples in different languages of 'The little dog bites the big man' have a certain amount of accidence in common, in that they have ways of indicating, for example, number and gender. It would be possible for a language to operate without accidence, or at least with very little. English has less than German. Languages such as Creoles and pidgins have much less than English. But leaving aside these special cases it appears that all traditional languages do have some accidence, and some rules for its use. Greenberg's work revealed the following rules (amongst others): 'If either the subject or object noun agrees with the verb in gender, then the adjective always agrees with the noun in gender'. 'If a language has a category of gender, it always has a category of number'. 'If in a language the verb follows the nominal subject and nominal object as the dominant order, the language almost always has a case system' (as in German or Latin).

7.3.3 Phonology

It may seem that, as far as phonology is concerned, there are few similarities between different languages. But on a level of greater generality these do exist. All language is primarily spoken (although it may also be transmitted through other means, such as writing). It is not a language of gesture. It does not proceed on one continuous steady note, or a varied wail like a siren, but is modified by intonation—pitch, stress, and jointure (pauses). Also it seems as if in all languages the phonology serves not just to transmit the message but also to add to its meaning at the same time. We may note, for instance, the effect of emphasizing each word in turn in a sentence like 'I will go now'.

7.3.4 Semantics

So far we have discussed lexical, grammatical, and phonological universals. Can we also speak about semantic universals? That is, are there any similarities in the way in which meaning is expressed in different languages? Very little is known about this. It does seem, however, that there are some correspondences in, for instance, metaphors, onomatopoeia, and euphemisms. Thus in many languages evil is associated with darkness, good with light, kindness with warmth ('warm reception'), hostility with cold ('cold disdain'). Phrases derived from parts of the body—'the heart of the matter', 'the neck of a bottle'— occur in many languages (Ullman, 1961).

7.4 Implications

What are the implications of our observations?

Consider two tribes of ape-men on separate islands, divided by thousands of miles of sea, with no possible means of contact over thousands of years. They gradually evolve to primitive human state and develop a means of communication. Why, instead of choosing gesture as a medium and producing sign language, do they choose sound? Why, having chosen sound, do they both choose to use it in the form of individual 'words'? Why are those words in classes like 'noun', 'verb', and so forth? For instance, why do they not choose a class of word to describe a whole event. Thus *pex* might mean 'dragon flying', or *slix* mean 'dragon eating'. Why do they arrange to have their subjects before their objects? And so on.

On these two islands both peoples walk upright. Why did not one walk on all fours, or upon their hands?

The answer to both sets of questions seems to be the same. It is natural to man to walk upright on two feet, and it is natural to him to develop language, and language of a particular kind. There has never been discovered a tribe whose members walk upon two legs and one hand, gesticulating with the other hand, or, if talking, doing so without using nouns, verbs, or adjectives (in, for instance, the form of a continuous yodelling).

7.5 Summary

We can speak of features common to all languages, known as linguistic universals. These features suggest that the capacity   to produce language is innate in man.

8

Basic language

8.1 How simple can you get?

There was a child standing in Nellie's shop in Barnt Green. His mother snapped at him: 'Don't you never touch none of them sweets'. The rebuke was well deserved, for the child's behaviour might well be described as pestilential, and he was in any case well gorged on chocolate crisp.

One might criticize the mother's language for its redundancy (it communicates a negative three times), although one sympathizes with her need to be emphatic. However, redundancy is not just confined to occasions such as this. It is part and parcel of language, even when language is being used 'correctly'. In the quotations from different languages in the previous chapter, for instance, there were many instances of this.

Let us take a fresh example: 'Yesterday a guest was arriving'. In this sentence we are told twice (by 'yesterday' and 'was') that it took place in the past, and we are told twice that there was one guest (by the singular form 'guest', and by the singular verb).

Let us cut out all unnecessary signals: 'Yesterday guest arrive'. Further, if it was clear from the context we were speaking of yesterday, all we need say is 'guest arrive'.

This is not a merely theoretical exercise, for it is in effect exactly what has happened with those forms of language called pidgins and Creoles.

8.2 Pidgin

On various occasions two people have come together and have had to communicate without a common language. European explorers, traders, and settlers throughout the world would not trouble to learn the language of the peoples they came into contact with; and these peoples had to begin to learn theirs, imperfectly, simplifying and perhaps modifying it with language habits from their own tongue. Europeans hearing the natives' attempts at English would attempt to simplify their language, sometimes using baby talk. In Africa, China, and Melanesia there are pidgins based on Portuguese, Spanish, French, and English (though this does not exhaust the list). The view that the term 'pidgin' is a mispronunciation of 'business' is not now widely held. It is sometimes said to come from *pidian* (perhaps meaning 'people'), a word probably from the local Indians which was used in the short-lived British colony at the mouth of the Oyapock river in South America in 1605-6. However, for various reasons, the Hebrew *pidjom* ('barter') seems more likely.

Here is an example of Papuan pidgin with a literal translation.

MERI HOLIM WORK
girl   obtains job
Wanpela yangpela Papuan meri bambai   holim wok olsem   namba
a   young   Papuan girl by and by obtain work all same (as) number
wan kuskus long Lokal Gavman   Asosiesin   bilong Papua Nuigini
one official of   Local Government Association of   Papua New Guinea
insait   long mun   Septemba long dispela yia
inside (in) of   month September of   this   year

Many of the words are only slightly changed from their English originals, but widened in meaning: *holim* is from 'hold' (the *-im* ending implies a direct object); *long, bilong* are from 'belong', and important prepositions, replacing words like 'of', 'for', 'at', 'with'. There is no future tense indicated in the verb: instead the word *bambai* ('by and by') is added. *Wanpela* was originally 'one fellow', but now is the equivalent of 'a' or 'one' (*sampela* is the plural, 'some').

Taim mun   Ogas   i   pinis Miss Loko bai   i   go kisim wanpela
time month August he finish Miss Loko by and by she go join   a
kos   bilong Lokal Gavman   long Vunadidir Lokal Gavman   Treining Skul
course on   Local Government at   Vunadidir Local Government Training School
i stap klostu long Rabaul
it stay close to   Rabaul

Whole phrases are sometimes used to do a job that in English might be carried by a single word. In the previous passage *namba wan kuskus* was used for 'secretary' and in this *i stap klostu long Rabaul* for 'near Rabaul'. There is the same simplicity of the future tense device: the verb stays the same whatever the subject (*i pinis* for 'it finishes'). Notice that *i* (originally 'he') is used for 'he', 'she', or 'it'.

8.3 Creole

A pidgin is not the native language of any race or people. It grows up when speakers of one language need to communicate with those of another, and is mainly a simplified version of the language of the dominant race. Thus most of the words in the examples we have looked at could be traced back to English. Often the chief contribution of the non-dominant language is from its phonology: pidgin speakers use much the same intonation and phonology as they would in their own language.

Sometimes the non-dominant people lose their own language in the course of time, and pidgin becomes their mother tongue. In this case it becomes known as a Creole language. It seems that West Africans, imported as slaves to the American continent in the seventeenth and eighteenth centuries, began by communicating with their masters in pidgin English, then lost their native language and spoke only pidgin, which thus became Creole. Once such a language becomes a mother tongue it tends to re-expand its structure and vocabulary; and if it continues to be spoken where the original dominant language is still spoken and has prestige, as, for instance, English does in the West Indies, it can be modified again in the direction of this language. Thus in Jamaica we find a spectrum of language ranging all the way from the very aberrant 'bongo talk' of isolated groups in the mountains, to the provincial standard English of town dwellers in, say, Kingston. Some differences between Creole as spoken, for instance, in Guyana and standard English are as follows:

A simple verb form whatever the subject ('I/you/he come')
A present tense whether meaning is present or past ('Nobody remember' for 'Nobody remembered')
Omission of verb 'to be' ('Mr. Arthur comin')
Plural of nouns same as singulars ('de mango')
No 's to indicate possessives ('Mr. Arthur fruit')
Subject case usually used for all personal pronouns, whether subject or object ('He told he'), though on occasion object case may be used in the same way ('Him told him')

It would be wrong to regard Creoles as debased versions of English: they are languages in their own right. We cannot, for instance, argue that, because Creole does not have the more complex way of indicating past and future tenses that English has, it cannot indicate time past and time future effectively, any more than we can argue that English is inferior to German on the same grounds. This is not to say that Creole is often as highly regarded as standard English in countries where it has grown up. But this is a matter of the status of a language and is different from the adequacy of the language itself. It is closely related to the prestige in the community of the group which speaks it.

8.4 Immigrant language

Quite apart from its linguistic interest the relevance of some knowledge of Creole is clear. Many West Indians immigrating to the United Kingdom speak an English which has characteristics of Creole to a greater or lesser extent; and the 'black dialects' of the United States developed in a similar way to the Creoles of the West Indies—from the English-based pidgins used for communication between the slaves on the southern plantations and their white masters.

Let us consider the problems of some West Indian children. The pronunciation of individual words and the intonation of the English teacher will be strange and be a cause of non-comprehension, as indeed the pronunciation of a Glaswegian is to many English people. The child's own pronunciation will be different from that of U.K. classmates. This seldom presents a serious and continuing problem, and in any case the way we speak is so much part of ourselves, and our group identity, that attempts to change it deliberately are ill-advised. For this reason the Schools Council project, *Teaching English to West Indian Children*, now renamed *Concept 7 to 9,* concentrated its efforts (in the 'Dialect Kit') on enabling the children to read and write standard English rather than to speak it.

In reading, all children face the problem that their spoken language and the standard written language do not match very well. The West Indian child will have added difficulties caused by the dialect. Progress can be good until the child needs to make use of phonic clues to the sound of a new word. 'The cat sat on the mat', for instance, could be pronounced 'Di kyat sit pan di mat' by a young Creole-speaking child. The central sounds in 'cat', 'sat', and 'mat' for him are all different from the sounds in standard English. Spelling difficulties are naturally linked with reading difficulties.

As far as writing is concerned there are grammatical differences between Creole and standard English, as we have seen. In the following

Jamaican Creole sentences, for example, the verb 'to be' is not expressed, and certain other differences will be noted.

Di bwai tomi veri big
The boy's tummy is very big
A no fi yu baal ya
It is not your ball—this

On the other hand it is included (presumably because of the influence of the standard language) in

Im de a yaad
He is at home (yard)
Dis uman-ya a di bwai momi
This woman is the boy's mother

It is clear that a West Indian child speaking forms such as these will have a greater difficulty than many U.K. children in writing standard English. It is important to realize that such children are not using 'bad grammar' but the proper forms of a language in some ways different from English.

8.5 Summary

Languages are redundant: they use more means than are strictly necessary for communication. Some languages, pidgins, originated from a deliberate stripping down of a redundant language, and in course of time became Creoles, developing features different from the original dominant language.

9

Functions of language

9.1 Linguistic ability

There is a common belief that our ability to express ourselves in words is related to the extent of our vocabulary. Not many years ago a publisher would advertize 'It pays to increase your word power' and would sell you books enabling you to do this. In principle these were vocabulary lists with definitions which you were expected to learn. Thus a word like 'hagiographer' would be printed, with its definition, 'a student of the lives of saints'. How often this was likely to come up in conversation was not stated. Someone wanting to describe such a man, but not knowing the word, could always say 'He studies the lives of saints'. The possession of a sizable, largely unused vocabulary is no guarantee of our ability to express ourselves well.

On the other hand it is undeniable that we need some vocabulary to avoid the word 'hagiographer', and we need to be able to choose the correct form of, and arrange, words like 'study', 'life', 'saint' to mean the same thing. It is, however, surprising how well we can express ourselves with few and simple words. Some years ago 'basic English' was devised for the benefit of foreigners learning English. This cut down vocabulary to about 850 words. Thus 'The demonstration occurred at night' could become 'The protest took place at night' and 'The private secretary corresponded with the men who owed the money' could become 'The private secretary sent letters to the debtors'. The English language possesses, for instance, words like 'get' which can be used in combination to avoid other words: 'get off' (dismount), 'get away' (escape), 'get away with' (avoid punishment), and so on. In fact these are often, particularly in the spoken language, the normal usages.

Nor is the ability to use long or complex sentences any guarantee of effective expression. Many passages of the authorized version of the Bible, or of poetry like much of Blake's, are written with great simplicity of vocabulary and grammar. Until comparatively recently it used to be common in tests of linguistic ability to award marks on the length of sentence, number and variety of adjectives, and so on, but this is only of limited use. With very young children such criteria can have some validity—a child at two will have shorter sentences, and fewer words than that child at four—but for older children such tests have to be treated with great circumspection.

What is now being realized is that people's linguistic ability depends not on the amount or complexity of the language they possess, but on what they can do with what they possess. Thus there is a kind of conversation which we call 'exchanging the time of day' or 'small talk'. This sort of language has the function of easing social relationships rather than exchanging information. It does not require a large vocabulary (in fact, a comparatively limited one will suffice, so long as you know the topics to talk on), but some people find it hard to manage. This is, of course, only one of many functions we use language for.

9.2 Functions of language in 4-year-olds

9.2.1 A conversation between 4-year-olds

Here is a conversation between two children aged 4, Edmund and Lois, preparing to play at zoos with the writer. They have on the floor between them a large 'zoo tray' in which, at the moment, the zoo equipment (animals, fences, buildings, trees, etc.) are piled higgledy-piggledy. Let us look at the uses they are making of their language:

Lois	can I have the giraffe
Edmund	(*deliberately funny voice*) no I'll have that/o da de da de doh doh/doh de do doooh . . . I'll have that/I want the teddy bear/right/eh were going to sleep today/ oh oh Im going to sleep today (*rhythmic*) eh eh fell in the house/Im going to sleep today
Lois	oh clear all this zoo out
Edmund	bash
Lois	Im going to clear this zoo up I am
Edmund	oh dont youll have a mess
Lois	pardon
Edmund	youll have a mess/dr wilkinsons got to do that/dont touch the microphone
Lois	why

Edmund	cause you cant
Lois	why cant you
Edmund	cause its uncle toms
Lois	why is it uncle toms
Edmund	because it stays here/hell take it back to uncle toms/its uncle/because its dr wilkins/its dr wilkinsons/ dont touch that/its poisoned (*she touches railway turntable*)
Lois	whats poisoned
Edmund	that turntable
Lois	it isnt/really
Edmund	it is/it is really
Lois	you can touch it sometimes cant you/going round fast isnt it
Edmund	eh eh youve got poison on your fingers/dont make that noise because . . . .

This is only a short sample, but a variety of language uses may be seen.

9.2.2 Discussion

The language is used to *carry on a relationship* between the two children. This is crucial to our social life, and much mental disorder seems to occur among people who are unable to use language in such a way. There are some children who cannot play together even though they are playing alongside one another.

Inseparable from a relationship is the *maintenance of identity*. Edmund is using language to assert his dominant role (he is a boy, it is his zoo, it is his house).

We may use language *to control or affect the behaviour of others*, be it by commands or the gentlest of persuasions. Edmund is clearly anxious to do this in the matter of why Lois shouldn't touch the microphone or the turntable.

The giving of reasons or explanations is another function of language. Edmund's reasons why Lois shouldn't clear the zoo up, or touch the microphone or the turntable clearly display imagination, and it is a pity that his master stroke about the turntable being poisoned fails to convince Lois.

For her part Lois is anxious to *find out the reasons, to explore by means of language*. Questioning ('Why can't you?') is one of the major means of *exploring and making discoveries* about people and the world about us.

Lois is not concerned to assert herself but to get on with the job in hand. She sets out her future: 'I'm going to clear this zoo up I am'.

This is related to, but rather different from, *speculation or hypotheses* about the possibilities. We see this in Edmund's prediction that if she clears up the zoo she'll 'have a mess'.

The early passage in which Edmund adopts a deliberately funny voice illustrates several uses of language. We can use language to *enter into the feelings of others*. This is what Edmund is doing when he takes the teddy bear, rocks it, and puts words into its mouth 'I'm going to sleep today' (he then lets it drop). Associated with this on this occasion is the use of *language for mimicry*. In addition, language is being used here largely for its own sake, as a sort of *celebration*, both in the part-sung nonsense words and in the words attributed to the bear—an activity associated with the delight children have in songs and nursery rhymes at this age. This is a function of language that poets often employ.

Of course, there is a certain *giving of information*, particularly by Edmund to Lois, but we can see that in this passage this is not a principal function of the language, but subordinate to other functions. The (entirely false) information that the recorder is Uncle Tom's is there to provide explanation.

There are other uses of language not represented here. For example, there is the very common one of *telling about some past event*, actual or fictional. Much gossip is of this kind ('So she said to me she said...') Members of families at the end of the day, or friends when they meet, often catch up on events which have happened since they last talked. In this way they use language to *make sense of experience*. Associated with this is an *analytical use of language* in which one may distance oneself from what is being thought about, be it even one's own feeling and behaviour.

These functions are not mutually exclusive. Several of them may be carried out even in one sentence: one can give information, explain, tell about a past event, and assert one's independence all at the same time. In any extended passage of language then, whatever the overall purpose being served, there are bound to be a variety of functions being carried out also. Thus in what we describe as passing the time of day, gossiping, having a conversation, having a discussion, giving a speech, talking in a committee, each word, phrase, or sentence may well demonstrate a further use, or further uses, of language.

We have said that people's ability to express themselves is not merely a matter of the amount of their vocabulary or the length of their sentences. We need to take into account how well they use the language they have in order to fulfil a variety of human needs. Most people can employ the above functions of language to some extent, but it is the extent to which they do so that constitutes the value of language for them. Everybody can hold a discussion we may say, but this is not necessarily true: some people argue rather than discuss, and they may even assert points of view without beginning to argue. This is often because the more detailed functions of language—to explain, explore, enter into others' feelings—are escaping them.

9.3 Summary

In some TV games one may be at a loss if, when asked the definition of, say, 'branchcephalic', one cannot reply 'a term used in ethnology in the description of skulls, meaning short headed'. But in the normal occurrences of life it is not the lack of particular vocabulary which causes people problems, so much as a difficulty in being able to handle language flexibly, in a variety of functions—to relate to others; to empathize with them; to be aware through language of one's own thoughts and feelings; to analyse, discuss, interpret; to hypothesize ('What would happen if . . . .'), and so on.

10

Descriptions of language function

Various people have made lists of language functions, but there is as yet no agreement as to how many significant uses we should take account of. It depends partly on the purpose for which we want to use the list, partly on how detailed we want to be. Thus in the previous section we've been talking about general categories—analysing, informing, speculating, and so on. The three accounts of language function given below are more detailed.

10.1 Models of language

10.1.1 Seven functions of language
M.A.K. Halliday (1973) gives a general account, in which he discusses seven functions or models—instrumental, regulatory, interactional, heuristic, personal, imaginative, and representational. (See Part 2, further work on Chapter 10.) He emphasizes that from an early age children have a knowledge of the nature of language: the child knows what language is because he knows what language does (1969, p. 27). And the child knows what language does because he does things with it. In another article (1971) he develops this, emphasizing that all our language is part of our social behaviour and expresses our attitudes. Thus in regulatory language (controlling the behaviour of others) the mother could have a range of choices from 'You're not to do that again' to 'I'd like you to stay and help me at home', 'Daddy doesn't like you to play rough games', 'We don't want people to think we don't look after you' or 'You might have hurt yourself on all that glass'.

10.1.2 Categories for writing
A second description of functions comes from J.L. Britton (1971), who devises them for application to written work. A large amount of our

speech is face to face, intimate, unrehearsed—walking a street with a friend, commenting on a shop or a new building, telling him of a past incident, exchanging a confidence. Britton calls this expressive speech. This sort of speech fulfils many of the functions described in the previous section. From it might develop, though there is no need for this to happen, 'poetic' language on the one hand and 'transactional' language on the other. By 'poetic' he means not just a poem, but any language which is shaped and organized into something in and for itself: a poem certainly, but also a novel, a play, an anecdote or joke skilfully told. By 'transactional' he means language for 'getting the world's work done', from that we use in buying hamburger and chips, or negotiating for a house, to that used in arguing a case in a report or a court of law. Britton argues that these second two, 'poetic' and 'transactional' language, only develop if there is experience of the expressive mode.

10.1.3 Ideational and relational uses

A third set of functions is used in the work of Joan Tough (1974), partly as a refinement of the Halliday categories. She feels it useful to divide language uses into two, the 'relational' and the 'ideational'. By the 'relational' she means those functions which 'maintain the self' (we saw how Edmund was doing this), and those which relate to other people in responding to them, taking them into account. By the 'ideational' she means those uses which are directional, directing one's own and other's actions; which are interpretative, organizing and reflecting an experience; and which are predictive, or hypothesizing, imaginative, or empathetic. It is interesting to note that she discerns class differences in some of these uses amongst children as young as 3 years of age. She writes:

The children of professional workers used language five times as often as the other group for predicting and for collaborating in action with others, three times as often for the interpretive use of language beyond the level of the monitoring of their experiences, and five times as often for projecting through the imagination to a scene not present except through the use of language. The children from the homes of unskilled and semi-skilled manual workers used speech almost three times as often to secure attention for their own needs and to maintain their own status by defending or asserting themselves in the face of the needs and actions of others, and twice as often to parallel or monitor their own actions, as the children of professional workers.

(Tough, 1969)

10.2 A classification of language functions

As we have indicated, there are various ways of classifying language functions. Each have their particular advantages. The categories below are drawn from young children's talk, such as the dialogue between Edmund and Lois in the previous chapter.

In any interchange it is likely that there will be three kinds of activity going on. One is concerned with the self-expression of the individual, the maintenance of his *amour propre*, the defence of his own territory. This is concerned with the question 'Who am I?' It is a matter of introspection, self awareness, as well as assertion. A second is concerned with the relationships with others: establishing contact, maintaining bonds, moving between intimacy and distance, co-operating. There are also matters of understanding, sympathizing with, getting inside the other, guiding the other. This language is concerned with 'Who are you?' A third kind of activity is concerned with exploring, describing, analysing, reflecting on, explaining the world that was, that is, that will be. This is concerned with the question 'Who or what is it, was it, will it be?'

An apparently simple question, 'Where are you going?', could be fulfilling all three kinds of activity: asserting the rights of the speaker to know; establishing or keeping contact with someone else, and attempting perhaps to alter his intention; and obtaining information. Here are the categories set out:

Who am I?	1	Establishing and maintaining self
	2	Language for analysing self
	3	Language for expressing self (for celebrating or despairing, etc.)
Who are you?	4	Establishing and maintaining relationships
	5	Co-operating
	6	Empathising, understanding the other
	7	Role playing, mimicry
	8	Guiding, directing the other
Who/what is he/she/it?	9	Giving information
	10	Recalling past events (past)

Descriptions of language function

11 Describing present events (present)
12 Predicting future events—statement of intention
statement of hypothesis,
what might happen

13 Analysing, classifying
14 Explaining, giving reasons for
15 Exploring—asking questions, but in other ways also, by
'sounding out' people
16 Reflecting on own/others' thoughts and feelings

11

Relationships of language and thought

11.1 Ways of thinking

Language is a system of symbols for representing thought. But what is thought, and is language the only way of representing it? Characteristically, thought is not the thing itself, but a representation of the thing itself. Thus the thought represented by 'Newcastle Brown Ale' is not the same as Newcastle Brown Ale; the statement 'Fred loves Nellie' is not the same as Fred actually loving Nellie. If we think of a landscape, kettle, or face of a friend, our mental representation is different from the landscape, kettle, or face itself. An interesting division of thought into three kinds has been made by Bruner (1964). Assuming that representation is a characteristic of thought he speaks of enactive, iconic, and symbolic representation.

11.1.1 Enactive representation
Perhaps it is easiest to take first some examples of enactive representation. There is a game in which a victim is blindfolded and given certain objects, ranging from soap to a pan scrubber or a jelly fish, to identify. To identify soap there must be some representation of it, as it were, in one's organs of touch, which enables one to recognize it. A more complex example would be the capacity people have to walk about a building or familiar streets with perfect confidence without having much of a mental picture of them. Witness the difficulty many people have in giving street directions. It is as though the body had some picture of them built into it. Driving and tying knots are other examples: few of us could visualize exactly what happened in changing gear, much less put it into words.

11.1.2 Iconic representation

By iconic representation is meant the mental pictures we have or can conjure up at will, and for which we may or may not have words. This may be of something simple like a table, or full of details like a football match; of something we know well like a banana, or something we have never seen, like a brontosaurus. It can be the 'picture' of a sound, as when a tune keeps running through our heads, or when we imagine the voice of a cuckoo or a well-known politician.

11.1.3 Symbolic representation

Symbolic representation can take various forms: traffic lights, for example, are visual symbols of 'stop', 'caution', 'go'. The most important symbol system is language. Linguistic representation is, of course, the putting of thought into words, and this distinguishes man from other animals. It enables him to deal with abstractions and generalizations and thus to develop his thinking to a higher level, as well as to communicate with others. It is possible to think about black puddings, Devon cream scones, or bangers and mash using iconic imagery, but the concept 'food', meaning all these and a lot more, seems to need the word itself; at least it is very helpful to have the word.

11.2 Roles of language

11.2.1 A regulatory function

The work of the Russian psychologist, Luria, stresses the importance of language in enabling us to *regulate* our behaviour. A pair of identical twins he studied were retarded in language compared with other children of their age because they communicated with each other (as twins often do) by 'synpraxic' means (a mixture of speech, gesture, and action) rather than by speech alone, and thus their speech did not develop greatly. He found that, when asked to carry out an instruction which was given in words—'Make a pattern with mosaics', for instance—they were unable to do so. Because they could not express the task in words themselves, they were unable to plan it, and persist in carrying it through. Presumably they had forgotten what they had to do. In Luria's words, 'constructive activity in accordance with a verbally formulated task was beyond our twins, who could not themselves formulate the task verbally and so provide a reinforcement when the corresponding activity began' (Luria and Yudevich, 1971, p. 82).

11.2.2 Language/thought interactions

Clearly language is important in the development of thinking. Nevertheless, it seems that thinking would develop without it. Piaget argues that, particularly in the earlier stages, thought and language develop parallel and gradually become more interlinked. That thought does develop without any or with very little language being associated with it is apparent from studies of children born deaf, though the degree to which their thinking is impaired, compared to that of hearing children, is a matter for debate. Language and thought are not the same. When we attempt to describe a scene to someone else we can only put part of it into words. And we have thoughts for which we cannot find the words: when we say something is on the 'tip of the tongue' it is not really there at all, but presumably on the 'tip of the mind'.

11.3 Thought and communication with others

11.3.1 Egocentric and socialized speech

There is a famous discussion by Vygotsky (1962) of a book by Piaget, which helps to clarify the role of communication with other people in the development of thought.

In his first book, *The Language and Thought of the Child* (1923), Piaget suggested that the most primitive forms of thought are 'autotistic': they are subconscious desires, wishes, or fantasies, which cannot be communicated by language. These make their first manifestations in the young child in what Piaget called 'egocentric speech'. Egocentric speech is that we often hear in young children when they are playing or before they fall off to sleep, a kind of monologue or running commentary, a speaking of thoughts aloud.

Piaget argued that such speech is not really concerned with communicating to others but with fulfilling immediate needs of the child, who cannot conceive the viewpoint of the listener, or even that he has one. Or course, no criticism is implied by the term 'egocentric': it is used to mean simply 'centred on the self'. On the other hand, Piaget distinguished socialized speech as speech whose function is to communicate with others. It is the normal use of speech after the early years of the child—in gossip, conversation, discussion. Piaget's position was that egocentric speech was gradually replaced by socialized speech, and that egocentric speech simply died away.

In his review of Piaget's book, Vygotsky considered that all speech is 'socialized' (he preferred the term 'communicative) in origin. It originates from attempts of the child to respond to the language of other adults round him. He conducted some experiments which showed that if the child had no audience he was less likely to use egocentric speech than if there were somebody in the room. Vygotsky argued that all speech is communicative. Egocentric speech is just one manifestation of communicative speech in which the child is attempting to understand for himself his environment as he explores it. Certainly egocentric speech disappears as Piaget said, but for Vygotsky it did not just fade away. Instead it became 'inner speech', that is, language in the mind, serving and interacting with the thought processes.

11.4 Summary

It is possible to regard thought as being of three kinds—enactive, iconic, and symbolic. Symbolic thought is characteristic of human beings and its most important symbol system is language. Language is not essential to the growth of thought but is certainly important in relation to it. This language which serves thought develops in the communicative relationships of children, and then grows silent because it has become internalized.

12

Influence of language on thought

12.1 Does language affect attitude?

It is quite clear that the words we use influence our thinking about the things they refer to. 'Adult human female', 'woman', 'lady'—these terms may refer to the same person but have a different flavour about them. In politics your own party plans, the other plots, yours is diplomatic, their is deceptive, yours is pragmatic and flexible, theirs 'staggers from makeshift to makeshift'.[1]

These are examples of uses of language for particular purposes, and are obviously designed to have an influence. But it can be argued that much of language itself communicates meaning despite or beyond the intentions of the user. Thus it has been said that much colour prejudice is built into language itself: black is a symbol of evil, white of goodness and purity. Blake put into the mouth of his Little Black Boy a protest against this: 'And I am black, but Oh! my soul is white'. Some advocates of women's rights see the usages of English as constantly confirming woman's second class status. For one thing the biological description of the species is 'man' (in evolutionary terms we speak of the descent of man). We say 'men and women', 'lads and lassies', 'boys and girls', 'a lover and his lass', 'male and female' (with the male always first). There is no singular third person pronoun to include both sexes, and 'he' or 'him' has to be used (man embraces woman, as the old joke has it). Thus in Blake's proverb 'If the fool would persist in his folly he would become wise'. The fool may presumably be of either sex, but the pronouns are such, it is argued, that we may scarcely think of this or other (more complimentary) statements applying to women, as though they were in some sense not worthy of consideration.

---

[1] The language of Watergate has recently revealed some interesting specimens: 'surreptitious entry'—burglary; 'increments in the form of currency'—bribes; 'My statement was inoperative'—'I was lying'.

Influence of language on thought

The various terms and usages in a language influence our thinking and, as one might expect, it seems that they may also influence speakers of different languages to think differently about particular topics. Abortion is a controversial subject in many countries, but workers on world population control are finding their difficulties increased in some countries where the term for abortion is the same as the term for murder in the local language. An interesting probable effect of the use of the pronouns *tu* and *vous* in French and *du* and *sie* in German, compared with the single 'you' in English, is mentioned by Slobin (1971, p. 128). Speakers of English are not having to make the difficult decision in almost every remark as to whether to use the polite more distant form rather than the friendlier more intimate; if they switched to French or German they could find themselves having to pay much more attention to aspects of social relations which were not previously of central concern. An interesting illustration comes from an experiment in which bilingual Japanese women were asked to complete sentences in both languages, on two separate occasions. One woman wrote in Japanese 'When my wishes conflict with my family's it is a time of great unhappiness', and in English 'When my wishes conflict with my family's I do what I want' (Ervin-Tripp, 1964).

12.2 Does language determine thinking?

It would be generally agreed that, in the way outlined above, language determines to some extent the way we think; and that different languages influence us to think differently. These two notions, *linguistic determinism* and *linguistic relativity*, are associated with the work of the notable U.S. linguist, Benjamin Lee Whorf. We have stated above what is known as the 'weak' form of the theories: that is roughly to say that language *influences* our thinking. But there is a strong form of the theories, which says that language *determines* our thinking, and that speakers of different languages may perceive the world differently. Our views arise because language has been a mould for our thoughts. By the term 'perceiving the world differently' we raise such questions as whether language causes us to have a different view of, for instance, colour, or more important, such things as time, space, and causality.

12.2.1 Perception

The Wolofs are an African people living in Senegal, which was a former French possession. Thirty Wolof children between 6 and 16 were given tests involving the arranging of pictures into groups (Greenfield, Reich, and Olver, 1966). This required, amongst other things, distinguishing red from orange (which is represented by one word, *hanka*, in Wolof), yellow from orange (one Wolof word is sometimes used for both) and blue from another colour (not named in the report). There is no word for blue in Wolof; the French *bleu* is used. If it is true that language affects our perceptions, we would expect the children who only spoke Wolof to make most mistakes, those who spoke Wolof and French to make fewer, and those who spoke only French to make fewest, since all the terms—*rouge, jaune, orange, bleu*—occur in French. This was found to be so, but mistakes were comparatively rare, and disappeared with increasing age, so that by the age of 10 there was virtually no difference. The authors comment: 'as a universal trend with age the constraints of reality increasingly overcome language if the one opposes the other' (p. 303).

12.2.2 Classification

As far as thinking about the world in terms of classes of things is concerned, it appears that children who have terms like 'colour' and 'shape' in their vocabulary may do better at appropriate sorting tasks than those who do not. From the same set of experiments with the Wolofs it was found that those who knew these terms could sort objects by colour (pick out all the same) or by shape (pick out those similar) better than those who did not. This is not just a matter of perception: it seems to imply that the subject first classifies by, for instance, 'shape' and excludes such categories as 'colour' and 'function' before seizing on individual shapes. Bruner (Bruner *et al*, 1966, pp. 83-4) tells us of a number of studies at Harvard where children were given sorting tasks. Younger children sorted on the basis of appearance—colour, shape, size, and so on. 6-year-olds might arrange 'scissors', 'bicycle', 'coat' together because 'they had holes in them', but older children would have the language of super-ordinates—'tools', 'transport', 'clothes', and would sort accordingly.

From these and other experiments it seems that in simple perception, for instance, of colour, language is not necessary, but if we once start arranging and classifying or analysing our perception, then .

language is important both to enable us to do this, and to influence the kinds of classification we make.

12.2.3 Grammar and thinking

So far we have been concerned with individual words. How far, however, does the grammar of a language create or help to create our view of the world, and our thinking about it? Whorf argues that grammar very largely determines thinking.

Class   In the language of the Hopi Indians of North America the Hopi verb extends into some of the things we call nouns—'lightning', 'wave', 'flame', for example. After all, they are things happening, at least briefly. The nearest we get in English is with participles like 'waving', 'flaming'. It may be argued that if our nouns were verbs we might be more aware of the world as continuous processes not static objects.

Tense   As far as tense is concerned, the Hopi verb expresses something not so much about the event, when it happened, as about the speaker—is it a memory for him? is it present before him? is he expecting it? Such usages seem to indicate psychological rather than mathematical time. Whorf illustrates this diagramatically (see Part 2, further work on Chapter 12).

We should be careful, however, in reading too much into the forms of a word. Take 'breakfast' in English. From this word we might assume that English speakers think of it as a more continuous process than 'dinner' or 'supper'—'breaking one's fast'—and that all English speakers are highly religious. Neither is the case.

Whorf believes that these variations between certain different languages are so profound that the speakers perceive a largely different universe, and argues that, for instance, Orientals such as the Japanese have been able to develop western type technology only by abandoning their own thought patterns and taking over those of the West.

12.3 Codability

Leaving aside for the moment the question of whether language determines our world view, it is clear that it is much easier in some languages to put an idea into words than it is in others. Thus Whorf tells us the Eskimoes have a variety of different words for snow, depending on its type. In English we could convey the same meanings, but more laboriously—saying, for instance, 'hard packed snow', 'soft slushy snow', 'brittle snow', and so on. The way in which a language can express certain ideas is known as their 'degree of codability', and will of course vary from language to language. It seems that what we can say easily we are more likely to think about and to say. The forms of language we habitually use have relevance not only to the study of differing cultures, but also to problems of linguistic advantage and disadvantage within a culture.

12.4 Summary

There is general support for the 'weak hypothesis' that language influences thinking, but less support for the 'strong hypothesis' that it determines thinking. Some would argue that the constraints of reality overcome language if the two are opposed. In everyday life we are often aware of both without conflict: for instance, we speak of the sun rising, as though the sun went round the earth, but of course this is quite false. Codability in a language (how easily a thing can be said) seems to be more important than the idea that language determines what we think.

13

Non-verbal communication in the classroom

13.1 What is communicated?

One important concern of the teacher is to further the learning of new understanding and new attitudes. Learning is by definition some change in the learner (knowing something he didn't know before, riding a bicycle he couldn't ride before), and thus understanding and attitudes must be different from what they were before. The first problem, therefore, is whether learning takes place; the second problem is whether the learning taking place is that the teacher intends.

As far as acquiring new understanding is concerned there are two possible failures: the pupil is simply confused; or he feels he understands when he doesn't. This last is by no means uncommon. The human mind tries hard to 'make sense' of new experiences. Thus the child who heard the hymn 'Gladly my cross I'd bear' and understands it as 'Gladly my cross-eyed bear' is doing this. It happens also when people abroad make sense of a language they don't understand—hearing a man speaking Serbo-croat say things like 'put down the tea pot, Gertie' in the middle of an otherwise unintelligible conversation.

By new attitudes we may mean, amongst many others, an interest in a subject or topic, or even an enthusiasm for it, which wasn't there before, a recognition of its significance, a willingness to look for evidence on which to base judgements (the so-called 'scientific attitude'), and so on. But it may be that opposite attitudes are encouraged: the teacher may communicate boredom towards a subject by his tone of voice, or the pupils may reject a subject because of his overbearing enthusiasm for it. Attitudes are conveyed by non-verbal means as much as by verbal—the para-linguistics of the voice, appearance, and stance of the teacher, the arrangement of the desks and chairs, and so on. (Of course, it sometimes happens that a subject is rejected by individuals in a class whatever its intrinsic merits, and however well it is presented, merely because it is offered in school, by a teacher.)

It is not only the teacher in the classroom who communicates attitudes to life and learning. As we saw in Chapter 1, communication is not necessarily intentional. The buildings themselves can present an atmosphere. The pattern of organization of a school, represented by, for instance, a timetable, can communicate attitudes, partly because it is a continuous pattern, going on from day to day and year to year. What the school teaches in this way has been called the 'hidden curriculum'. Jackson (1966) argues provocatively that this curriculum teaches denial, delay, and interruption. To break off from one lesson to go to another interrupts and frustrates our interest in it, causes delay before we can next pursue it. These are features of life itself, but Jackson argues that schools, as organized at present, exaggerate them.

13.2 Classroom communication

Leaving aside now the very large question of the total communication of a school, let us look at the nature of the non-verbal communication in relation to the verbal in some specific classrooms.

13.2.1 Communication in the infant school
A group of 5 to 6-year-olds talking to a visiting adult; other groups and individuals at work in the room.

Physical environment   Modern school, large windows, child-sized tables and chairs in groups, pictures, children's own work displayed, wendy houses, cage containing gerbils. One girl says 'They smell like pictures'. 'No they don't', a boy says, and nobody seems to know what she means. Most think they smell 'nice' but others don't appear to think they smell at all. The atmosphere is friendly and informal.

Linguistic

Amanda	guess what/after bonfire night were going to have a baby and guess what were going to call him/if its a boy or girl/Julia/but if its a boy were going to call him rubbish
Adult	rubbish
Amanda	yes
Adult	well thats a strange name

68

Christopher	its a silly name
Adult	why
Christopher	because its rude/its rude and its a word that normally/ rubbish is a word for cardboard and all drop out things that you don't need and you chuck it away and its called rubbish
Adult	youre not serious are you Amanda
Amanda	yes

Paralinguistic   Amanda uses the phrase 'guess what' with a pause to attract the adult's attention, and then proceeds, in a matter of fact, continuous tone, which conceals the surprise she intends to produce in the adult. The adult reacts appropriately with exaggerated surprise, which gratifies her and draws the rest in. Christopher is contemptuous and speaks with speed and passion. He uses loudness rather than variation in intonation to convey the emotion. Amanda's final avowal that she is serious is flat and unruffled.

Visual   Children of both sexes neatly, brightly dressed; adult wearing a dark suit.

Proxemic   The adult is sitting on a chair intended for an infant. This brings his head level with those of the ten children who press around him. Their bodies make a wall, giving intimacy and privacy to the group, cutting it off from the other group and individual activities going on in the room. Amanda has placed herself near the adult.

Tactile   The bodies of members of the group are touching, one or two of them have their hands on the shoulders of those in front as they lean towards the speaker. One boy eases himself onto the adult's knee.

Kinesic   Amanda uses eye contact to take the adult's attention and with it that of other members of the group. Having got all eyes upon her she looks away while she speaks, shyly, but also as though relying on the power of her words to hold them. She holds the hem of her dress and sways slightly. In any case the adult's attention assures her of an audience. Her expression remains solemn. Christopher talks 'publicly', from the outskirts, head up, without looking at any one in particular. His expression is bright, but otherwise not mobile. The expressions of both, and the comparative lack of eye contact, may be a reaction to the presence of a strange adult in the group, but not necessarily so. They may, for instance, represent a stage in the learning of facial gesture in relation to words.

The nature of the communication   The physical environment presents a pleasant informal atmosphere. It is a classroom where the furniture is child-sized, easily moved for various activities. Aspects of the children's psyche are on the walls in writing and drawing. In this room groups can form and change easily. The children come round a comparative stranger and, by his positioning himself and by the close contact between themselves and him, are able to establish quite a personal conversation very quickly. It is obvious that the small group supports Amanda and Christopher in a way that a large class would not. Information about trust, confidence, participation, and security is passing all the time. The context strongly supports and influences the linguistic communication. And, of course, that communication is very much richer in context, not only from the paralinguistics of the speakers, but also from, for instance, the expressions of the listeners— impassive, credulous, puzzled, frankly disbelieving.

13.2.2 Communication in the primary school

Physical environment   Two sides of the room are almost entirely windows, on which are silhouettes of animals or flowers in coloured tissue paper. Children's work on the walls. Class of twenty eight 8 to 9-year-olds. Tables usually with four children to each. Smell of floor polish.

Linguistic

Teacher	now/pay attention/I want you to stop what you are doing/ and come round the table
Children	(*variously*)
	what is it . . . whats that . . . (*statuette*[1] *on table, covered by pillow case*)
Teacher	Id like to introduce you to a friend of mine/Nigel/dont you want to meet this/friend of mine

[1] The statuette was of Blind Joe, the blind bell-man of Oldham in the 1860s, still very much a living legend in the town.

70

Nigel	yes miss (*statuette unveiled*)
Children	(*variously*)
	its a little man . . . hes got a top hat hes got a stick
Derek	hes got a bell
Malcolm	its not a bell/its not a bell is it miss
Teacher	yes
Derek	yer/told yer
Jacky	you can touch cant you Mrs. Holmes
Teacher	yes
Jane	Mrs. Holmes/where did you get him/
Teacher	(*covers him up again*) well what did you notice . . . (*various characteristics elicited*) yes and his stick
Amanda	its a walking stick miss
Teacher	what else about it
Jane	miss miss miss/its white miss

Paralinguistic   The teacher is experienced and relaxed. Her tone is gentle: it is not a tone which would be used to adults, but it is in no sense patronizing. She restores Nigel to order by a touch of mild incredulity in her voice. She obviously enjoys talking about the statue, and the children become instantly enthusiastic.

Visual   Teacher in grey pinafore dress, blue jumper, with hair recently set. Smiles easily but with a firm chin. Children all but two in grey uniform (girls green jumpers).

Proxemic and tactile   The children are first of all working at their tables; the teacher is sitting attending to the work of a girl who is standing by the desk. The teacher rises to attract attention. The unveiling of the statuette heightens interest. The children experience it by feeling as well as by seeing and questioning. They are very close together, often touching. One boy moves round the back of the group to get a closer look.

Subsequently the children are asked to bring their chairs round. The teacher sits with them in front of the desk. There is a slight jockeying for the position nearest the teacher on the part of three girls.

Kinesic   They all sit with big eyes shining as they listen to more about the statue; one or two of them hug themselves as though anxious to prevent their limbs from creating as interruption. The teacher's eyes

71

move backwards and forwards over their eyes, constantly covering the
group as she talks.

The nature of the communication   The room suggests brightness and
openness and the pictures indicate that it 'belongs' to the children. The
teacher, however, is exerting more control in directing attention to the
learning task than in the infant school.

13.2.3 Communication in a secondary school

Physical environment   A classroom of a former municipal grammar
school built in the late twenties or early thirties. One wall contains tall
windows. There is a board for notices near the door. Hardboard has
been placed along the back wall for display, but is not being used (the
room is not a 'subject' or 'specialist' room). Desks of wood with steel
frames (purchased in the sixties) are arranged in rows; table at front
for teacher's books and papers. There are thirty pupils (14 to 15 years
old); even so the room is overcrowded, with little circulation space.

Linguistic   The teacher has written on the board and the pupils are
copying:

Physiology. Yeast is a saprophyte which can carry out anaerobic
respiration, i.e. respiration occurring in the absence of atmospheric
oxygen. As in mucor enzymes are involved in digestion, so here
numerous complex enzymes are present in yeast and these are collectively
termed zymase.

John	please sir is that mucor
Teacher	yes what did you think it was
John	mucus sir
Teacher	*(shrugs and raises his eyes heavenwards; slight laugh fron one boy)*
	werent you here when we did mucor
John	yes sir
Teacher	now these enzymes bring about fermentation/you start off with $C_6 H_{12} O_6$ on this side *(writes on board)*/what do you end up with/nobody/well its $2CH_5OH + H_5OH + 2CO_2$/ *(writes on board)* write that down

Paralinguistic   There is a good deal of silence in this lesson, punctuated by the squeak of the chalk on the blackboard. The teacher is a youngish man, with a quickfire delivery, who pushes his lessons along rapidly, impatient of pauses or digressions. His first question to John is ironic but not unkindly.

Visual   Teacher eaglefaced, black hair strictly curtailed at collar. Belted leather jacket. Formal shirt and tie. Pupils, boys and girls, in a variety of dress.

Proxemic   The pupils are sitting in tight rows, boys and girls strictly segregated (not from any official policy). Their shoulders are bent most of the time; they glance up at the board to copy. Few look up at John's question. They put their pens down to watch the board for the equation, one or two boys stretching a little.
The teacher is standing in front. He often walks up and down restlessly.

Kinesic   The teacher's eyebrows are expressive, but the class is not responding to him so much as to the work task. When he talks he looks at a point in the air beyond them. A few pupils twist their lips or look puzzled when asked to complete the question; most look impassive. He is not responsive to these looks and, instead of helping them with the answer by, for example, leading them step by step in chemical or layman's terms (alcohol, gas given off), he merely supplies the answer.

Tactile   There is no tactile communication. People take especial effort to avoid touching others.

The nature of the communication   The physical environment has a slightly unkempt air, and contributes less positively to the learning situation than that of either of the other classrooms. The teacher's stance and behaviour signify pressure and more pressure.

13.3 Summary

The nature of the learning is obviously related to the non-verbal as well as the verbal messages in each case. A general atmosphere is provided by the building, the room, the furnishing, the decoration, pictures or their absence. A message about the degree of freedom is obviously sent by the closeness or otherwise of the chairs or desks. A message about the responsibility of the learner is sent even by such matters as the amount of talking they do, leaving aside its content. The tone of the teacher is communicating about attitude to a subject, and so on. The messages are complicated: at any one moment in time they are going out by several means from teacher to taught and vice versa. More important, however, is the fact that the messages are continuous, if changing. In their continuousness lies their effect.

14

Language in the classroom

We have seen that non-verbal communication plays a part in classroom learning. Obviously, however, a good deal of learning goes on by means of language, and recently there has been much interest in the role of language in the classroom.

14.1 Analysis of classroom language

14.1.1 Studies of classroom language

There have been various studies of classroom language, together with attempts to analyse it according to some scheme or other devised by the investigators. These schemes have differed from each other partly because they were used to investigate different facets of the language: the nature of the interaction (Flanders, 1970), the types of meaning conveyed (Bellack *et al.*, 1966), the description of the language in relation to its use (Sinclair *et al.*, 1975), the language of specialist subjects (Barnes, 1969). Most of the schemes have one thing in common: they are far too complex for use by any but the original investigators. Barnes's is an exception, and, as far as teachers are concerned, his studies are clearly the most important yet. Inevitably analysis of classroom language is a long job, as good recordings have to be obtained, and then transcribed, before the language itself can be studied.

14.1.2 An approach to classroom language

To be useful, a study of language must have reference to some specific aspects of a situation. Although we will not attempt a full-scale 'analysis' here, we will look at three different lessons, bearing in mind the following aspects of work in the classroom:

What determines the course of the lesson?

Language and education

In what way does the learning take place?
What is the role of the type of language used?

14.2 A language lesson

These are third-year boys in a city comprehensive, who have just
listened to a tape of a broadcast interview with a Tynesider who has
found he may be well-connected.

Teacher	Now then let's start by thinking what sort of people these are.
Terry	One's old and the other young.
Tony	Hark at brain box.
Terry	What's wrong with that?
Barry	He's not young he's about 30.
Teacher	Which is the younger one?
Two or three voices	The interviewer.
Teacher	How do you know?
Chris	He sounds it, sir, and the other chap says he's 56.
Teacher	What else about them? (*Silence*). Where do they come from?
Barry	Yorkshire, sir. The old chap comes from Yorkshire.
Tony	No he doesn't.
Terry	Yes he does, my grandad comes from Yorkshire and he talks like that.
Tony	You can't tell where they come from by how they talk.
Barry	Yes you can we went to my sister's in London and everybody said 'you come from Birmingham don't you'. (*With an attempt at a cockney accent*).
Chris	Sir, sir don't you change sir—if you live in different places you talk like them.
Terry	Malcolm Webb used to live in Scotland but he don't talk Scotch.
Tony	He talks brummie—like you.
Teacher	Where is he? All right Tony (*addressed to Tony to restrain his grimaces at Terry*).
Barry	He's not here today. Got a cold.
Tony	Working for his uncle.
Teacher	Are his parents Scots?
Terry	I can't tell what his dad says it's like foreign like.
Teacher	How long have they lived in Aston?

Chris	He went to't infant school with me sir.
Teacher	So they've been here about ten years. Malcolm speaks brummie but his mum and dad don't. Why do you think that is?

14.2.1 What determines the course of the lesson?

This lesson has started with the playing of the tape. The teacher is guiding the lesson. There are some signs of constructive discussion from the pupils, but the teacher probably feels, at this stage at any rate, that he needs to have all the contributions passed through him because there is a quarrel lurking between Terry and Tony. Tony does make positive suggestions ('You can't tell where they come from by how they talk'), but his hostility to Terry threatens to disrupt the lesson. Previously the teacher has dealt with it by ignoring it; now he issues a mild restraining aside ('All right Tony'), so as not to interrupt the flow of the lesson. He also ignores Tony's 'treacherous' remark that Malcolm Webb is truanting. He brings this first phase of the lesson to a point with a summary intended to push on the discussion further.

14.2.2 In what way does the learning take place?

The teacher's technique is to initiate one aspect of the topic—'what sort of people these are'—and to pick points out of the discussion which he wants to use. Apart from his opening sentence, and his summary at the end, all his utterances are questions, and even this last is a summary for the purpose of a question. One of his questions fails ('What else about them?') and he has to rephrase it. Otherwise they seem successful. He has told the pupils nothing, but has nicely prepared the way for a discussion of the relationship of accent to identity. He thus facilitates the learning by bringing into sharp focus the problems involved, so that the pupils can attempt solutions of them.

14.2.3 What is the role of the type of language used?

There seems to be no communication problem brought about by the language. None of the questions cause any difficulty in themselves and the teacher seems careful, whilst using a standard grammar, to avoid any terms which might seem alien to the class. He refers to 'brummie' and 'mum and dad' (not 'mother' and 'father'). The general tone seems fairly relaxed. The pupils' language is under no undue restraints. Chris is most anxious the lesson shall go well and is supportive of the teacher (notice his 'sir, sir'). Barry's mimicry of Londoners is an amusing retaliation for his apparent humiliation.

14.3 A science lesson

A science class of first-year pupils in a mixed secondary school.

Teacher	All right then now, can you now please pay attention? You remember what happened when we burnt a candle under a bell jar. What happened? Well?
Jane	The water came up sir.
Teacher	Yes, but why did the water come up?
Jane	Because er there was er a vacuum.
Teacher	Yes, but why was there a vacuum? Yes?
Kenneth	Well the candle kind of sucked up the water sir.
Teacher	(*with inoffensive irony*) How did it do that? Yes?
Dan	Some of the air got burnt up.
Teacher	That's not right is it?
Geoffrey	Sir, sir oxygen sir.
Teacher	It was the *inactive* air that was left, the oxygen that was used up. What's the oxygen called? Come on. (*Silence*). Its called the *reactive* part, isn't it. What's it called, Jane?
Jane	Reactive.
Teacher	Why is it called reactive? (*Silence*). Its called reactive because it *reacts*, isn't it?

14.3.1 What determines the course of the lesson?

Here the course is firmly set by the teacher, and the purpose at this stage is revision. No questions of class control arise. The personality of the teacher and the material itself seem, at least on the surface, to set the directions for learning.

14.3.2 In what way does the learning take place?

The questions are not open, as in the previous discussion. There is only one possible right answer and this the teacher seeks. Since the purpose is revision of information there is no reason why it should be otherwise.

The problem, however, is that the teacher is so set on the right answers, even formulated in particular words, that he rejects, or perhaps does not hear, any others. Thus he wants the word 'oxygen', and does not have time for an answer like 'Well the candle kind of sucked up the water sir'. This may be metaphorical, but how much or how little understanding does it reveal? The teacher doesn't stop to find out. Again, he brusquely rejects 'Some of the air got burnt up'. On what grounds he rejects is not quite clear—perhaps because it was the oxygen rather than the air that was burnt. But the oxygen is 'some of the air' too. Is that what the pupil intended? And if so will he be confused now?

14.3.3 What is the role of the type of language used?

The teacher is very concerned with the exact language of science as he conceives it. Thus, after he has got the answer 'oxygen', he straightaway mentions the 'inactive air that was left' though he hasn't asked about this. And he rushes on to his next technical term 'reactive' without having sufficiently prepared the ground for it, so the pupils are baffled by 'What's the oxygen called?' There would seem to be several answers possible to the question in this form. He has to supply 'reactive'. He can't get an explanation of the name, and so tells them that it 'reacts'. But if the pupils don't understand 'reactive' it is at least possible they don't understand 'react' either.

14.4 Discussing a poem

A second-year class in a mixed secondary school. The pupils are in groups discussing the line 'they used to laugh with their hearts' of the following poem by Gabriel Okara.

> *Once Upon A Time*
>
> Once upon a time, son,
> they used to laugh with their hearts
> and laugh with their eyes;
> but now they only laugh with their teeth,
> while their ice-block-cold eyes
> search behind my shadow.

There was a time indeed
they used to shake hands with their hearts;
but now that's gone, son.
Now they shake hands without hearts
while their left hands search
my empty pockets.

'Feel at home', 'Come again',
they say, and when I come
again and feel
at home, once, twice,
there will be no thrice—
for then I find doors shut on me.

So I have learned many things, son
I have learned to wear many faces
like dresses—homeface,
officeface, streetface, hostface, cock-
tail face, with all their conforming smiles
like a fixed portrait smile.

Ian	It means you know shake with laughter.
Pauline	All hearty like.
Carol	Yes.
Susan	No it doesn't, not shaking like a jelly. It means kind of you mean it.
Pauline	I like that bit about the faces. He says the faces are like dresses. You know you put a different dress on when you feel different.
Ian	I don't.
Carol	I put on this one to come to school and when I get home I can't wait to get out of it. (*Sympathy*)
Pauline	You feel a different person.
Susan	If you have too many things its showing off. Sally Turner even has a special dress for (*inaudible*). (*Laughter*).
Carol	Give me the chance.
Ian	What do you need a lot for? Waste of money.
Pauline	Girls need more clothes than boys.
Sean	Why do they?
Carol	Course they do, everybody knows that ....

(The teacher intervenes to steer the discussion back.)
　　　　　　. . . homeface, you know, like this (*Carol, who is an*
　　　　　　excellent mimic, puts on a surly expression). (*Laughter*)
Pauline　　What abour officeface? (*She makes one.*)
(The teacher hovers.)
Susan　　　(*After the laughter has died*) I like the next line, about a
　　　　　　fixed portrait smile. You know when your photo has a silly
　　　　　　grin on you didn't want.
Ian　　　　It's like your face begins to ache when you try to keep up a
　　　　　　smile for people, relatives and that.

14.4.1 What determines the course of the lesson?

A class has been split into groups to discuss the poem. In this group of
five, teacher guidance is absent except for one intervention. There is no
apparent leader in the group. Perhaps no-one wants to manage the
discussion, and it begins to turn to a topic which is not in the poem,
but which is triggered off by the expression 'like dresses'. The teacher
does not feel that they would get back on course by themselves and
intervenes briefly. She hovers again when the group gets rather excited
over the mimicry performed (very effectively) by the two girls, but the
group moves back to the topic of its own accord. By now they are
really interested in the poem and begin to look at it again in terms of
its exact meanings.

14.4.2 In what way does the learning take place?

The task here is to experience the poem and to be articulate about it. In
the opening passage the group works out together the meaning of
laughing with one's heart. Later the various public faces are understood
and appreciated from the mimicry of the girls. In the last two speeches
they are beginning to sound out meaning in terms of their own
experiences—of having their picture taken, and of the difficulties of the
'social smile'. Their insights are shared with the group. Only Sean contributes little to the dialogue, and how far he is following the discussion
cannot really be judged from this short extract.

14.4.3 What is the role of the type of language used?

The language is informal. It's being used to explore the poem, and to explain it. Thus in dealing with 'laugh with their hearts' Pauline comes up with 'all hearty like' which gets the image but not the flavour of the phrase. Susan refines this, describing Pauline's view by an analogy ('like a jelly'), and comes to the essential quality of sincerity ('you mean it'). With the 'bit about the faces' Pauline again attempts to explain in terms of a girl's experience of dress. The language is used supportively: they try to help each other to arrive at the meaning (except where a male-female argument about clothes begins). Towards the end they are trying to find common experiences through which to explain—'It's like when your face begins to ache'.

14.5 Discussion

14.5.1 Guidance
In contrast to a conversation, which may change direction as the interests or impulses of the participants dictate, a lesson is concerned with exploring a particular area of skill or knowledge. The teacher is responsible for guiding this exploration.

In the discussion about the interview, the teacher guides the lesson fairly indirectly, by asking questions which make use of the pupils' ideas. In contrast, however, to the group discussion about the poem, all the discussion here is channelled through the teacher, who thus maintains considerable control both over the incipient quarrel and the course of the lesson.

Control in the science lesson is entirely in the hands of the teacher. He is anxious to get on fast, and is not really listening for any answers other than the one he wants. The problem of the discussion moving away from the subject does not occur, but the teacher is insisting that the pupils not only deal with the subject, but also with the correct vocabulary. Thus many pupils who have some understanding of the subject, but lack the vocabulary, are unable to participate.

The pupils discussing the poem largely determine the direction of the discussion, although the teacher does bring them back to the poem when there is a possibility of the topic being abandoned altogether. Unlike the science lesson, which requires revision of specific material, this lesson allows pupils to initiate their own ideas about the poem, and rely relatively little on direction from the teacher.

14.5.2 Learning

It is fashionable to commend 'open questions', since they encourage
pupils to think for themselves, but not all questions can be open: some
must be closed. There is no room for a difference of opinion on the
name of the capital of the U.S.A., the formula to calculate the area of a
circle, or the present tense of *être*. To say this, however, is not to agree
with the old-fashioned type of lesson where facts were recited and
copied from the blackboard: those lessons contained too many facts
and too little thinking about the facts.

Obviously the type of learning must be suited to the task: revision in
the science lesson requires right answers from the pupils, in some form
or another; the class discussing the interview attempts to solve problems
set by the teacher; the discussion of the poem involves exploration of
the subject through personal experiences. The lessons succeed to
varying degrees in what they are trying to achieve, but it is probably the
case that least is being learnt where the teacher seems to be teaching
most and having a bigger share of the words spoken.

14.5.3 Language

There is a variety of language used in the three passages. The teachers
are affecting the behaviour of their pupils in more or less direct ways:
language is used to inform, support, explore, and so on. It is susceptible
of analysis in terms such as those of Chapters 9 and 10, but it is more
useful here to consider some general aspects of the language used.

In the discussion of the interview there is no gap between the
language used by teacher and taught. This does not mean that the
teacher's language is in any way ineffective, or that he deliberately
adopts phrases alien to him, but that he chooses language which is
common to him and his pupils. In contrast the science teacher uses
a special vocabulary. The point is not whether at some stage a
specialized vocabulary for science isn't necessary (it clearly is), but
whether, in the earlier stages, and with some children, it isn't interfering
with their learning. In the science lesson, the children probably have at
least some understanding of the concept, but the lack of specialized
vocabulary prevents them either showing or developing this understanding. (See Chapter 15.)

A special vocabulary may cause an interference with learning, and so
too may everyday words. A pupil learning to read was failing at 'set' in
'The sun had set', and the cause of this was that he had never met the

word. He understood 'went down' readily enough. He might alternatively have met 'set' in the sentence 'The jelly had set', and have been confused by the sun apparently doing the same as the jelly.

Other difficulties are brought about by the teacher having a different set of language usages from those the child is acquainted with. It is true that a 'middle class' accent can alienate some children. Leslie Stratta found pupils were rejecting arguments put forward by a psychiatrist in a taped discussion because of his accent, and they later discovered that they agreed with him almost entirely (Wilkinson, Stratta, Dudley, 1974, pp. 73-6). As far as the language itself is concerned, to conduct the discussion in terms of the 'middle class code' of the teacher and the 'working class code' of the children is to vulgarize it.

Thus Joan Tough (1973, p. 44) points out that children entering infant school may not understand indirect instructions like 'Would you like to (pick up the bricks)' or 'Would you mind (picking up the bricks)' to which the answer might seem to be 'yes' or 'no', since they have been used to a direct command at home, 'Pick up the bricks'. By teaching the child to understand and to use the first form the teacher is not imposing a middle class usage, but is teaching a more complex language, which regards the other person not as a servant but rather as having a right to consideration. Presumably this is not a matter of class, though it can be a cause of real misunderstanding, particularly at the change from home to school, infant to primary, primary to secondary schools, when different language usages may be met with.

14.6 Summary

Methods of analysing the 'language of the classroom' vary with what they seek to discover. Certainly a useful approach can be made by considering the means by which the lesson is made to progress, the nature of the learning taking place, and the types and functions of language employed.

15

Language in education

15.1 Registers of English

We all change our style of speaking or writing according to the circumstances. We use a different sort of language for writing to a personal
friend from that we use for an essay or report, or letter to the local
authority about the non-arrival of a grant or about a rates bill to which
the computor has madly added noughts. We speak in one way to little
children, in another to adult strangers, and so on. In addition we are all
aware that, whether we use them or not, there are special usages
associated with, for instance, law, science or religion. These differing
usages for differing occasions are known as 'varieties' or 'registers' of
English.

15.2 The registers of education

People writing and talking about education use a particular register or
group of registers. Education has its own need for technical terms—
'readiness', 'IQ', 'vertical grouping', 'comprehensive', 'phonic method',
and so on. Many of these terms are drawn from the subjects on which
educational theory draws—psychology, sociology, linguistics, philosophy.
Such terms are necessary to save time. To have to say 'a method of
learning to read whereby the child sounds aloud individual letters from
which he builds up the sound of the whole word', instead of 'phonic
method', would be tedious in the extreme.

Sometimes ordinary words are given a somewhat different meaning:
'code', 'reinforcement', 'reward', 'drive', 'goal', 'response', 'bland', and
so on. Sometimes words are invented because there is no existing word
which adequately describes an idea that the inventor feels is important.
'Numeracy' is an example; so is 'feedback'. Sometimes, like other
writers, educationists seek metaphors in which to express their ideas:

thus 'halo effect' is our tendency to attribute other virtues to 'good' students. Sometimes these departures from general practice are fully justified; on other occasions they may have the effect of confusing the listener or reader.

Let us examine a sentence from a report on some 'microteaching'[1] experiments.

In the initial microteaching clinic at Stanford it was found that some sort of systematic exposure to teaching strategies was needed to help acquaint trainees with a repertoire of useful behaviour and also help provide a focus for critiquing trainees' microteaching lessons.

(McKnight, 1971).

A student rewrote this as follows:

In the first microteaching experiment at Stanford it was found that students needed to learn about various ways of microteaching so that they could practise them, and so that their tutors could comment on their lessons in the light of them.

Asked to justify her version, the student wrote:

I didn't see the need for all the special words. Why a 'clinic'—it suggests the children are diseased? Why 'strategies'—are teachers at war with children? The word 'repertoire' made me think the teachers were going to burst into song. Why 'exposure'—it suggests the teachers are passive like photographic plates: 'trainees' does the same. 'Critiquing' made me shudder! I couldn't find it in the dictionary . . . . Rereading my version it seems to make the whole thing sound matter of fact, but perhaps this is no bad thing.

Readers will be able to form their own views about the student's version, and her justification of it. It should be said that the term 'clinic' was in use at Stanford and is not a coinage of the writer of the sentence (though that does not, of course, alter the point she is making). At any rate the student draws attention to the way the language used, particularly the metaphors chosen, may influence our thinking, a point we have already touched on in Chapter 12, and which we may now look at with specific reference to education.

[1] 'Microteaching is a scaled down but realistic classroom context which offers a helpful setting for a teacher (experienced or inexperienced) to acquire new teaching skills and to refine old ones. It does so by reducing the complexity and scope of such classroom components as the number of pupils and the length of lessons, and by providing trainees with information about their performance immediately after completion of their lesson.'   (McKnight, 1971).

15.2.1 Metaphors in education

In a very interesting article W.J. Cheverst (1972) draws attention to
three groups of metaphors which are often to be found in educational
writing. In that which is *child-centred* we find words like 'growth',
'harmony', 'discovery', 'assimilation', 'readiness'. In that which is
knowledge-centred we find words like 'store', 'foundation', 'stock',
'cells', 'bricks', 'structure'. In that which is *teacher-centred* there are
words like 'guiding', 'shaping', 'moulding', 'directing', 'imparting'. He
examines official reports on primary education from 1905 to 1968 and
shows how the change in attitude is represented in the metaphors used
(see pp. 200-2).

Metaphors can be helpful in thinking about education. They give
vividness to the writing, and draw our attention to something which
perhaps we had not previously known. Thus in the eighteenth century
when Rousseau (1957, p. 6) compared children to growing plants
('Plants are fashioned by cultivation, men by education') he was drawing
attention to them, not as passive recipients of knowledge, but as having
a potentiality within themselves. But, of course, the analogy breaks
down if pushed too far. For instance, plants on the whole don't need
other plants to interact with. Again plants can only develop one way: a
rosebud can only become a rose, but a child can develop in countless
different ways. The danger arises if the metaphors become so much part
of our thinking that we do not realize their limitations.

It is not possible to list even the most frequent metaphors currently
used in education. *Horticultural* metaphors such as that just quoted are
very common, often indicated by 'growth', 'development', 'roots',
'fruitful', 'favourable climate', 'springs'. Then there are a group of
military metaphors ('attack', 'assault', 'tactics', 'strategy') and a group
of *medical* metaphors ('clinical', 'diagnosis', 'consultant'); and a group
of *building* metaphors ('word/vocabulary building', 'curriculum construction', 'bricks', 'tools', as in 'words are tools'). Metaphors from
science include especially 'model'. A model is a simplified version of
something which helps us pay attention to certain features of it (as in a
diagram). Unfortunately it is a term which often confuses rather than
explains. A well-known curriculum scholar writes: 'The details of this
model serve little purpose here. But its broad outline provides a framework which, if only glimpsed, may reduce somewhat the extent to
which I talk past you' (Goodlad, 1968). A model is an 'outline' or a
'framework' by definition. So this writer is really saying 'I hope my

model will help you to understand me'. Under the circumstances it seems doubtful.

15.3 Language in school

A very large amount of language is used in a school each day. For convenience we may classify it as:

(a)   the language for running the school,
(b)   the language for personal interaction,
(c)   the language for teaching.

Under the first heading we may include such matters as letters to parents, and school reports to parents, which go out from the school rather than contribute internally to its running. We may include fire regulations ('When the bell sounds stop what you are doing at once . . .') and school rules ('Except on wet days no one is to be in the classroom without permission of a teacher . . .'). In the same category we can place fixture lists, team lists, house points, honours boards, lists of library times and dinner sittings, and to some extent notices of theatre trips, club activities, and so on.

It is interesting to note the variety of types of language used in one particular school during a short period. Here are some snippets from a primary school assembly:

Good morning children . . ., it's a very nice bright morning . . ., the hymn we're going to sing suits the day very well . . ., we'll sing all three verses. . . .
Morning has broken/like the first morning. . . . (*singing, with piano*)
Oh Heavenly Father friend of all children/bless our school/help us to do our best. . . .
We've had people going into classrooms not their own during the dinner hour/which is not allowed. . . .
I'll ask Mrs. Jessop to give us the result of yesterday's netball match. . . .
I'm very glad to say that after a bad start to the season we won yesterday's match by 7 to 2/it was disappointing that a member of the team did not turn up/and we were lucky to have such a good reserve to take her place. . . .
Thank you staff. Will you carry on Mr. Forster.
Will you turn please/(*music on piano*) lead on first years.
(*as children leave, various teachers to individuals*)
No talking . . . don't push . . . what happened to your hymnbook . . . why have you got your outdoor shoes on . . . thank you Mark (*to boy holding door open*)

This language is predominantly concerned, in various ways, with running the school and guiding children in a particular direction: this use of language even applies to the prayer, and the report of the netball match.

The assembly opened with a different type of language, however, a more personal kind. The head is re-establishing a friendly relationship with the children. This is, of course, difficult to do with a large group, and will happen much more easily when he talks to individual children. In this particular school, as in many others, there is an informal contact between staff and pupils which makes relationships easy outside the classroom. Language is used constantly—pupil to pupil, pupil to staff, in and out of the classroom. It forms part of the daily, unofficial—but essential—interacting in a school or any other institution. This use of language is not, however, our particular concern here, though we may mention in passing that the nature of the relationships is very relevant to the type of learning going on.

The third type of language, that used in teaching, we ought to spend a little more time on. In the secondary school we tend to find a wider variety of registers than in the primary school, many of them associated with the traditional school subjects. There is also a register for giving instructions in teaching, often to be found in textbooks and examination papers. The variety of registers used in teaching has recently become known as 'language across the curriculum'.

15.3.1 Language in examinations

In 'O' level papers set in 1974 the following were some of the instructions: (Biology) 'Describe. . . .', 'Distinguish between. . . .', 'Explain why. . . .', 'Make a sketch map. . . .'; (English Literature) 'Read the following passage. . . .', 'Give an account. . . .', 'Show the importance of. . . .', 'Say concisely. . . .'; (Domestic Science) 'State the composition of. . . .', 'List five important foods. . . .', 'Compare. . . .', 'Name the ingredients. . . .', 'How would you. . . .'; (History) 'Why did. . . .', 'What was. . . .', 'What were the causes. . . .', 'What problems were. . . .', 'How did. . . .', 'Describe and explain. . . .', 'Show how. . . .'; (English Language) 'Write a composition. . . .', 'You should understand that the question is designed to test your accuracy in the writing of English. ... .'

Examiners adopt a no-nonsense approach. In some questions there is even a tone of moral indignation lurking: 'You should understand. . . .', and if you don't, you can jump in the lake. But to be more serious, it is clear what kind of language is required from the examinees—a cognitive language, in which to state and explain. Even where imaginative work is required the line is the same: 'Write a composition. . . .' No help is given in setting the atmosphere for the candidate as would be done in a good lesson. The subjects are merely listed after this instruction: 'The island', 'The problem of noise', and so on. That the instructions of examiners need not be so abrupt has been demonstrated by John Dixon and his associates in a pamphlet published by NATE (*Criteria of Success* n.d.)

15.3.2 The language of subjects

Here are some brief quotations from the exercise books of a 14½-year-old girl:

(a) The tapeworm attaches itself to the intestine of its host by suckers and hooks on its head. It has segments covered in thick cuticle to protect it from the host's digestive juices. It has no mouth but is surrounded by the digested food of the host which it absorbs along its whole surface

(b) Scarlatti Sonata in A. Analysis
Section A, Bars 1 - 6 A major (tonic)
Section B, Bars 6 - 14 A major. Ends in E major (dominant)

(c) French seam
1 With RS together pin, tack and machine ¼″ from raw edge
2 Trim close to stitching, press seam flat in one direction
3 Turn so that RS are together, pin, tack, and machine on seam line

(d) I like the passage by Alan Sillitoe because I enjoy reading the style in which he writes. I have had the loneliness of the long distance runner and liked it very much. His style is simple and unemotional. He leaves the reader to make his own opinion of characters and there is little give away of what they are like.

(e) 3 America is by far the greatest producer of hydro-electric power in the world.
4 All the potential hydro-electric capacity is not used. The total potential capacity is about 2,800 kilowatts. In fact there is only 160 million kilowatts installed.

(f)   *Sick of the Palsy*

>   Hidden away,
>   Unknown to us
>   He was
>   Kept dark
>   Playing
>   With himself.
>   We didn't know
>
>   We heard him
>   moan but he didn't
>   say anything
>   Because
>   He couldn't
>   His mouth opened silently
>   Along with his helpless soul
>   He didn't know.
>
>   We saw the limbs
>   rocking to and fro
>   Without purpose or control
>   Flesh and bones moving
>   in union but some how
>   Without it.
>
>   And when he's no longer here
>   only a little will
>   remain, in a vision
>   of his mother's,
>   The love
>   And the thought
>   Of what might have been.

(g)   There are two forms of energy. One is kinetic energy when something is moving. When a man pedals a bicycle down a hill it is
kinetic energy. A body possesses potential energy if we force it
to change shape. When we wind up a clock we force the spring to
change shape.

In this last case the girl was making her own notes based on the
following passage from J.S. Strettan's *Outlines of General Science*
(1960):

There are two forms of mechanical energy. A body has Kinetic Energy
when it is moving; the more massive the body and the faster it moves,
the more energy it has. A body possesses Potential Energy if a force has
been applied to it to change its position or shape. A bicycle at the top

91

of a hill and the wound-up spring of a clock have potential energy. Potential energy is stored energy.

These seven extracts illustrate some of the demands made upon the abilities of secondary school children to use and to understand language (not including a second language such as French or German). The uses of language vary, in Britton's terms (10.1.2), from the 'poetic' to the 'transactional'. Thus in (f) we have an example of 'the poetic', a shaped piece expressing a state of feeling. The others in their various ways are transactional: less in (d), most in (c) which gives instructions for direct action.

In terms of two of the three levels of language discussed in 6.2 (phonology is ruled out in written work), the girl has to employ a variety of grammatical usages. In (d) and (f) she can use personal constructions and active verbs ('We didn't know', 'I like the passage'). In others she has to be impersonal: (e), for instance, has the potential construction, 'is not used' (not 'we do not use. . .'). In (b) (c) and (e) the connection between the sentences is not so much grammatical or logical as successive: a list presentation is given. This may seem to indicate clear thinking but in (e) it is not clear whether 4 refers to America alone as mentioned in 3. In (c) there is an absence of subjects, just verbs of command, and the object is only implied (what do you pin, tack, and machine?)

The vocabulary has a high technical element—A major dominant, RS, hydro-electricity, kilowatts, kinetic energy. Many of the words have a special meaning or connotation different from their ordinary usage. We hope that the host at a party or inn is not the same as the host of a tapeworm. A major (tonic) is not the same as a major tonic, with or without gin. A massive body is not the same for the physicist as for the all-in wrestler.

There is a serious point here, however. A comparison of the two passages under (g), the girl's own written version and the passage she was basing it on, reveal misunderstandings brought about by the interference caused by the everyday meanings of the words. Thus when she explains 'when a man pedals a bicycle down a hill it is kinetic energy' she is thinking of the power produced by his muscles (he's energetic) and this is not the point. Again she seems to have misunderstood the scientific use of 'force' (something which acts upon something else), and is trying to make the common meaning of 'force' (to act violently) fit the situation ('force the spring to change shape'), and this is once again the wrong meaning. It seems clear that in this case the specialist language used is actually hindering the understanding of the concepts.

It so happens that in this passage we can discern the nature of her misunderstandings. But this is by no means always the case. For instance, in (e) it is not clear whether she realizes that the kilowatt capacity is just for America. Indeed we do not know what she understands by America (north and south, north only, U.S.A. as distinct from Canada). Does she understand what kilowatt means? The phrase 'there is only 160 million kilowatts installed' suggests she is very vague about it: one does not 'install' a kilowatt. Again there is no indication of whether the figures are per minute, per hour, per day, per week, per year. The fact that she does not put this in may indicate a further confusion. Of course, we have no means of knowing whether she understands what she writes in (a), (b), and (c) either, but there are no obvious gaps or inconsistencies.

Douglas Barnes has pointed out that there is a particular concern to teach vocabulary on the part of science teachers. He quotes from a teacher in a science lesson:

We're going to cut the grass into small pieces and then we're going to put it into the . . . what we call a mortar . . . this is what we call a mortar . . . this bowl . . . and anyone know what we call the other thing which we're going to pound it in?

and comments:

The act of giving a technical name seems for many teachers to have taken on a value of its own in separation from its utility; in this case the naming activity is totally irrelevant to the process which it interrupts (Barnes, 1969, p. 48)

In both (e) and (g) the source of her difficulty seems to lie to a large extent at any rate in the registers used. Passage (d) does not indicate any such problems. But she has been set a very difficult task—to say why she likes the passage by Sillitoe—and the fact that her answer is limited to 'I like . . . because I enjoy . . .' is a reflection of this. There is no indication that she has misunderstood the original.

These passages indicate a few of the many demands that the language we use in school makes upon children. The girl whose work we have used was above average in ability, and yet a few quotations reveal misunderstandings brought about to some extent by the very registers which, it is sometimes argued, aid accurate thinking. Whatever their

positive merits, and we would not question these, the use of special
registers is not here encouraging accuracy.

15.4 Summary

The language used about education, particularly the metaphors, may
influence (or even confuse) our thinking about it. In the school itself
there is a wide variety of language uses which we may class as being for
the organization of the school, for interpersonal relationships, and for
teaching and learning. By the time a pupil reaches his teens he may have
a range of registers to cope with, which may be helpful in or,
alternatively, a hindrance in his learning.

16

Communication in early childhood

16.1 Tha'rt welcome bonny brid[1]

There are various ways in which it is possible to damage human beings
psychologically: by annoying them, insulting them, threatening them,
persecuting them. But often it is far more effective to do none of these
things: to do nothing to them, to leave them entirely alone. So in
prison solitary confinement is recognized as a severe punishment. So in
big cities anonymous lonely people put an end to their own loneliness
because no-one speaks to them, no-one cares for them. If this is true for
adults, how much more so is it true for little children, whose
personalities are yet to be formed? It seems that neglect in the early
years has a permanently detrimental effect upon their lives.

The baby comes from the warmth and protection of the womb
where every need is catered for by his physical connection with his
mother's body. He comes into a world which is cold and hostile:

> 'Into the dangerous world I leapt
> Helpless, naked, piping loud'

as Blake says in 'Infant Sorrow'. And he must be welcomed into this
world, made to feel warm, friended, secure. And this welcoming and
cherishing must go on continuously over months and years. If it does
not, the chances are that the child will never join the human family,
will always in some sense remain an alien to it.

The communication which says 'I welcome you', 'I cherish you' is
obviously not primarily a matter of words. In a poem by Anne Sexton,
a woman muses over her new born child:

---

[1] The first line of a Lancashire dialect poem by Samuel Laycock, written in the
cotton famine of 1861-5, welcoming a new-born child   (Laycock, 1910).
brid bird

Yours is the only face I recognize.
Bone at my bone, you drink my answers in.
Six times a day I prize
your need, the animals of your lips, your skin
growing warm and plump. I see your eyes
lifting their tents.

Communication is taking place by a variety of means, and we shall look at these in more detail later. In the meantime let us look at the general process of welcoming and sustaining the child in the world.

16.2 Mothering

This process is known as 'mothering' (though it is not necessarily confined to the mother). Michael Rutter surveys the research, and comments: 'Six characteristics have usually been said to be necessary for adequate mothering: a loving relationship, which leads to attachment, which is unbroken, which provides adequate stimulation, in which mothering is provided by one person, and which occurs in the child's own family' (Rutter 1972, p. 16). Presumably we do not need research evidence to tell us how important love is to the young child. Indeed the psychologists have a good deal of difficulty defining and measuring it; they are happier with terms like 'warmth'. Their findings suggest that 'warmth' is important for the child not only in his relationship with his mother but throughout the other close family relationships.

'Attachment' is a technical word for a special relationship or bond which a child establishes with an adult. This has parallels with 'imprinting' in the animal kingdom. Orphan animals will 'imprint' on a human being. In the nursery rhyme Mary's little lamb which 'followed her to school one day' is an example. For obvious reasons the child will usually establish a bond with his mother, and some people would argue that this is crucial. But there seems to be evidence that the father could serve in this way. Children often establish subsidiary bonds with adults and siblings.

Certainly with most children mothering is provided by one figure, usually the natural mother. This is not to say that an adopted mother could not serve the same function; indeed in some communities it is Granny who does the mothering, whilst the mother is working. There is also some evidence that a child can relate to a few women who have the responsibility for caring for him (as in Kibbutzim) as long as they remain the same and pay him close and personal attention. What is damaging is discontinuity. Many situations involving various mother figures are in fact discontinuous, and thus unsatisfactory. There has been a tendency of recent years to consider that a bad home was better than no home at all for children, and not to move them to institutions. But this can only be rule of thumb. There are some very bad homes, and some institutions which are good as institutions.

That the mothering relationship should be continuous seems to be indicated by the association between broken homes and delinquency, and by the distress caused to young children by separation from their parents, such as that occasioned by hospital treatment. Some writers suggest that the effects of being separated from parents in such a way for any length of time produce consequences extending into adult life. In a famous film by the Robertsons, 'John' goes into care for nine days at the age of 17 months. He at first 'protests' (acute distress and crying) and this is followed by 'despair' (misery and apathy). It is as though he is mourning for the death of his parents. At last he becomes 'detached', and seems to lose interest in his parents, even when they reappear. It is as though he has become reconciled to their death. What has perhaps been damaged permanently is his ability to love, because it seems to him that his love has been betrayed. However, the long term effects of separation are obviously difficult to determine.

The effects of John's separation would be described as 'deprivation'. Children who have never known love and responded to it are said to be suffering from 'privation'. Their case is indeed serious, for they do not form lasting relationships or display love. This is the origin of the 'psychopathic' personality.

That the mothering relationship should include stimulation of the child is important. He must be encouraged to explore the environment, to manage his body. Play, particularly with adults, is one of the principal means by which he is stimulated. He must learn to use language. And the development of language is associated with the development of mental processes. The dialogue of children and adults is a crucial one. The retardation of children in unstimulating environments such as orphanages illustrates just how crucial it is. As far as the forming of bonds is concerned, it seems to be the quality and intensity of the interaction that is important, and not just the presence of an adult. Similarly a dog in a family may show much more preference for the 10-year-old son who occasionally romps with him and teases him than for the adult to whose lot has fallen the continuous task of feeding and exercising him.

We can look at 'mothering' as fulfilling two functions. One is making the child feel loved, secure, protected. The other is in a sense the opposite—stimulating him, challenging him, making demands on him, presenting him with problems he must solve. In this way he grows, mentally as well as physically.

16.3 Means of communication

Early communication between mother and child is continuous with that within the womb. He feels the warmth of her body and its softness. An American research worker, Harlow (1969), gave 'substitute mothers' to young monkeys. One was a frame of wire, in which a bottle could be placed and milk sucked from it. The other, which could also provide milk, was also a frame of wire, but covered with sponge and towelling. The monkeys with this 'mother' developed without apparent ill effects, but those with the wire mother could not, at a year old, associate with monkeys of the opposite sex. When a few did become pregnant they appeared to be without maternal instincts, and abandoned their offspring. We must not push the parallel between the animal and the human situation too far, but the comparison is certainly suggestive.

The human baby tastes the mother's body and her milk. Probably he relates to her by smell also. She is constantly handling him, dressing, undressing, rocking, cuddling him, kissing him. Wordsworth thought she might sometimes overdo it—'Fretted by sallies of her mother's kisses' ('Immortality Ode'). But another line of Wordsworth's in the same poem draws our attention to a further means of communication in mothering —the eyes. He speaks of the young child 'With the light upon him from his father's eyes', thus reminding us that other members of the family are involved. Looks and smiles seem important to the child and he communicates by smiling himself at six weeks. The first social smile can have an electrifying effect on the mother and it seems to make her altogether more responsive (Bowlby, 1971, p. 298). An advantage for the child of attachment to a single figure is that this person is likely to be more sensitive to the signals which he gives and more skilled at interpreting them.

It is very common for children to be talked to before they can understand the meaning of words. Many adults talk nonsense or coo or sing to them, and clearly the children often find it pleasurable, however such 'conversation' may seem to a dispassionate observer. In their turn children can communicate before they can use words: a child at a year old may use, say, a double grunt to mean a variety of things, depending on how he grunts.

16.3.1 Class differences in early communication

In a U.S. experiment, middle-class and working-class (white) mothers were observed at home with their 10-month-old daughters. Differences were minimal in non-verbal communication, including physical contact. In contrast there was much more talking with the children in the middle-class homes. The experimenter suggested that the working-class mothers felt their infants weren't capable of communicating and thus there was no point in conversing with them (Tulkin and Kagan, 1972).

Another U.S. experiment (Smith, 1970) hypothesized a negative relationship between talk and other means of communication. Those who find words easy use them, those who don't use the other means more. Pairs (a mother and child in each) were observed carrying out two tasks, a manipulative and a practical one, requiring them to tell each other stories. They were recorded on video-tape and the incidence of 'body contact', 'body closeness without contact' (for example, inclination), and 'glancing behaviour' was noted. It appears that the hypothesis was confirmed with body contact, partly because the working-class mothers, with less language, tended to steer their children physically rather than by words in the first task. There was no difference in the incidence of bodily inclination. However, middle-class mothers, with more language, nevertheless used more eye contact and reciprocity than working-class mothers.

We might speculate on the significance of this. Physical contact and closeness are saying things like 'I love you', 'You are secure with me', 'I will help you'. Eye contact is not only saying this. To look a person in the eyes is often a mark of respect and approval. But it is also a method of control: more particularly it often means 'Over to you', 'It is your turn to contribute'. We see this in adult conversation when a speaker looks at the listener as a signal that he expects a reply. We may regard eye contact, therefore, as related to the linguistic and other demands which are made constantly on children in many middle-class households, but are made less frequently in working-class homes. The obligation to answer is reinforced by the eye contact.

It should be stressed that there are as yet few experiments in this field and we must be careful not to overgeneralize from the two we have described.

16.4 Talking to young children

A good deal of the stimulation we have spoken about comes from the conversation of the mother with the young child. The father and any other children often take a part but, by the nature of things, it is usually the mother who is in continuous contact with her child.

In many households children are talked to from the moment they are born, and long before any response can be expected. At feeding time, which occurs five or six times in the twenty four hours, a particularly intense interaction may go on between mother and child. Mr. Stephen Wrigley recorded the talk of his wife with their 6-week-old son at the 10 p.m. feed. Here is part of the transcription.

(*The baby awakes and is carried into the lounge for feeding*)
Where were you when the lights went out/hey/golly/yes/stay down there for one second (*bib is put on*) what have we got for Benjie Bear tonight/there we are/(*baby begins to feed and seems to notice, as usual, the black beam set in the white ceiling over his head*/that's my friend/ beamy/oh/have you been scratching your face again/oh, dear me.

The mother's talk may seem hurried as read in this transcription, but this was far from the case: it was gentle, relaxed, punctuated by long periods of silence. The whole feeding session lasted just over an hour. A fuller transcription is given in Part 2, further work on Chapter 16.

Wrigley points out the variety of features in it. How the mother uses repetitions, utters some phrases in sing-song, sings a snatch of a song. There are some signs of the language being simplified, and alliterative terms like 'Benjie Bear' being used, which might be expected to have a special appeal to the child a little later in his development. But there are also 'adult' sentences both those addressed to the baby ('Have you been scratching your face again') and those really intended for the husband ('Where were you when the lights went out').

Here we touch on a somewhat controversial matter. It is certainly true that adults often simplify their sentences, and slow them down when talking to young children: they often use rhyme, repetition and alliteration which they think will appeal to children. But we do not in fact know whether children are specially helped by these simplifications; perhaps they learn language as much from the adult usages they normally have all around them, though this seems unlikely. One thing is clear, however: the enjoyment of the mother we have quoted in using language must surely convey itself to her baby and stimulate his own interest in responding.

There has been some investigation of ways of talking to children. Adults may use *simple words and sentences* ('eat your pobbies/there you are'). They may use particularly *explicit* sentences, as when giving a running commentary ('let's put this bib round your neck'). Here they may even substitute nouns for pronouns (as when the mother says 'mummy's got to get baby's supper'). They may *repeat* ('got to go to the shops/got to go to the shops haven't we'). The way adults *expand* children's sentences has often been noted (the child's 'name doggie' may be expanded to 'What's the name of the doggie?'). Sometimes children's sentences are *commented upon* (the child says 'nice flower', the adult 'Yes, it's red isn't it'). Children are *prompted* to say more ('What did you eat?'). They are sometimes *echoed* with the same purpose ('You ate what?').

An experiment by Cazden (1965) with 2½-year-olds suggests that expanding is less effective than commenting upon what the child says in developing his language. Cazden calls commenting 'modelling'. Examples would be

child: doggie bite   *adult*: Yes, he's biting (*expansion*)
Yes, he's mad (*modelling*)

However, this remains an open question until more evidence is available; and indeed another experiment by Feldman and Rodgon (1970) showed just the opposite—that expansion was superior to modelling. These two experiments are mentioned merely to show how little we know at the present time of how children learn language, and how difficult it is to attain exact knowledge.

16.5 Summary

Communication with young children is the means by which we welcome them into the world, the means by which we sustain them in it, and the means by which we further their development. We may call this communication 'mothering' and it must be both supportive and challenging. If it is lacking, then prospects for the child in the short and the long term seem gloomy. Communication is total: it goes on by both verbal and non-verbal means. There are hints that there may be class differences in the way it is carried out. Talking to young children frequently goes on long before they can understand; and it is important that it should, for a variety of reasons, an important one being that this is the way they learn language, though we are by no means clear about how this happens.

17

How is language acquired ?

A very young child knows no language. He must acquire it. What is involved in doing this?

17.1 The nature of language

Language consists of words, which are organized in terms of grammar, phonology, and meaning.

As far as grammar is concerned, he must learn the rules of syntax for arranging words in relation to one another. He must know that words cannot go in any old order. 'We're only here for the beer' is acceptable, but 'Only for beer here the' is not. Some of the rules involved here are: subject precedes verb; 'only' must be adjacent to 'here' (not 'only we'); the preposition phrase 'for the beer' follows the rest; 'for' precedes 'the', which precedes 'beer'; 'we are' may be contracted to 'we're'; and so on.

The other group of grammatical rules concerns accidence, whereby words themselves alter, either by having additions, or by changing their form (in number, tense, and possession particularly). Thus the learner must discover that 'break' and 'broke' are connected, but not 'break' and 'steak', or 'broke' and 'coke'; and that there must be agreement between subject and verb ('we eat', not 'we eats') but that (unlike French) there is no agreement between adjectives and noun ('fat ladies' not 'fats ladies').

As far as phonology—the sound and sound patterns of the language— is concerned, the learner must master its phonemes, or individual sounds; its intonation, or sequence of pitches; its compulsory and optional stresses. He must be able to recognize which sounds are English and which aren't, even with nonsense words ('glo' is English, 'nglo' isn't). But he must also learn more complex rules, such as when 'you're not' is pronounced as a question, or as a prohibition, and when it is pronounced to mean 'don't be silly' or 'others might'.

103

The child must also learn meaning. In an elementary sense this involves knowing which name—'mummy', 'book', 'table'—belongs to which concrete object. Much more difficult, because they do not refer to concrete objects, are abstractions like 'love', 'hate', or 'cleanness'. There are also words for actions: actions which are comparatively simple and visible; actions which are neither, like 'I think', 'I believe'. Many words have no content at all; they are concerned with relationships. Thus in 'There's an old mill by the stream', only 'mill' and 'stream' have any content, but 'by the' has the job of relating 'mill' to 'stream'.

17.2 The child's problem

Let us put ourselves in the position of a young child who knows no language. He is surrounded by language, some designed for his ears, much not. He has to make sense of this language, not only to understand it but also to use it. It must be like it is for us as adults being in a foreign country whose language we do not understand. In some ways his situation is worse than ours in that he does not know even the basic facts about language, such as that it consists of words.

For instance, he hears sounds which we may represent on paper as follows:

> cee cee coirl tiffk bive vet uty zoop
> zet tis zet tis liuff caaz gum

He does not know that language is made up of individual words. For all he knows it may consist of long stretches of undulating noise. He does not know whether any, some, or all pauses are significant. He does not know which sounds are significant and which aren't. Thus there is a different sound represented by the *i* in 'coirl' from the one in 'liuff', but we take no notice of it in English; whereas two similarly close sounds represented by *th* and *d* in 'there' and 'dare' represent important distinctions.

Again he may notice certain parts are stressed, others not:

> c̄ee c̄ee c̄oirl t̄iffk b̄ive vĕt ūtў z̄oop
> z̄et tĭs z̄et tĭs luiff cӑaz ḡum

Does a stress mean a unit? What pattern can he deduce from

How is language acquired?

$$- - - - - \cup - \cup -$$
$$- \cup - \cup \cup \cup -?$$

We as adults are aware that language has certain patterns: for instance, those of simple sentences. The child may be aware of this, and seek the patterns, for it is from examples of these that he must deduce the rules for making others. He might then hypothesize that words which sound alike (begin with the same letter, for example) are related:

cee cee coirl . . . caaz

or he might wonder whether repetition didn't point to basic patterns

cee cee
zet tis zet tis

Now neither of those things would be true of this piece of language. It consists of a disguised form of:

Baa baa, black sheep, have you any wool?
Yes sir, yes sir, three bags full.

It contains no straightforward simple sentences, only an inversion as a question. Nor do the two following lines:

One for the master, and one for the dame,
And one for the little boy who lives down the lane.

It could be argued that 'three bags full' means 'I have three bags full', but this argument is only valid for somebody who already knows the simple sentence patterns. A good deal of what the child hears will not be in a form to suit his learning: it will perhaps be too complex or fragmentary. This makes the comparative ease with which he acquires language even more puzzling.

17.2.1 Comment

Of course, not all the language he encounters will be in a form unsuitable for learning: some of it will be simplified quite deliberately by his parents or other adults. A great deal of it is met with in context, linked with objects or actions. 'You want to get down' is accompanied almost immediately by the lifting down of the child, whose ear acquires 'down' and something of its significance. Nevertheless, even considering these

105

things, the dramatic progress he makes in learning language seems something of a mystery, which we shall have to look at further.

17.3 Summary

In language learning, lexis and the grammatical, phonological, and semantic conditions for its use are acquired. This seems a difficult task, and the explanations for it are not obvious.

18

Theories of language acquisition

18.1 Imitation

It is often assumed in casual conversation that children learn language
by 'imitating' their elders. But a moment's consideration shows us that
there is much more to it than that.

Let us take a parrot or budgerigar who imitates and nothing more.
He can say, for instance, 'Fifteen men on a dead man's chest' and can
perhaps supply the next line, 'Yo, ho ho and a bottle of rum'. But he
cannot, when the mood takes him, change it to 'Ya ha hoo and a barrel
of beer'. Nor can he use the line in the right situation. If the family
were drinking gin, if they were watching Tom and Jerry, or spying on
the neighbours, he would continue to use it unchanged. Still less could
he take the individual words and use them with other words ('You're
a rum lad', 'I want a hot water bottle'). He would need to have been
taught these phrases separately.

18.2 Classical conditioning

The parrot's ability to imitate is inborn. If he did not imitate the
human voice, he would imitate the sounds made by other birds and
animals. We can, however, train animals and birds to do things they
would not do naturally. It would presumably be impossible to teach an
elephant to jump through a hoop of fire because this is too far from her
natural behaviour, but we could (given sufficient skill, patience, and
courage) teach her to sit on a circular dais. In principle the way we
would do this is to show her the dais and urge her to mount it. Every
time she did this correctly we would reward her with a lump of sugar
or more substantial food, and pat her encouragingly. Soon she would
climb the dais when she saw it, because she now associated it with a
reward. Psychologists would regard the dais as a *stimulus*, the elephant

mounting it as a *response*, and the sugar as *reinforcement*. A bond is established between the stimulus and the response by means of a reward, or positive reinforcement.

stimulus S $\qquad\longrightarrow$ *response* R
dais   squatting on dais

as a result of *reinforcement*
sugar and praise

If the elephant showed a tendency to do other things at the sight of the dais, such as rolling it like a skittle ball at the trainer, this response would be discouraged by not providing the sugar, by a sharp reprimand or even a slap, so as to *extinguish* the undesired response. This would be known as negative reinforcement.

This principle is certainly involved in language learning. Martin, aged 16 months, is looking at a book with his mother. She shows him pictures (S), and when he responds by naming them correctly (R), she rewards him with praise.

Mother	yes it's a candle darling very good/what's that
Martin	(*noise*)
Mother	pardon darling
Martin	ock
Mother	no/yes it's not that's right/yes and what's that
Martin	deiyorog
Mother	yes frog/that's right

This theory doesn't get us far. 'Apple' or 'table' can be learnt in this manner, but obviously we can't hold up 'love' or 'honour' as a stimulus and reinforce a response to them. Much less can we go beyond single words or ideas. Where would we begin to teach a sentence like the one just used: 'This theory doesn't get us far' (remembering that the learner must know its meaning as he knows the meaning of 'frog', not just be able to recite it parrot-like)?

This (S→R) is the simplest theory in behavioural psychology. It is known as classical conditioning, but it is not the only theory.

18.3 Operant conditioning

No one would seriously argue that classical conditioning theory explains language acquisition beyond the earliest stages. A further theory, 'operant conditioning', associated with the name of B.F. Skinner (1957), is offered by the behaviourists as a complete explanation. Skinner distinguishes between two types of conditioning—respondent and operant. In respondent (classical) conditioning it is held that if there is no S there can be no R. But there seems to be other behaviour—for example, an infant crawling on the floor—in which the original stimulus is not known and not clearly observable. No one prods him to crawl, he just crawls, sometimes at meteoric speed. By bumping his head he learns not to crawl into walls (negative reinforcement); by being comforted by his father he learns to crawl to him (positive reinforcement).

Skinner argues that the production of noises (which become language) is a similar sort of behaviour. Let us suppose that Martin, in the conversation just quoted, had not been trying to say 'hot', but that 'ock' was one of the many noises children produce before they can speak. His mother reinforces (and corrects) the sound 'hot' by her approval, establishing a connection between the word and the picture of the candle, and presumably Martin will be more likely to use the sound in that connection in future.

The noise the child makes is not a response (R) to anything in the first place. Skinner calls it an operant. When the noise is uttered and reinforced, the child is more likely to use it in that particular circumstance again. Take another example. If the word 'food' is uttered, and is rewarded by the appearance of food, then the child will be much more likely to use the word 'food' again. The diagram below shows the simplest form of operant conditioning.

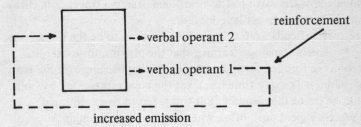

If it is said that simple processes like this scarcely go any distance at all in explaining our adult language, such as the language of this book, Skinner would argue that complex behaviour may be built up on these elementary bases. His famous experiments with pigeons, for instance, demonstrate how comparatively soon they can be taught to move in a figure of eight. (Every time a pigeon moves in the desired direction, but only then, it is fed corn.) And we can, of course, see how longer responses to stimuli could be acquired by conditioning. Thus when we hear 'How are you?' we very soon learn to respond with 'Very well, thank you' (whether it is true or not).

18.4 Critique of behaviourist theory

Strict behaviourists attempt to explain all human behaviour in terms of stimulus, response, and reinforcement. Skinner's famous experiments with the pigeons provide a good illustration. We might assume the pigeon is conscious of what it is doing, when it walks in a figure of eight. But this assumption is quite wrong: it is just responding to stimuli. We do not need to assume it has a mind which 'understands' or is aware of what it is doing. Behaviourists consider that there is no difference in *principle* between human behaviour and animal behaviour, despite the apparent complexity of the one compared with the other. Both, they say, can be explained in terms of stimulus, response, and reinforcement. There are, however, certain difficulties about behaviourist theories applied to language learning.

1. One is that the learner must have heard something said (S) before he can repeat it (R) and it can be reinforced. Now the number of words and combinations of words in the form of phrases and sentences is immense. It has been commented that there are at least 10^{20} sentences 20 words long, and, since it would take perhaps 1000 times the estimated age of the earth just to hear them, learning language in this way would be a somewhat lengthy task.

2. A second difficulty is that there does not seem to be the immediate reward for correct language learning that the pigeons, for example, received in the form of corn. An adoring mother hanging over her baby may give him milk every time he makes the noise represented by 'milk' and thus he learns the meaning. But this seems to be exceptional. Children talk a great deal, often when no one else is listening.

It is obviously impossible for the child to have heard every sentence he uses. Suppose he has learnt 'The elephant likes a bun'. What use can he make of this knowledge to generalize it to 'The elephant likes a cake'? If we assume a mind which recognizes that both bun and cake are nouns and that their meaning is similar, despite the appearance of the words, it is easy. But the behaviourist cannot assume this kind of awareness. We may illustrate from dogs again. A well trained dog would probably respond to 'talk' as he responds to 'walk', but would not respond to 'stroll', although their human meaning is closer. In other words, unless we can presume understanding the ability to generalize doesn't get us very far. Let us take a further example, the two sentences:

> John is eager to please
> John is easy to please.

The learner acquires the first sentence, and assumes by generalizing that the second can be used in a similar way. He is, of course, wrong. The sentences are only superficially similar. We cannot learn that from the words themselves but only from a deeper knowledge that in the first 'John' is the subject but in the second John is the object:

> John is eager to please
> It is easy to please John

18.5 Summary

It seems that in our present state of knowledge behaviourist theory is only somewhat more adequate than 'imitation' to explain language learning. These theories do not explain the creative elements in our use of language whereby we can produce sentences we have never heard before.

19

The creation of language

The theories we have examined so far do not explain how human beings are able to make sentences they have never heard before. We might ask a question which is in some ways similar: how can we play a game of monopoly which we have never played before (because no game of monopoly is like any game of monopoly that we have played before)? The answer in both cases is the same. We can do it because we know the rules—in one case the rules of monopoly, in the other the rules of grammar.

19.1 Theories of grammar

A grammar is a system of rules for arranging and adjusting words (see 6.2). In his book *Syntactic Structures* (1957) Noam Chomsky describes three grammars.

19.1.1 A finite state grammar

Let us suppose that we can give an alien from outer space some rules for using English. We might say that a basic rule is that one word is related to the next. Thus in the sentence, 'Beer is best', 'Beer' is related to 'is' as its subject, 'best' is related to 'is' as its complement. 'Beer' is related to 'is' also because both are singular (compare 'Beers are best').

But to say this does not get us very far. We very soon come up against sentences in which this is not true. 'Picture if you can a winkle'. There is no connection in 'Picture/if' or 'can/a' but there is in 'Picture/a'. Obviously, then, a grammar with rules saying there is a connection between one word and the next is not adequate.

19.1.2 A phrase structure grammar

We need a grammar in which there are rules which can cope with such apparent discontinuity between one word and the next. We need a grammar which has rules about groups of words, not just single words, and which has rules for inserting one group of words inside another. The traditional school grammar has such rules. It would explain the sentence as follows:

Picture . . . a winkle   main clause
if you can   subordinate adverbial clause of condition

Since an adverbial clause relates to a verb, it may be inserted next to a verb.

    Chomsky would regard such traditional grammar as 'phrase structure' grammar, but his terminology would be somewhat different:

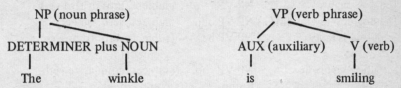

In the older terminology a 'phrase' was a group of words without a main verb; in modern terminology a phrase is a group of words dominated by a noun or a verb (and in the latter case it may have a main verb).

19.1.3 A transformational grammar

Such a grammar is still not satisfactory, however. We can make a separate analysis for each sentence admittedly. But when we have done this we are no nearer a definition of the connection between the following:

(a)   The winkle smokes a pipe.
(b)   The winkle does not smoke a pipe.
(c)   Does the winkle smoke a pipe?
(d)   Doesn't the winkle smoke a pipe?
(e)   The pipe is smoked by the winkle.
(f)   The pipe is not smoked by the winkle.
(g)   Is the pipe smoked by the winkle?
(h)   Isn't the pipe smoked by the winkle?

And yet we sense some connection. They are all forms of the same sentence, but certain changes have been made to them. Chomsky calls these changes 'transformations': they are changes into negative, interrogative, or passive, or various combinations of these. (These are (b) negative; (c) interrogative; (d) negative and interrogative; (e) passive; (f) passive and negative; (g) passive and interrogative; (h) passive, negative, and interrogative). Chomsky's 'transformational' grammar gives some explanation of this connection.

The argument is as follows. We all acquire two sets of rules. The first set of rules is for making 'basic phrase structures' or, to put it in everyday language, simple sentences. These rules are concerned with the basic order of subject, verb, and object or complement. The rules produce four basic patterns:

The dog gnaws	NP VP	(subject, intransitive verb)
The dog gnaws grandma	NP VP obj.	(subject, verb, object)
Grandma is tasty	NP VP be	(subject, verb 'to be', complement)
Grandma seems upset	NP VP cop. Comp.	(subject, copulative verb, complement)

The second set of rules are 'transformational rules'. The kernel sentence, such as 'The winkle smokes a pipe' or 'The dog gnaws', is 'transformed' to various combinations of interrogative, negative, or passive states. The rules for changing tense ('The dog gnawed') and number ('The dogs gnaw') are also a form of transformation.

19.2 Innate language ability

The theory of transformational grammar makes it possible to understand how human beings can produce language they haven't heard before. It is not because they are just conditioned to reproduce words and sentences they have heard in appropriate situations, but because they have rules for making more sentences. And these rules are not limitless. One set of rules produces the simple sentences; the second set enables us to adapt our sentences in various ways.

The question becomes, therefore: how do young children acquire these rules? Normally they hear a large amount of language daily, and it seems that they have to learn the rules from this. In 17.2 we spoke of the nature of the problem of acquiring language. If we regard the mind as a kind of 'data processing machine' which examines the probabilities of occurrence of certain features, then there are difficulties. For instance, to deduce the rules for making a simple sentence pattern such as one of those above, we might expect the child to hear a considerable number of these. He may do so, but they are frequently in disguised form—expanded, fragmented or 'transformed', or with parts of them 'understood'. (Thus 'Yes', in answer to 'Are you going?', means 'Yes, I am going', the last three words being 'understood'.) The occurrence of what Chomsky calls 'well-formed sentences' seems to be limited.

Chomsky therefore argues that the mind has a built-in Language Acquisition Device (LAD) which 'knows' what to look for in the mass of language around. The mind is not a blank on which language stamps itself: instead, it is *predisposed* to pick out the rules of language. To some extent we may compare it to a magnet which will pick out metal items from a mass of materials, but not wooden or plastic ones. Children acquire the rules of language quite quickly, and the acquisition of grammar precedes that of meaning (as we use the term), although this does not mean that a sentence he uses does not 'make sense to the child'.

This view that human beings are innately constituted to acquire language receives support from a biologist like Lennenberg, who compares it to man's innate ability to walk upright on two feet. Lennenberg argues that there is little variation within the species. All natural languages resemble one another, in that they all make use of similar features. Thus they all string together individual words, and have a syntactic structure; they draw on a comparatively small number of sounds (phonemes), some 40 or 50. It follows that either all languages, many completely separated from one another in remote parts, acquire by chance the same features (this seems very unlikely) or man is somehow predisposed to acquire a language which has such features.

He also sees language learning ability as innate because it seems to depend, not on any specific experiences that a child has had, but on certain organic developments of the brain. Even when conditions are unfavourable it develops. Thus deaf children learn to read and write even though they fail to develop vocal communication at the normal rate. And man always seems to have had language, more or less as we know it. There does not seem to have been an earlier stage at which a non-syntactic language was used (Lennenberg, 1964).

19.3 Summary

Theories of conditioning do not seem adequate to explain man's ability to learn language. A more likely explanation is that children learn rules for making language, rather than learning forms of language. According to Chomsky, these rules are of two kinds: phrase-structure rules and transformational rules. How do children acquire these rules? A 'data processing' method seems inadequate. It is more likely that the capacity is innate, that man possesses a 'Language Acquisition Device' which predisposes him to select the rules from the language around him.

20

The development of language

20.1 Stages in language development 1 - 5

During the first five years when a child is learning language we may
reasonably speak about definite stages in his language development, as
long as we are content to confine ourselves to the grammar he uses,
because that is reasonably easy to study. There are, however, no definite
stages by which his vocabulary increases. We can certainly say that the
vocabulary of a child at 5 years will be greater than it was at 18 months.
It is, however, increasingly difficult as the child gets older to know the
extent of his vocabulary: he may know many words he does not use, or
we do not hear him use. As far as semantic development is concerned, it
is often very difficult to be sure what he means by what he says; though
we hope he talks more interestingly—'talks more sense'—at 5 than at
1½.

20.2 Acquisition of grammar

There are three aspects of grammar to be acquired—the phrase structure
rules, the transformational rules (see Chapter 19); and the rules of
accidence.

20.2.1 Holophrases
Children begin with single words. These need not be words in our
sense. A child can get a long way with a single sound combination like
'uhuh' to mean a variety of things. Sometimes they are more than
single words to an adult, but the child learns them as one: 'what's that'
is one example of what is known as a 'giant word'. These single word
equivalents are called *holophrases.*

117

They are used in a variety of ways: linked with action ('down' meaning 'I want to get down'); as a name ('dindin'); to express emotion, such as approval or disapproval ('uhuh'). It is interesting to note that the child's use of a holophrase may indicate a greater grammatical knowledge than is immediately evident. Thus, when he uses 'door' to mean 'open door', he is using a noun to mean verb plus noun in our terms.

20.2.2 Phrase structures

(*a*) *Pivot and open classes*   The next stage seems to be when the child uses words in combinations, and can change the combination. Thus we can only regard 'what's that' as a holophrase until we know the child can use 'what's this', 'what's book', etc. It seems that children have a small number of words (pivot class) that are frequently employed, which they use along with a larger number of others (open class) that are less frequently employed. Thus, 'allgone' or 'see' or 'my' could be pivot words, used alongside 'milk', 'shoe', 'hand', 'sock', 'apple', and so on. Pivot words seldom occur in combination with each other, but open words may do so ('horsey, cow').

This notion is useful in indicating how children do combine words; but it may also be doing them an injustice to run all such combinations together as a pivot/open class. It seems that in effect they may be using a form of adult grammar. A child saying 'allgone milk' is using adult terms *verb and noun*, whereas in 'my sock' he is using possessive pronoun and noun.

(*b*) *Further phrase structures*   Further combinations that occur are more in accordance with adult grammar, often in stripped down or telegraphic form. Thus Susan, aged 2½, is looking at a picture book with her mother:

Mother   Shall we find a picture of your dolly?
Susan   yes/there dolly/there dolly (*book falls*) oh dear/dolly gone/
            get dolly mummy/get dolly/I get dolly

We find here two complete sentences syntactically speaking ('get dolly mummy', 'I get dolly'), though the definite article is not yet used. The verb 'to be' is also missing ('there dolly').

20.2.3 Early transformations

Emerging rather later than the first phrase structure are some transformations, such as questions with a word like 'where' or 'what' (known as '*wh*-transformations'), in a sentence like 'Where mummy gone?' Auxiliary verbs are not used (for example, 'Where *has* mummy gone?'). The child will also use a negative transformation using 'no' or 'not', for example, 'No mummy go' (with the negative probably used in front of the sentence).

Here is part of a dialogue between Guy, who is nearly 3, and his mother. They are playing with his toys, principally a 'wheel van' and model animals. The van is loaded and is supposed to be going to school.

Mother	Where's the school bus? Is this the school bus in the car park?
Guy	No the wheel van, wheel van.
Mother	That can't be a school bus.
Guy	No a the wheel van. Where school bus mummy? Where school bus? Where school bus? ...
Mother	Which way is it to school? Which way is the bus going?
Guy	That my wheel van. Open it. Daddy do that. Daddy do that.
Mother	Daddy's opened the doors.
Guy	Here school mummy. Here school.
Mother	Good, you'd better stop there then.
Guy	Pig get out/pig/pig get out.
Mother	Let him get out.
Guy	Yes, wheel van. Going brm. Doing writing.
Mother	He's doing writing at school. He's a very clever pig.
Guy	Sit down. Sit down. Sit going down. School bus in here. This one. This one wheel van going this. This one going school. This one. This one going school. This horsey going school. In school, this horsey.
Mother	Can he get in?
Guy	Yes.
Mother	Yes, just about.
Guy	Going school, your school, going school. Get out, get out lamb. Err ... get out. Doing writing, writing.
Mother	Do they do anything else at school?
Guy	Yes. Sums. Sums. Going school Zoe, going school, going school. That one going wheel van, in wheel van. No. Brm. Legs in it. Going school. Going school. That little, little big

119

lamb going school. That big lamb. Go school Zoe, go school. No touch it. Doing writing. Go away. Go away. No touch it. Here school. Here school. Yes. Brm here—that—that school. No touch it. Go away. Go away. Play daddy. What's that for? What's that for?

Mother	What's it for?
Guy	Look out. Look out.
Mother	Yes, that't the lookout, that's the windscreen.
Guy	Yes.
Mother	What are you going to use it for?
Guy	To look out. Drive, driving. Me driving.

It is clear that Guy's understanding is considerable: he may not know the word 'windscreen', but he knows the concept and its function. As far as his grammar is concerned, to judge from this sample he can use *wh*-transformations ('Where school bus?' 'What's that for?'), and negative transformations by inserting 'no' ('No touch it'), neither of which, of course, are accurate in terms of adult grammar. He uses some verbs ('touch') but not auxiliaries ('This one going school', not 'is going'), and the verb 'to be' is omitted ('Here school'). He is moving to the stage of being able to use some prepositions ('Legs in it'), but is not secure in this ('going school'). He can use the definite article ('the wheel van').

At this stage, at least in this passage, there is no evidence that he can use rules of accidence (for example, tense, number, possession).

20.2.4 Further transformations and accidence

Between the ages of 3 and 4 many children acquire auxiliary verbs which enable them to carry out interrogative transformations (for example, 'you think' becomes 'do you think?'). Sentences become less telegraphic in form as words such as definite and indefinite articles and prepositions are used. Features of accidence (for example, agreement of singulars, tense other than the present) appear. Sentences may become more complex.

The following is a transcription of part of a conversation with Francesca, aged 3, about her tortoise. Pet tortoises are a pretty torpid lot, but Francesca's is a toy powered by the dynamos of her imagination, so there is very little it can't do.

yes he does/he eats/and he eats a apple/ he eats lots of things/to eat/in the winter/eats leaves cabbages vedables and apples and nanas and grapes and he eats/hollies/they won't prick/his teeth/won't prick it teeth/and and/and he eats flowers and roses/and petals/no he doesn't eat the stalks up/no he don't make his teeth/he don't pick the flower up off/the stalk/he doesn't/no he only eats petals/and they fall off the flower/and he like them/and he/and he picks them up to eat . . . that's what he wants to eat . . . *cat enters* hallo/hallo/going to go in your room/I don't know where he's going to go/do you think he's going to go on your bed.

At this stage later and earlier forms of accidence exist side by side ('he eats', 'he picks them up', 'they fall off', as against 'he like them'). There are assured negatives ('he doesn't eat the stalk up'), and interrogatives ('do you think he's going to go on your bed'). The most advanced feature is what is now known as 'embedding', where a sentence (or subordinate clause) is included in another ('I don't know' and 'he's going to go where' as 'I don't know where he's going to go').

There are no signs in the passage that Francesca can yet handle tense by means of inflections, but she can certainly handle a future meaning in 'going to go'. Could she also have said 'will go'? There is insufficient evidence on this. Certainly Amanda, who is just 4, in this next transcript has no difficulty with past inflections.

Once upon a time mousie lived/and he couldn't have a hole because/he was so fat/and he didn't have a time to spare because he was so happy/ and I didn't know what to do/so he had an idea/I've giving him a new home so I did/that was in my mummy and daddy's room/there was a little mouse hole.
was there?
and they/there really is.

Command of inflections is apparent, as well as the ability to use complex embedded constructions ('I didn't know what to do'). The unacceptable forms ('I've giving') are doubtless slips.

20.2.5 Almost complete command

By Francesca's age (just over 3), and certainly by Amanda's age (4), many children have got a considerable command of English grammar—the phrase structure, the transformational rules, and the rules of accidence. They may be said to 'know' English grammar.

There are, however, some syntactic rules which children do not seem to master until they are older. Carol Chomsky, the wife of Noam

121

Chomsky, has investigated these in *The Acquisition of Syntax in Children from 5 to 16* (1969). Take, for instance, a sentence like 'John is eager to see'. Children will easily understand that it is John who wants to do the seeing. But if we take 'John is easy to see', they will not readily grasp that it is John who will be seen. They need to realize that the subject of the second sentence is 'to see John'. (Every adult realizes this, even though he might not be able to formulate it in this way.) Thus children were shown a blindfold doll and asked 'Is this doll easy or hard to see?' A child who answered 'hard to see' would be asked to make it easy to see; the typical response of the younger children would be to remove the blindfold.

Again, children may be confused about who does the shovelling in a sentence like 'John promised Bill to shovel the driveway'. The younger children think that Bill shovels, on an analogy with, say, 'John told Bill to shovel the driveway', where it would be Bill. Similarly, distinctions between 'ask' and 'tell' present problems. In all these cases the 5-year-olds predominantly got the wrong answers, but improved as they grew older so that by the age of 10 nearly all of them understood the constructions.

It should be added that, as far as accidence is concerned, many regional and class dialects have forms of their own, different from the standard forms. Forms such as 'I done it', 'us be going', 'we'm going', 'I told he' are commonly used in such cases. Such forms almost never result in any confusion in understanding, though they are often stigmatized as 'bad grammar'. 'Us isn't doing nothing' breaks three rules of accidence (but none of syntax) and the meaning is never in doubt except to the pedant who wishes to score a debating point.

20.3 Summary

It is possible to trace the stages in the acquisition of grammar from holophrases (single 'words') to combinations of words, first organized according to the child's own syntax, and then increasingly along the lines of adult grammar. In the later stages variation on simple patterns ('transformations'), and alterations to individual elements for particular purposes, accidence, are learned. By the time they enter school, children normally have a considerable (though not complete) mastery of grammatical rules.

21

'Good at English'?

21.1 Competence and performance

A knowledge of the rules of grammar, particularly phrase structure and transformational rules, is what Noam Chomsky (1900, p. 4) has described as one's 'competence' in language. This term may be misleading as it just refers to the intuitive *knowledge* of the rules a person possesses, and not to his ability to use language on this or that occasion: these uses he refers to as 'performances'. 'We thus make a fundamental distinction between *competence* (the speaker/hearer's knowledge of his language) and *performance* (the actual use of language in concrete situations).' It is important to keep Chomsky's special use of the term 'competence' in mind, because normally we use it to mean 'performance' ('He gave a competent speech'). Chomsky says that in fact one's competence is never truly realized in one's performance: 'A record of natural speech will show numerous false starts, deviations from the rules, changes of plan in mid-course, and so on'.

Obviously there is much more to 'performance' than a knowledge of grammatical rules. A personal letter, a government report, a funny story about Wigan, gossip in a fish and chip shop, all demonstrate the user's knowledge of grammar, but the language of the report is different in register (15.1) from that of the gossip and that of the story. Spoken language will also vary according to the different non-linguistic means of communication which accompany it.

The idea of competence says nothing about these aspects of communication. It is helpful in that it makes us realize that we cannot speak of children who just 'haven't got any language' if they don't use it in front of us, but in itself it doesn't get us very far. It says nothing about our ability to communicate: all that Chomsky classes rather vaguely under 'performance'. Del Hymes (1971) suggests that little purpose is served by the distinction between competence and performance. We need a term concerned with both our knowledge of language,

123

and our ability to use it, and he does not see why the term 'competence' should not be used for this. Competence in language could thus be called *linguistic* competence. But we cannot ignore other means of communication (silence, for instance, can be used meaningfully with words) and thus he uses the term *communicative* competence. The matter of communicative competence is too complex to be tackled here, as it concerns the projection of a total personality by linguistic and non-linguistic means. We will confine ourselves to a narrower topic, which is still complex: what do we mean by linguistic competence, or what do we mean when we say someone is 'good at English'?

21.2 'Good at English'

'Oh yes, she's good at English', the teacher may tell the parents. Or the parents may be confronted with a school report which, under the heading 'English' reads 'Only fair' (is this the same as 'Fair only'?) or 'Excellent', or perhaps 'Poor/very poor'. Whether or not the parents know what these terms mean, the teachers must, otherwise they wouldn't use them.

But do they? At one time 'good' for some teachers meant an ability to do clause analysis, but certainly not an ability to speak English, for which there was little opportunity. A few years later it meant ability in creative writing (the expression of intense personal feelings from the viewpoint of a haddock, for instance). For many parents and many employers (who object to their typed letters beginning 'Dear Sire or Madman') it means formal correctness in spelling and punctuation. Other people comment on language ability negatively. Edward Blishen once said that many children suffer from 'verbal starvation'. One infant teacher was heard to say recently that some of her children 'just don't have any language'. More fashionably, some children, we are told, suffer from a 'restricted code'. It is obviously important to examine the topic.

21.3 Language and situation

We commonly find that we are better at using language on some occasions than on others. We all know people who dry us up, or topics on which we have nothing to say, or occasions when we don't quite know how to put things (boasting modestly at an interview, for instance). So often it's not that we 'lack language' in the sense that we do not know the words and phrases required; it is that we are not able to use them in a particular circumstance. One is often surprised what command of language apparently inorate children display in the right situation. Of course, we can understand more than we are normally called upon to say.

Teachers, like Chomsky, have often felt that the children's grammar was in reasonably order. What was needed, therefore, was to add to their vocabulary. To teach children lists of words isolated from their experience is, of course, bad practice. They can effectively increase their vocabulary only in relation to the experiences they need to express. A large vocabulary in itself is no guarantee of linguistic ability. Profound things may be said simply, even parsimoniously, yet effectively. And the understanding of a joke like

Child   Mummy, Mummy, can I play with Grandma?
Mother   Oh no, we can't keep digging her up.

is dependent on understanding two slightly different usages of the term 'play with' and not on knowing several words for 'play'.

Whether a speaker or writer is successful or not will depend on the function for which he is employing language, and these functions are various. Language, of course, communicates, but if this means passing information from A to B, then it is a very limited account of what language does. Language enables us, for instance, to influence, to interact by means of, to explore, to celebrate, to explain ourselves to ourselves as well as to others, to establish, assert and maintain our identity (Chapter 9).

Teachers set up situations with which to elicit language from the children. If these situations are too difficult, they only have the effect of discouraging the children: thus to write about a happening might have this effect, to talk about it the opposite. The tasks must be such that the child is able to express his thoughts and feelings, with reasonable success, which will spur him on on a further occasion.

21.3.1 Situation—spoken and written
Let us consider the major division into spoken and written tasks which may be given to pupils. Here is a written account given by Jenny, aged 9, of her holiday in Pisa:

125

The leaning tower pisa

We went to pisa. We all had an ice-cream. It was a very hot day I had a chocolate one. then we went to the tower I was the first one to the top. Pisa is a very small town.

The sentences are short and the thoughts are unconnected. It may be that she is striving for formal correctness, though without complete success. The piece lacks life and interest. Contrast her spoken account of the same holiday:

it was a few months ag ago/about half a year/I think it was/we went we went I think/it was in italy/and we/we went to a big tower and it/one of the seven wonders of the world and it was crooked it went like that and/there were 200 steps and we had to go all the way up and/I was the first one up and we/I I almost got blown off the side when the bells went/we had it was about you had to put earplugs in mm but we didnt have any/cause we didnt know they were going to go/then then we had to go down again/and then/just across/across the road there was another place when mm/I think it was a/it was round with a/long round roof on/and and/somebody came in it made such an echo/it was very very loud/he was talking softly and when/when he went in it made a very loud echo/and then after that we went out again and we went down to the graveyard/I dont know if we were allowed in but we did go in/and mm/there was a few graves and/I wish Id seen some bones but I didnt/I looked in every single grave that hadnt a grave top on/ but I didnt find any

The transcription cannot do justice to the spoken presentation, and the way it held the audience, a small group of friends, rapt. There is a whole dimension of excitement, humour, and emotion which is missing. But what we have is interesting, with vivid details. A sentence like the last is quite complex, even though she had no time to think about it.

From the written version we would probably have concluded that this girl is 'poor at English': from the spoken we know that she is not. It's too easy to say the spoken is 'better' than the written. Writing is in some ways more difficult: we have to conjure up the whole scene by using vivid language; we do not have the qualities of our voice and our presence to help. (In this sense, as Vygotsky (1962, pp. 98-101) says, written language is abstract.) Even so, we would expect less of a discrepancy between spoken and written versions. One of the reasons for this may be the expectations she thinks she has to fulfil. Has she been told 'I don't mind if you write only a little, as long as it's right'? But even granted this, why does she not choose some of the interesting details—the noise of the bells, or the graves—rather than the trivial ones?

126

It seems clear that she has not learned to use written language as a means of expressing her thoughts and feelings. There is no doubt that we as teachers partly create the language our pupils produce.

21.4 Summary

The notion of 'communicative competence' for our total ability to communicate is a useful one, but difficult to consider: the notion of what we mean when we say someone is 'good at English' is more manageable. The 'same' linguistic task may produce very different language in different situations such as the spoken and written. To some extent the situation creates the language.

22

'Good at English': some criteria

22.1 The language of an 8-year-old

22.1.1 Toni's spoken language

Toni is 8. She is a diffident, 'not-very-able' girl who has few companions of her own age, but will relate to adults who gain her confidence.

We have been considering how the situation in which children perform has an effect on the nature of the English they produce. Let us look at several pieces of spoken and written language from Toni and ask ourselves how successful they are. Were the tasks too difficult so that she failed, with consequent discouragement, or were they just challenging enough to cause her to reach out for words to give meanings she might not otherwise have expressed?

What criteria of success do we use? She must communicate, certainly, and this implies that she must make an imaginative identification with the listener or reader to see what her words are meaning to them. It also implies that she has a choice of language in which to offer the meanings she thinks appropriate.

Toni had partial success in telling a trusted adult about some birds in her garden:

once I could remember/about a little bird/he was just born/in the little nest/by our gate/and/you see when he was grown up he learnt how to fly/and he kept popping out of the hedge so we kept putting him back in/soon he grown up into a bird and he still kept doing it so we/had to keep putting him back in/and then he flew away/and a new one came see/so/we/kept putting this nother little bird in/he kept doing the same/ so when/a bird came/I kept putting him back in and he came/kept coming out on another side of the hedge

There seems to be a slight confusion about time, and about the number of birds, which is probably in the language rather than in her mind.

This task, arranging from her past experience, she found more difficult than when she was asked to give an account of a prearranged sequence such as a TV Boss Cat cartoon:

so boss cat/went away/and he suddenly realized that on saturday/there would be a race and/he on saturday he went to the race/and he made the horse go into the race/and the horse didnt win

Here she is confident, obviously seeing the events clearly, and she deliberately emphasizes the day, and repeats 'the horse', so that the listener will not feel it is boss cat who enters the race.

22.1.2 Toni's written language

On the other hand, her retelling of part of a Hobbit story that had been read to her the day before was disastrous. She confused the order of events, and did not understand action and motive. She could not make it clear to herself and thus could not begin to make it clear to others. In her written version of the same episode she gave up even the attempt to understand, which the presence of a listener had provided her with:

Then want water round the outste of the HOBBIT. In the cave it was cold. The HOBBIT was a very good HOBBIT. Some Time. The HOBBIT was going to go in the water for 10 day. The HOBBIT did not like it. It is not a very good cave.

It is clear that the tasks, spoken and written, could not succeed because the summary of a section of a very literary book, heard once before, was beyond her (and many others of her age).

On the other hand, she obviously found real satisfaction in writing her diary for that week. There is quite a long entry, of which this is only part:

Sunday I went to the Hospital. And I went to picked Some flowers for Mommy and Daddy. and I Play with my frinds. And my frind is Lisa, My Brother play with Lisa Brother—it is funny for my and Lisa Brother because Lisa Brother nemy is the sames at Brother nemy Because my Brother nemy is neil. and Lisa Brother nemy is neil.

If we conventionalize the spelling and punctuation we have a joke with the reasons for it very carefully and effectively explained in simple vocabulary. Her own chuckle comes through, as it were, perhaps even better than it would in her spoken language. Unlike the Hobbit passage this diary is not constrained by the idea of having to write 'good sentences' or to spell and punctuate correctly, with the consequent depression of ambition.

The Time Machine story is interesting from other points of view:

and I found myself go backwards to the ole day when Jesus was born. the people was poor in those day. But I was not poor. and God help the people to Be not strong. The people Did not have clothes like me. The Time Machine fell fo the rocks. and I could not get Back to my home. Jesus was a boy when when I come to Bethlehem. and Jesus Play with me. and I live with Jesus. and Jesus help me build a Time Machine. But I could not build a Time Machine. but God make me Strong. In the end I made my Time Machine.

In some ways it is an allegory of Toni. 'Jesus play with me' she says. No one else did. 'God make me strong', she says. There was need for this as her father often deserted her mother. This piece was serving for Toni other functions which we tend to forget when we identify English too crudely with communication. It is noticeable that it is in her writing, where she has more privacy, more time to reflect, that she is, albeit unaware, attempting to deal with some of her deeper problems.

Obviously 'good at English' cannot be defined in terms of spelling and punctuation alone, nor in such over-simple ways as the amount of vocabulary, nor in performance of any particular task, though we would regard someone who could use English for a variety of functions in a variety of situations as having more linguistic ability than someone who could not. One thing we certainly require is that people shall be able to externalize their thoughts and feelings in a form we can share, and this demands some recognition of what words are likely to mean to us. Toni is learning to do this. But, of course, it is not the only function of language, as we saw in the Time Machine. If Toni is not conspicuously good at English, at least English is good for her.

22.2 Context free language

In the past 'good at English' has usually meant 'good at written English', such as compositions.

Written English tends to be 'context free': the whole of the meaning is carried in the words; there is no speaker to convey emotion in his voice or gestures; and he is not supported by an audience. Kevin, aged 9, tells his classmates:

and so he put him/in with him/and he was about this long/and he ate
him up

He is talking about his pet goldfish, eaten by a lamprey (brought to the
classroom), and they understood perfectly. But in his diary Kevin has
to explain more because the audience is absent and presumably does not
share the background of his friends.

We caut a long worm in the cannal it was yellow it ate all the stickle-
backs. My little brother put it in the tank the worm ate him up

What written English requires the writer to do is to make an imaginative leap into the reader's mind and to try to conceive how things will
appear to him. In this Kevin doesn't quite succeed. The goldfish is 'it'
and 'him' in the last sentence but the identity is not quite clear. It is not
that he lacks the vocabulary, but he cannot conceive the reader's
difficulties. On the other hand, he succeeds in doing so in his description of the creature.

The fact that he can describe it as a worm does not mean that his
conceptual grasp is complete. As one of his classmates said, 'It's not a
worm. Worms don't cat tiddlers'. For an exact description he would
need the word 'lamprey', but this lack does not prevent his finding
words to tell us about the animal. In fact, his very ignorance of the
name gives us a more vivid description than we might otherwise have
got. In a sense much written English is for an 'audience of strangers': it
has to be more explicit because the writer cannot assume too much.

Spoken English tends, however, to be 'context bound': we almost
always speak to some one present, from whom we get immediate
reaction (if only looks, nods, grunts) to tell us if we are making the
right guesses about his understanding, and there is much we convey by
our personalities. Often the things we talk about are immediately
present. How explicit our language should be will still depend, of
course, on how far the listener shares our knowledge of words and
things. Thus an American might be puzzled by being directed to 'the
bottom of the road where the church used to be', not only because he
would be ignorant of the church, but also because 'bottom' for 'end' is
not U.S. usage. But it is true that on the whole it is easier for nearly
everyone to use the spoken rather than the written language.

Certainly the written language can be a good test of our ability to
communicate through words and nothing else, and no one would
deprecate that. But in fact written words are less than words in that
they are stripped of the sounds, stresses, and intonations properly

belonging to them (as well as the attitudes and emotions which inevitably come out when we speak). Most of our communication goes on in speech, so if we are to judge someone good at English we must take into account their spoken language also. This is not easy as people's performances vary, probably even more than with the written language, from situation to situation.

22.3 Vocabulary and language

One thing which prevents people from performing well in some situations is their uncertainty about the appropriate language conventions, or 'registers' to use. On the one hand, there are social conventions, but to call them conventions does not imply they are necessarily trivial. There is a range of relationships implied by the differences between 'Shut the door', 'Would you mind shutting the door?' 'Put t'wood in t'hole', and to vary the tone of each one of these introduces more. On the other hand, there are necessary intellectual or technical conventions. It is his interest in its chemical properties, not obscurantism, that causes a scientist to refer to common salt as sodium chloride.

Even so, it is easy to lay too much emphasis on the vocabulary people possess. It is not so much what their language *is* but what they can *do* with it—its functions—which seems to be important. For instance, Joan Tough, in her Schools Council project, 'Communication in the Early Years', shows that, despite apparently having a similar quantity of language, 3 to 5-year-old 'disadvantaged children' were, compared with others, less able to report on the past, collaborate, explain, create imaginatively, justify their own behaviour, and so on. They had not *got into the habit* of using language in certain ways.

22.4 Linguistic ability

Clearly we need to reconsider the meaning of 'good at English'. We can assume that every normal native English speaker will have the basic grammar and vocabulary of the language. What more do we look for?

First, that a person can make an imaginative leap into his listener's mind so as to choose language that has meaning for the listener. Strangely, this second person is sometimes oneself, as when one talks speculatively or writes a poem so as to find words in which one can understand something.

Second, that a person can choose with discrimination from his stock of words and phrases which is the best word to put next to the other. This does not necessarily imply a huge vocabulary. When Blake speaks of the 'Sick Rose' he relates two simple words to produce a third thing, profound and vivid. Choice brings about the creation of a relationship between words.

Third, that a person can use language to carry out a variety of functions. We all have muscles, but cannot all embroider, tight-rope walk, or belly dance. We all have language, but may not have acquired the habit of using it in certain ways. Some people can assert but not argue, argue but not discuss, talk but not listen. Of course, these are habits of mind as well as language.

Fourth, that a person can use language in a variety of situations. People said to have a 'restricted code' are considered to be limited in the situations in which they can perform effectively. Such situations tend to be context bound because it is explicit language these speakers find difficult. They might also find some of the functions of language hard to operate.

22.5 Summary

The study of Toni's language brings out strongly the relationship of her performance to the task she is expected to undertake. It is clear that certain tasks are so far beyond her that they can only result in discouragement; but other tasks stretch her sufficiently to give her a feeling of achievement.

The ability to produce a context free language is certainly one of the criteria we use to judge someone's linguistic ability; but there are others, such as use of language to serve a variety of functions; and, particularly, the ability of the speaker to adjust his language to the listener's frame of reference.

23

'I's in difficults miss'

23.1 Difficulty with language

23.1.1 Language and class

There is a good deal of debate as to whether 'working-class language' is inferior to, or just different from, 'middle-class language'. Certainly in the past it has often been thought inferior, partly because its accidence was not standard (see 20.2.5). As we have seen, however, no particular accidence is essential to language, and some languages get along with very little at all (Chapter 8). We have also seen that language and thought interact and are related, but they are not the same (Chapter 12). It seems that language privation should not be described in class terms at all, but in some such terms as we have outlined above: what people can or cannot do with their language; how far they can make a leap into the minds of others so as to choose the language which has meaning for them.

23.1.2 Linguistic privation

To argue that one form of language or 'dialect' which serves the need of a group is not inferior to another merely because, say, its accidence or paralinguistics are different is one thing. To say that everyone has a language adequate for their needs, if only we could view it freed of preconceptions, is quite another, and is clearly false.

Ben, the boy whose cry for help, 'I's in difficults miss', forms the title of this chapter, is in no sense the victim of 'middle-class' deprecation of 'working-class' language. His language privation is only too genuine. He is a 'remedial' pupil, with a verbal IQ 70-80. He is alarmingly big for a boy of 11, and his resorts to violence seem related to his frustrations in other forms of expression. The conversation discussed below was recorded with a sympathetic adult in a familiar environment—a corner of his classroom—with the rest of the class

134

pursuing other activities. It could be argued that the classroom situation was likely to show his language in an unfavourable light. But the opposite is likely to be true. The adult took great pains and spent a good deal of time listening to what he had to say. This certainly did not happen outside school. Often his classmates misunderstood what he said to them.

23.2 Features of Ben's speech

23.2.1 Information

In response to an invitation to talk about himself, where he lived, his interests, and so on, he spoke as follows, with much incidental support and encouragement from the adult.

I live Stratfield . . . . its some/bricks house/its a bricks house . . . . I we got/we got/some (*rooms*) up the front/we got two up the front/mm/ its one not very old and one best one (*incoherent section*) . . . . we got a colour telly (*preferences*) tarzan and football (*talking of Tarzan*) he always go (*begins as though to do gesture of breast beating*) I can't do it . . . . he got a knife/by his (*gesticulates to thigh but can't find this word or equivalent, accepts prompt of 'leg'*).

Many features of Ben's speech are indicated here.

(a) The phonology and paralinguistics cause difficulties. There is a strong local accent, but even within that certain pronunciations cause confusion. Certain parts are incoherent noises and it is difficult to tell whether the problem lies in the phonology and paralinguistics only, or in the underlying language as well.

(b) The syntax here is acceptable in that there are 'well-formed sentences' ('I can't do it'; 'we got a colour telly'), but these are 'old-organized' phrases (see 4.2.4). 'I live Stratfield' indicates an uncertainty about the use of prepositions like 'in', whereas 'up the front' is a dialect idiom.

(c) The accidence is inconsistent. As far as concord is concerned, he senses there is something wrong with 'its some bricks house' but the best he can do in remedy is 'its a bricks house'.

(d) The active vocabulary is limited. On two occasions he resorts to gesture when he cannot find the words; but in the second case clearly knows the word 'leg' which would have served. The contrast between the living room and the best room defeats him. It was carefully elicited from him subsequently that what he was

135

trying to put into words was something like 'the older
furnishings are in the living room and the newer in the best room'.
In fact in speaking of the living room ('its one not very old') he
says roughly the opposite of what he means.

23.3.3 The past
The task of describing matters of fact and information well known to
him presents less difficulty to Ben than recalling a past event.

oh yes/I er/on Saturday/on Saturday/I went to Launton and(... ? ...)
off my friend/and she called Madeline. .... and/she went in to the
station for the train. .... up the platform and she get on and I really
left and we left/and we come home/and/we/when I came home/I was
asleep and my dad/we stopped/for my sister she not a very good
traveller/she feel ill/and/and/and/and then/she was all right we
(*incoherent*) tow-er (*told her*) tow-er/tell me when you want to stop/
she said please stop now please dad/and she went out/mummy and dad/
then and my sister and dad went out for a walk I wake up/and look and
back I fall asleep.

The account has more coherence transcribed than delivered orally, when
it was hard to follow. The problem of organization is greater and the
average listener would probably be confused about what was happening.
It is interesting to note that the syntactic arrangement is orderly,
particularly with phrases which are idiomatic or may have been
remembered verbatim ('tell me when you want to stop', 'my sister and
dad went out for a walk'). Ben seems to recognize the need for an
indirect construction (told her to tell us when she wanted to stop) and
perhaps this is indicated by his hesitations, but he is not capable of the
transformations required and gives instead a direct quotation. The
omission of the verb 'to be' ('she called Madeline', 'she not a very good
traveller') seems to occur in the present tense (with he and she, but not
with its—'its some bricks house') but not in the past ('I was asleep').
Common verbs ('went') may be used in the past form, whereas less
common ones are in the present even where past is needed ('I wake up'),
but this is not consistent ('she get on' where 'got' would be expected).

The major problem, however, for Ben is not one of particular forms
or even of vocabulary; it is a failure to organize what resources he has.
The general arrangement of incident is chronological, and this does not
seem to present him with much difficulty: his thought sequence is
clear. But it is almost completely context bound. Ben is in effect

assuming that we know the incidents as well as he does, and is not aware of the listener's confusion when a visit to Madeline mentioning a train becomes a car trip involving his sister. There are no explanations. 'Mummy' only appears in a single false start phrase 'mummy and dad'.

23.2.3 Speculation

The thinking in the last passage is at the level of recall. That Ben can think speculatively is shown in his response to a question about what would happen if the fire alarm sounded.

Ben	we go out this/out that playground and call the fire brigade
Adult	who would call the fire brigade?
Ben	the/headmaster/think
Adult	supposing both gates into the playground were locked/what would they do/
Ben	they got/a/axe and open it
Adult	what if he hadn't got his axe?
Ben	I dunno
Adult	guess
Ben	they ask for the key

Questions about a picture of a baker and housewife received specific replies—not, for instance, 'she's buying bread', but 'she's touching the bread'—but Ben was able to supply a conversation for both parties with prompting.

Ben	can I have/a fruit cake please
Adult	and what will the baker say?
Ben	yes
Adult	and what would she say then?
Ben	she/how much is it
Adult	what would he say/have a guess
Ben	thirty three pence

Another feature of Ben's language which should be noted was its literalness. To a question 'What is he feeling?', of a boy in a picture, he indicated the bicycle frame.

137

23.2.4 Discussion

With Ben and thousands of children like him it is difficult to dissociate problems of linguistic privation from problems of conceptual and psychological development. The frustrations associated with a lack of verbal fluency are often associated with other frustrations and contribute to them. The recording quoted shows that in the appropriate situation and with sympathetic guidance Ben was using language to carry out a hypothesizing function beyond what he would normally be required to do, but this was in a one to one relationship which a busy teacher with other such children could not possibly provide regularly.

About the nature of his privation we should be clear. It is first phonological and paralinguistic: it is difficult to tell what he says. Second, it is grammatical (though this is a social problem rather than one of communication). Third, it is lexical: certain words he does not have, or at least cannot command when necessary. Fourth, it is cognitive, in his inability to arrange his ideas, to answer other than literally, or at a general rather than a specific level. Fifth, it is functional: his ability to carry out certain linguistic tasks is limited though not non-existent. And sixth, it is imaginative: his language is context bound; he does not seek to meet the listener's frame of reference.

23.5 Summary

The debate about whether 'working-class language' is inferior or just different from 'middle-class language' is in some ways about trivialities, and turns attention away from genuine linguistic privation. Some of the features of this privation are exemplified in the language of 'Ben', whose cry for help, 'I's in difficults miss', is the cry of so many similar children.

Part 2

Further work

Chapter 1

1.1   What, and to whom or what, do the following communicate?
(Consider whether the communication is overt or covert, intentional or
non-intentional, coded or uncoded.)

'Lovely day again, isn't it?'
A tower block of flats.
'Would you like to get your books out?'
'I turn first right, then third on the left.'
Physical contact is a crowded underground train.
Autumn leaves.
'Get in lane.'
Policemen in uniform.
Multi-storey car park.
'You have been selected for our special privilege offer. . . .'
Holly berries.
'Could I see your driving licence please, sir?'
'Cuckoo.'
'Do you think the Battle of Bosworth marked the end of the Middle
Ages?'
'Well if you feel you really must go.'
'Tax-free bonus after five years, guaranteed by Her Majesty's Treasury.'
Exterior of a cathedral/town hall.
'Cock-a-doodle-doo.'
Indian girl in sari.
'Excuse me; would you mind if I smoke?'
'You have hissed all my mystery lectures.'

1.2   A simple communication model is explained in Wilkinson (1971a, pp. 37-39). A useful description of various types of communication model is to be found in DeVito (1970, pp. 94-107). See also Smith R.L., in Barker and Kibler (1971, pp. 16-43), and Parry (1967, pp. 24-29).

*1.2.1   The limitation, mentioned in this section, of some communication models ignoring function, is not present in the following extract from an important article by Roman Jakobson (1960). He shows how the elements in the model determine a different general function of language. The extract is relevant not only to this chapter but to several others, particularly Chapter 9, where it should be looked at again in relation to the model of language proposed by Britton. It is from 'Concluding statement: Linguistics and Poetics' in Sebeok (1960).

Language must be investigated in all the variety of its functions. Before discussing the poetic function we must define its place among the other functions of language. An outline of these functions demands a concise survey of the constitutive factors in any speech event, in any act of verbal communication. The ADDRESSER sends a MESSAGE to the ADDRESSEE. To be operative the message requires a CONTEXT referred to ("referent" in another, somewhat ambiguous, nomenclature), seizable by the addressee, and either verbal or capable or being verbalized; a CODE fully, or at least partially, common to the addresser and addressee (or in other words, to the encoder and decoder of the message); and, finally, a CONTACT, a physical channel and psychological connection between the addresser and the addressee, enabling both of them to enter and stay in communication. All these factors inalienably involved in verbal communication may be schematized as follows:

CONTEXT

ADDRESSER   MESSAGE   ADDRESSEE

                       CONTACT

CODE

Each of these six factors determines a different function of language. Although we distinguish six basic aspects of language, we could, however, hardly find verbal messages that would fulfill only one function. The diversity lies not in a monopoly of some one of these several functions but in a different hierarchical order of functions. The verbal structure of a message depends primarily on the predominant function.

But even though a set (*Einstellung*) toward the referent, an orientation toward the CONTEXT—briefly the so-called REFERENTIAL, "denotative," "cognitive" function—is the leading task of numerous messages, the accessory participation of the other functions in such messages must be taken into account by the observant linguist

The so-called EMOTIVE or "expressive" function, focused on the ADDRESSER, aims a direct expression of the speaker's attitude toward what he is speaking about. It tends to produce an impression of a certain emotion whether true or feigned; therefore, the term "emotive" launched and advocated by Marty (1908) has proved to be preferable to "emotional"). The purely emotive stratum in language is presented by the interjections. They differ from the means of referential language both by their sound pattern (peculiar sound sequences or even sounds elsewhere unusual) and by their syntactic role (they are not components but equivalents of sentences). "*Tut! Tut!* said McGinty": the complete utterance of Conan Doyle's character consists of two suction clicks. The emotive function, laid bare in the interjections, flavors to some extent all our utterances, on their phonic, grammatical, and lexical level. If we analyze language from the standpoint of the information it carries, we cannot restrict the notion of information to the cognitive aspect of language. A man, using expressive features to indicate his angry or ironic attitude, conveys ostensible information, and evidently this verbal behaviour cannot be likened to such non-semiotic, nutritive activities as "eating grapefruit" (despite Chatman's bold simile). The difference between [big] and the emphatic prolongation of the vowel [bi:g] is a conventional, coded linguistic feature like the difference between the short and long vowel in such Czech pairs as [vi] 'you' and [vi:] 'knows,' but in the latter pair the differential information is phonemic and in the former emotive. As long as we are interested in phonemic invariants, the English /i/ and /i:/ appear to be mere variants of one and the same phoneme, but if we are concerned with emotive units, the relation between the invariant and variants is reversed: length and shortness are invariants implemented by variable phonemes. Saporta's surmise that emotive difference is a non-linguistic feature, "attributable to the delivery of the message and not to the message," arbitrarily reduces the informational capacity of messages.

A former actor of Stanislavskij's Moscow Theater told me how at his audition he was asked by the famous director to make forty different messages from the phrase *Segodnja večerom* 'This evening,' by diversifying its expressive tint. He made a list of some forty emotional situations, then emitted the given phrase in accordance with each of these situations, which his audience had to recognize only from the changes in the sound shape of the same two words. For our research work in the description and analysis of contemporary Standard Russian (under the auspices of the Rockefeller Foundation) this actor was asked to repeat Stanislavskij's test. He wrote down some fifty situations framing the same eliptic sentence and made of it fifty corresponding messages for a tape record. Most of the messages were correctly and circumstantially decoded by Moscovite listeners. May I add that all such emotive cues easily undergo linguistic analysis.

Orientation toward the ADDRESSEE, the CONATIVE function, finds its purest grammatical expression in the vocative and imperative, which syntactically, morphologically, and often even phonemically deviate from other nominal and verbal categories. The imperative sentences cardinally differ from declarative sentences: the latter are and the former are not liable to a truth test. When in O'Neill's play *The Fountain,* Nano "(in a fierce tone of command)," says "Drink!"—the imperative cannot be challenged by the question "is it true or not?" which may be, however, perfectly well asked after such sentences as "one drank," "one will drink," "one would drink." In contradistinction to the imperative sentences, the declarative sentences are convertible into interrogative sentences: "did one drink?" "will one drink?" "would one drink?"

The traditional model of language as elucidated particularly by Bühler (1933) was confined to these three functions—emotive, conative, and referential—and the three apexes of this model—the first person of the addresser, the second person of the addressee, and the "third person," properly—someone or something spoken of. Certain additional verbal functions can be easily inferred from this triadic model. Thus the magic, incantatory function is chiefly some kind of conversion of an absent or inanimate "third person", into an addressee of a conative message. "May this sty up, *tfu, tfu, tfu, tfu*" (Lithuanian spell, Mansikka, 1929). "Water queen river, daybreak! Send grief beyond the blue sea, to the sea-bottom, like a grey stone never to rise from the sea-bottom, may grief never come to burden the light heart of God's servant, may grief be removed and sink away." (North Russian incantation, Rybnikov, 1910). "Sun, stand thou still upon Gibeon; and thou, Moon, in the valley of Aj-a-lon. And the sun stood still, and the moon stayed ..." (Josh. 10.12). We observe, however, three further constitutive factors of verbal communication and three corresponding functions of language.

There are messages primarily serving to establish, to prolong, or to discontinue communication, to check whether the channel works ("Hello, do you hear me?"), to attract the attention of the interlocutor or to confirm his continued attention ("Are you listening?") or in Shakespearean diction, "Lend me your ears!"—and on the other end of the wire "Um-hum!"). This set for CONTACT, or in Malinowski's terms PHATIC function (Malinowski, 1953) may be displayed by a profuse exchange of ritualized formulas, by entire dialogues with the mere purport of prolonging communication. Dorothy Parker caught eloquent examples: " 'Well!' the young man said. 'Well!' she said. 'Well, here we are,' he said. 'Here we are,' she said, 'Aren't we?' 'I should say we were,' he said, 'Eeyop! Here we are.' 'Well!' she said. 'Well!' he said, 'well.' " The endeavour to start and sustain communication is typical of talking birds; thus the phatic function of language is the only one they share with human beings. It is also the first verbal function acquired by infants; they are prone to communicate before being able to send or receive informative communication.

A distinction has been made in modern logic between two levels of language, "object language" speaking of objects and "metalanguage" speaking of language. But metalanguage is not only a necessary scientific tool utilized by logicians and linguists; it plays also an important role in our everyday language. Like Molière's Jourdain who used prose without knowing it, we practice metalanguage without realizing the metalingual character of our operations. Whenever the addresser and/or the addressee need to check up whether they use the same code, speech is focused on the CODE: it performs a METALINGUAL (i.e., glossing) function. "I don't follow you—what do you mean?" asks the addressee, or in Shapespearean diction, "What is't thou say'st?" And the addresser in anticipation of such recapturing questions inquires: "Do you know what I mean?" Imagine such an exasperating dialogue: "The sophomore was plucked." "But what is *plucked*?" "*Plucked* means the same as *flunked*." "And *flunked*?" "To be *flunked* is *to fail in an exam*." "And what is *sophomore*?" persists the interrogator innocent of school vocabulary. "*A sophomore* is (or means) a *second-year student*." All these equational sentences convey information merely about the lexical code of English; their function is strictly metalingual. Any process of language learning, in particular child acquisition of the mother tongue, makes wide use of such metalingual operations; and aphasia may often be defined as a loss of ability for metalingual operations.

We have brought up all the six factors involved in verbal communication except the message itself. The set (*Einstellung*) toward the MESSAGE as such, focus on the message for its own sake, is the POETIC function of language. This function cannot be productively studied out of touch with the general problems of language, and, on the other hand, the scrutiny of language required a thorough consideration of its poetic function. Any attempt to reduce the sphere of poetic function to poetry or to confine poetry to poetic function would be a delusive oversimplification. Poetic function is not the sole function of verbal art but only its dominant, determining function, whereas in all other verbal activities it acts as a subsidiary, accessory constituent. This function, by promoting the palpability of signs, deepens the fundamental dichotomy of signs and objects. Hence, when dealing with poetic function, linguistics cannot limit itself to the field of poetry.

"Why do you always say *Joan and Margery*, yet never *Margery and Joan*? Do you prefer Joan to her twin sister?" "Not at all, it just sounds smoother." In a sequence of two coordinate names, as far as no rank problems interfere, the precedence of the shorter name suits the speaker, unaccountably for him, as a well-ordered shape of the message.

A girl used to talk about "the horrible Harry." "Why horrible?" "Because I hate him." "But why not *dreadful, terrible, frightful, disgusting*?" "I don't know why, but *horrible* fits him better." Without realizing it, she clung to the poetic device of paronomasia.

The political slogan "I like Ike" /ay layk ayk/, succinctly structured, consists of three monosyllables and counts three dipthongs /ay/, each of them symmetrically followed by one consonantal phoneme, /. . l . . l . . k/. The make-up of the three words presents a variation: no consonantal phonemes in the first word, two around the dipthong in the second, and one final consonant in the third. A similar dominant nucleus /ay/ was noticed by Hymes in some of the sonnets of Keats. Both cola of the trisyllabic formula "I like / Ike" rhyme with each other, and the second of the two rhyming words is fully included in the first one (echo rhyme), /layk/–/ayk/, a paronomastic image of a feeling which totally envelops its object. Both cola alliterate with each other, and the first of the two alliterating words is included in the second: /ay/–/ayk/, a paronomastic image of the loving subject enveloped by the beloved object. The secondary, poetic function of this electional catch phrase reinforces its impressiveness and efficacy.

As we said, the linguistic study of the poetic function must overstep the limits of poetry, and, on the other hand, the linguistic scrutiny of poetry cannot limit itself to the poetic function. The particularities of diverse poetic genres imply a differently ranked participation of the other verbal functions along with the dominant poetic function. Epic poetry, focused on the third person, strongly involves the referential function of language; the lyric, oriented toward the first person, is intimately linked with the emotive function; poetry of the second person is imbued with the conative function and is either supplicatory or exhortative, depending on whether the first person is subordinated to the second one or the second to the first.

Now that our cursory description of the six basic functions of verbal communication is more or less complete, we may complement our scheme of the fundamental factors by a corresponding scheme of the functions:

REFERENTIAL

EMOTIVE   POETIC   CONATIVE
                PHATIC

METALINGUAL

Chapters 2 and 3

Photographs 1—6, between pp. 182 and 183, can be revealing in terms of the categories given in these chapters. It is helpful to attempt to supply the words which might be used if the people in them were speaking. Consider particularly dress, stance, distance, gesture, expression. What are those people thinking? What are their attitudes and feelings towards one another? How much of their communication is conscious? What sort of people are they (their age, their character)? What do they think of themselves? What do others think of them?

A useful study would be to collect examples of one or more means of communication used in daily life. For instance, people in general use a large number of gestures which they are not aware of, and which have no rational basis—to scratch one's head does not lessen one's puzzlement, to stroke one's chin does not guarantee one will come up with the answer.

As far as the U.K. is concerned, the major work in the field has been done by Michael Argyle. *The Psychology of Interpersonal Behaviour* (1967) is a very readable Penguin. For a somewhat different classification of means of communication to that given here, see Argyle's chapter 'Non-verbal communication in human social interaction' in Hinde (1972). Goffman is the leading American writer, and his *The Presentation of Self in Everyday Life* (1969) is another readable Penguin. See also Laver and Hutcheson (1972) and Cook (1971).

Chapter 4

Work on stereotypes associated with voices can be carried out on the lines of some of the experiments in this chapter. For instance, it is comparatively easy to make a tape in which people with different English accents read the same few sentences. Members of a group may then be asked to assign such matters as age and occupation to the owner of each voice. Judgements of character are obtained by the subjects rating each speaker on a five point scale such as the one below:

	1	2	3	4	5	
generous	–	–	–	–	–	mean
sociable	–	–	–	–	–	unsociable

A subject ticking 3 would indicate that he thought the speaker was neither very generous not very mean, and so on. Strongman and Woozley (1967) devised a number of scales for measuring reactions to regional accents:

generous/mean   ambitious/*laissez-faire*
sociable/unsociable   unpopular/popular
good-looking/unattractive   self-confident/shy
serious/frivolous   unreliable/reliable
talkative/restrained   determined/unsure
irritable/good-natured   entertaining/boring
dishonest/honest   kind-hearted/hard
imaginative/hard-headed   industrious/lazy
sense of humour/humourless

*Further reading: Robinson (1972, section 5); Laver and Hutcheson (1972), pt. 3 (papers by Allport and Cantril, Kramer, and Laver). Both these books have been drawn on in writing this chapter.

Chapter 5

*5.2   There is a critical discussion of von Frisch's work in Wenner and Wells' paper 'Do Honey Bees have a Language?', in which it is argued that smell rather than the dance guides bees to their food (Wells and Wenner, 1973).

5.3   The table on the next page compares Washoe's grammar with that of young children. What similarities and what differences are there?

Further reading: In *A First Language* (1973) Roger Brown evaluates the findings so far of the linguistic apes

***5.4 Design features of language**

Hockett and Altmann (1968) have devised a list of characteristics ('design features') which distinguish human language from animal 'language'. It is interesting to look at these features in relation to the communication of some different animals—say, a dog, a parrot, and a chimpanzee—but the extract by Edward Sapir in further work on Chapter 6 should be read first.

DF1	Vocal-Auditory Channel.
DF2	Broadcast Transmission and Directional Reception.
DF3	Rapid Fading. (The sound of speech does not hover in the air.)
DF4	Interchangeability. (Adult members of any speech community are interchangeably transmitters and receivers of linguistic signals.)
DF5	Complete Feedback. (The speaker hears everything relevant of what he says.)
DF6	Specialization. (The direct-energetic consequences of linguistic signals are biologically unimportant, only the triggering consequences are important.)
DF7	Semanticity. (Linguistic signals function to correlate and organize the life of a community because there are associative ties between signal elements and features in the world; in short, some linguistic forms have denotations.)
DF8	Arbitrariness. (The relation between a meaningful element in a language and its denotation is independent

Parallel descriptive schemes for the earliest combinations of children and Washoe (from Gardner and Gardner, 1971)

Brown's (1970) scheme for children		The scheme for Washoe	
Types	Examples	Types	Examples
Attributive Ad + N	big train, red book	*Object–Attributable* *Agent–Attribute*	drink red, comb black Washoe sorry, Naomi good
Possessive: N + N	Adam checker, mommy lunch	*Agent–Object* *Object–Attribute*	clothes Mrs G., you hat baby mine, clothes yours
N + V	walk street, go store	*Action–Location*	go in, look out
Locative N + N	sweater chair, book table	*Action–Object* *Object–Location*	go flower, pants tickle baby down, in hat
Agent–Action: N + V	Adam put, Eve read	*Agent–Action*	Roger tickle, you drink
Action–Object: V + N	put book, hit ball	*Action–Object*	tickle Washoe, open blanket
Agent–Object: N + N	mommy sock, mommy lunch	*Appeal–Action* *Appeal–Object*	please tickle, hug hurry gimme flower, more fruit

of any physical or geometrical resemblance between the two.)

DF9   Discreteness. (The possible messages in any language constitute a discrete repertoire rather than a continuous one.)

DF10   Displacement. (We can talk about things that are remote in time, space, or both from the site of the communicative transaction.)

DF11   Openness. (New linguistic messages are coined freely and easily, and, in context, are usually understood.)

DF12   Tradition. (The conventions of any one human language are passed down by teaching and learning, not through the germ plasm.)

DF13   Duality of Patterning. (Every language has a patterning in terms of arbitrary but stable meaningless signal-elements and also a patterning in terms of minimum meaningful arrangements of those elements.)

DF14   Prevarication. (We can say things that are false or meaningless.)

DF15   Reflexiveness. (In a language, we can communicate about the very system in which we are communicating.)

DF16   Learnability. (A speaker of a language can learn another language.)

DF1 indicates that language production and reception requires little energy and the body is free for simultaneous activities; DF4 that the speaker can usually reproduce any message he can understand (whereas it is often the male bird who gives the mating call, which the female cannot copy); DF5 that we can hear our own vocal communication (whereas we cannot see our own visual communication, such as a smile); DF6 that paralinguistic noise, such as breath, is unimportant *linguistically*; DF8 that a long thin person is not represented by a long thin word; DF9 that similar sounds do not indicate any relationship between meanings ('smock' and 'smog' have no connection); DF13 that the sounds of a language are meaningless in themselves and it is only when combined that they acquire meaning (for example, *sig + nals*). Thorpe in Hinde (1972 , pp. 27-47) discusses the applicability of the features to non-human communication.

Chapter 6

There are many books on language. The best short general introduction
is Jean Aitchison, *General Linguistics* (1972); on a larger scale in
R.H. Robins, *General Linguistics: An Introductory Survey* (1964). See
also Fowler (1974), Elkins (1974), and Lepschy (1970).

6.3   Here is an extract from the opening chapter, 'Language Defined',
to Edward Sapir's seminal book, *Language* (1949). In it Sapir
demonstrates the essential differences, as he sees them, between human
language and distinctive cries. Sapir's definition brings out that language
is: purely human; non-instinctive; a means of communicating;
systematic; symbolic, auditory; produced by the speech organs.

Speech is so familiar a feature of daily life that we rarely pause to
define it. It seems as natural to man as walking, and only less so than
breathing. Yet it needs but a moment's reflection to convince us that
this naturalness of speech is but an illusory feeling. The process of
acquiring speech is, in sober fact, an utterly different sort of thing from
the process of learning to walk. In the case of the latter function, culture,
in other words, the traditional body of social usage, is not seriously
brought into play. The child is individually equipped, by the complex
set of factors that we term biological heredity, to make all the needed
muscular and nervous adjustments that result in walking. Indeed, the
very conformation of these muscles and of the appropriate parts of the
nervous system may be said to be primarily adapted to the movements
made in walking and in similar activities. In a very real sense the normal
human being is predestined to walk, not because his elders will assist
him to learn the art, but because his organism is prepared from birth,
or even from the moment of conception, to take on all those
expenditures of nervous energy and all those muscular adaptations that
result in walking. To put it concisely, walking is an inherent, biological
function of man.

No so language. It is of course true that in a certain sense the
individual is predestined to talk, but that is due entirely to the circumstance that he is born not merely in nature, but in the lap of a society
that is certain, reasonably certain, to lead him to its traditions.
Eliminate society and there is every reason to believe that he will learn
to walk, if, indeed, he survives at all. But it is just as certain that he will
never learn to talk, that is, to communicate ideas according to the
traditional system of a particular society. Or, again, remove the new-
born individual from the social environment into which he has come
and transplant him to an utterly alien one. He will develop the art of
walking in his new environment very much as he would have developed

151

it in the old. But his speech will be completely at variance with the speech of his native environment. Walking, then, is a general human activity that varies only within circumscribed limits as we pass from individual to individual. Its variability is involuntary and purposeless. Speech is a human activity that varies without assignable limit as we pass from social group to social group, because it is a purely historical heritage of the group, the product of long-continued social usage. It varies as all creative effort varies—not as consciously, perhaps, but none the less as truly as do the religions, the beliefs, the customs, and the arts of different peoples. Walking is an organic, an instinctive, function (not, of course, itself an instinct); speech is a non-instinctive, acquired, "cultural" function.

There is one fact that has frequently tended to prevent the recognition of language as a merely conventional system of sound symbols, that has seduced the popular mind into attributing to it an instinctive basis that it does not really possess. This is the well-known observation that under the stress of emotion, say of a sudden twinge of pain or of unbridled joy, we do involuntarily give utterance to sounds that the hearer interprets as indicative of the emotion itself. But there is all the difference in the world between such involuntary expression of feeling and the normal type of communication of ideas that is speech. The former kind of utterance is indeed instinctive, but it is non-symbolic; in other words, the sound of pain or the sound of joy does not, as such, indicate the emotion, it does not stand aloof, as it were, and announce that such and such an emotion is being felt. What it does is to serve as a more or less automatic overflow of the emotional energy; in a sense, it is part and parcel of the emotion itself. Moreover, such instinctive cries hardly constitute communication in any strict sense. They are not addressed to any one, they are merely overheard, if heard at all, as the bark of a dog, the sound of approaching footsteps, or the rustling of the wind is heard. If they convey certain ideas to the hearer, it is only in the very general sense in which any and every sound or even any phenomenon in our environment may be said to convey an idea to the perceiving mind. If the involuntary cry of pain which is conventionally represented by "Oh!" be looked upon as a true speech symbol equivalent to some such idea as "I am in great pain", it is just as allowable to interpret the appearance of clouds as an equivalent symbol that carries the definite message "It is likely to rain." A definition of language, however, that is so extended as to cover every type of inference becomes utterly meaningless.

The mistake must not be made of identifying our conventional interjections (our oh! and ah! and sh!) with the instinctive cries themselves. These interjections are merely conventional fixations of the natural sounds. They therefore differ widely in various languages in accordance with the specific phonetic genius of each of these. As such they may be considered an integral portion of speech, in the properly cultural sense of the term, being no more identical with the instinctive cries themselves than such words as "cuckoo" and "killdeer" are identical with the cries of the birds they denote or than Rossini's treatment of a storm in the overture to "William Tell" is in fact a storm. In other words, the interjections and sound-imitative words of normal speech are related to their natural prototypes as is art, a purely social or cultural thing, to nature. It may be objected that, though the interjections differ somewhat as we pass from language to language, they do nevertheless offer striking family resemblances and may therefore be looked upon as having grown up out of a common instinctive base. . . .

What applies to the interjections applies with even greater force to the sound-imitative words. Such words as "whippoorwill", "to mew," "to caw" are in no sense natural sounds that man has instinctively or automatically reproduced. They are just as truly creations of the human mind, flights of the human fancy, as anything else in language. They do not directly grow out of nature, they are suggested by it and play with it. Hence the onomatopoetic theory of the origin of speech, the theory that would explain all speech as a gradual evolution from sounds of an imitative character, really brings us no nearer to the instinctive level than is language as we know it today. As to the theory itself, it is scarcely more credible than its interjectional counterpart. It is true that a number of words which we do not now feel to have a sound-imitative value can be shown to have once had a phonetic form that strongly suggests their origin as imitations of natural sounds. Such is the English word "to laugh." For all that, it is quite impossible to show, nor does it seem intrinsically reasonable to suppose, that more than a negligible proportion of the elements of speech or anything at all of its formal apparatus is derivable from an onomatopoetic source. However much we may be disposed on general principles to assign a fundamental importance in the languages of primitive peoples to the imitation of natural sounds, the actual fact of the matter is that these languages show no particular preference for imitative words. Among the most primitive peoples of aboriginal America, the Athabaskan tribes of the Mackenzie River speak languages in which such words seem to be nearly or entirely absent, while they are used freely enough in languages as sophisticated as English and German. Such an instance shows how little the essential nature of speech is concerned with the mere imitation of things.

The way is now cleared for a serviceable definition of language. Language is a purely human and non-instinctive method of communicating ideas, emotions and desires by means of a system of voluntarily produced symbols. These symbols are, in the first instance auditory and they are produced by the so-called "organs of speech". There is no discernible instinctive basis in human speech as such, however much instinctive expressions and the natural environment may serve as a stimulus for the development of certain elements of speech, however much instinctive tendencies, motor and other, may give a predetermined range or mold to linguistic expression. Such human or animal communication, if "communication" it may be called, as is brought about by involuntary, instinctive cries is not, in our sense, language at all.

I have already pointed out that the essence of language consists in the assigning of conventional, voluntarily articulated, sounds, or of their equivalents, to the diverse elements of experience. The word "house" is not a linguistic fact if by it is meant merely the acoustic effect produced on the ear by its constituent consonants and vowels, pronounced in a certain order; nor the motor processes and tactile feelings which make up the articulation of the word; nor the visual perception on the part of the hearer of this articulation; nor the visual perception of the word "house" on the written or printed page; nor the motor processes and tactile feelings which enter into the writing of the word; nor the memory of any or all of these experiences. It is only when these, and possibly still other, associated experiences are automatically associated with the image of a house that they begin to take on the nature of a symbol, a word, an element of language. But the mere fact of such an association is not enough. One might have heard a particular word spoken in an individual house under such impressive circumstances that neither the word nor the image of the house ever recur in consciousness without the other becoming present at the same time. This type of association does not constitute speech. The association must be a purely symbolic one; in other words, the word must denote, tag off, the image, must have no other significance than to serve as a counter to refer to it whenever it is necessary or convenient to do so. Such an association, voluntary and, in a sense, arbitrary as it is, demands a considerable exercise of self-conscious attention. At least to begin with, for habit soon makes the association nearly as automatic as any and more rapid than most.

But we have travelled a little too fast. Were the symbol "house"—whether an auditory, motor, or visual experience or image—attached but to the single image of a particular house once seen, it might perhaps, by an indulgent criticism, be termed an element of speech, yet it is obvious at the outset that speech so constituted would have little or no value for purposes of communication. The world of our experiences must be enormously simplified and generalized before it is possible to make a symbolic inventory of all our experiences of things and relations and this inventory is imperative before we can convey ideas. The elements of language, the symbols that ticket off experience, must therefore be associated with whole groups, delimited classes, of experience rather than with the single experiences themselves. Only so is communication possible, for the single experience lodges in an individual consciousness and is, strictly speaking, incommunicable. To be communicated it needs to be referred to a class which is tacitly accepted by the community as an identity. Thus, the single impression which I have had of a particular house must be identified with all my other impressions of it. Further, my generalized memory or my "notion" of this house must be merged with the notions that all other individuals who have seen the house have formed of it. The particular experience that we started with has now been widened so as to embrace all possible impressions or images that sentient beings have formed or may form of the house in question. This first simplification of experience is at the bottom of a large number of elements of speech, the so-called proper nouns or names of single individuals or objects. It is, essentially, the type of simplification which underlies, or forms, the crude subject of, history and art. But we cannot be content with this measure of reduction of the infinity of experience. We must cut to the bone of things, we must more or less arbitrarily throw whole masses of experience together as similar enough to warrant their being looked upon—mistakenly, but conveniently—as identical. This house and that house and thousands of other phenomena of like character are thought of as having enough in common, in spite of great and obvious differences of detail, to be classed under the same heading. In other words, the speech element "house" is the symbol, first and foremost, not of a single perception, nor even of the notion of a particular object, but of a "concept", in other words, of a convenient capsule of thought that embraces thousands of distinct experiences and that is ready to take in thousands more. If the single significant elements of speech are the symbols of concepts, the actual flow of speech may be interpreted as a record of the setting of these concepts into mutual relations.

Chapter 7

*7.3.1   In this extract, 'Formal and substantive universals', from *Aspects of the Theory of Syntax*, Noam Chomsky divides syntactic universals into two groups. The 'substantive' universals include such matters as that languages draw on a (limited) number of sounds, which they arrange in groups. The 'formal' universals are certain types of grammatical rules which languages may have in common, such as transformational rules (see 19.1.3).

A theory of linguistic structure that aims for explanatory adequacy incorporates an account of linguistic universals, and it attributes tacit knowledge of these universals to the child. It proposes, then, that the child approaches the data with the presumption that they are drawn from a language of a certain antecedently well-defined type, his problem being to determine which of the (humanly) possible languages is that of the community in which he is placed. Language learning would be impossible unless this were the case. The important question is: What are the initial assumptions concerning the nature of language that the child brings to language learning, and how detailed and specific is the innate schema (the general definition of "grammar") that gradually becomes more explicit and differentiated as the child learns the language? For the present we cannot come at all close to making a hypothesis about innate schemata that is rich, detailed, and specific enough to account for the fact of language acquisition. Consequently, the main task of linguistic theory must be to develop an account of linguistic universals that, on the one hand, will not be falsified by the actual diversity of languages and, on the other, will be sufficiently rich and explicit to account for the rapidity and uniformity of language learning, and the remarkable complexity and range of the generative grammars that are the product of language learning.

The study of linguistic universals is the study of the properties of any generative grammar for a natural language. Particular assumptions about linguistic universals may pertain to either the syntactic, semantic, or phonological component, or to interrelations among the three components.

It is useful to classify linguistic universals as *formal* or *substantive*. A theory of substantive universals claims that items of a particular kind in any language must be drawn from a fixed class of items. For example, Jakobson's theory of distinctive features can be interpreted as making an assertion about substantive universals with respect to the phonological component of a generative grammar. It asserts that each output of this component consists of elements that are characterized in terms of some small number of fixed, universal, phonetic features (perhaps on the order of fifteen or twenty), each of which has a substantive acoustic-articulatory characterization independent of any particular language.

Traditional universal grammar was also a theory of substantive universals, in this sense. It not only put forth interesting views as to the nature of universal phonetics, but also advanced the position that certain fixed syntactic categories (Noun, Verb, etc.) can be found in the syntactic representations of the sentences of any language, and that these provide the general underlying syntactic structure of each language. A theory of substantive semantic universals might hold, for example, that certain designative functions must be carried out in a specified way in each language. Thus it might assert that each language will contain terms that designate persons or lexical items referring to certain specific kinds of objects, feelings, behaviour, and so on.

It is also possible, however, to search for universal properties of a more abstract sort. Consider a claim that the grammar of every language meets certain specified formal conditions. The truth of this hypothesis would not in itself imply that any particular rule must appear in all or even in any two grammars. The property of having a grammar meeting a certain abstract condition might be called a *formal* linguistic universal, if shown to be a general property of natural languages. Recent attempts to specify the abstract conditions that a generative grammar must meet have produced a variety of proposals concerning formal universals, in this sense. For example, consider the proposal that the syntactic component of a grammar must contain transformational rules (these being operations of a highly special kind) mapping semantically interpreted deep structures into phonetically interpreted surface structures, or the proposal that the phonological component of a grammar consists of a sequence of rules, a subset of which may apply cyclically to successively more dominant constituents of the surface structure (a transformational cycle, in the sense of much recent work on phonology). Such proposals make claims of a quite different sort from the claim that certain substantive phonetic elements are available for phonetic representation in all languages, or that certain specific categories must be central to the syntax of all languages, or that certain semantic features or categories provide a universal framework for semantic description. Substantive universals such as these concern the vocabulary for the description of language; formal universals involve rather the character of the rules that appear in grammars and the ways in which they can be interconnected.

On the semantic level, too, it is possible to search for what might be called formal universals, in essentially the sense just described. Consider, for example, the assumption that proper names, in any language, must designate objects meeting a condition of spatiotemporal contiguity, and that the same is true of other terms designating objects; or the condition that the color words of any language must subdivide the color spectrum into continuous segments; or the condition that artifacts are defined in terms of certain human goals, needs, and functions instead of solely in terms of physical qualities. Formal constraints of this sort on a system of concepts may severely limit the choice (by the child, or the linguist) of a descriptive grammar, given primary linguistic data.

The existence of deep-seated formal universals, in the sense suggested by such examples as these, implies that all languages are cut to the same pattern, but does not imply that there is any point by point correspondence between particular languages. It does not, for example, imply that there must be some reasonable procedure for translating between languages.

In general, there is no doubt that a theory of language, regarded as a hypothesis about the innate "language-forming capacity" of humans, should concern itself with both substantive and formal universals. But whereas substantive universals have been the traditional concern of general linguistic theory, investigations of the abstract conditions that must be satisfied by any generative grammar have been undertaken only quite recently. They seem to offer extremely rich and varied possibilities for study in all aspects of grammar.

Chapter 8

8.2 The Lord's Prayer in Melanesian pidgin. By comparing this with the Authorized Version, attempt to discern the way the writer has translated it. Read the prayer aloud, and look for English words in disguised form.

Papa bilong mipela, yu stap long heven.
Ol i Santuim nem bilong yu. Kingdom bilong yu i kam,
Ol i harim tok bilong yu long graun olsem long heven.
Tude givim kaikai bilong de long mipela.
Pogivim rong bilong mipela, olsem mipela i pogivim rong
ol i mekim long mipela. Yu no bringim mipela long traim
tekew samting nogut long mipela. Amen.

8.2 Newspaper. Study the English and pidgin versions of this page of a newspaper (pp. 160-61) in relation to each other, with a view to drawing up a vocabulary and a grammar.

The vocabulary will be a list of words each with their English equivalent(s). The grammar should contain the essential rules: those concerned with tense (how does pidgin indicate past, present, or future); number (how does it indicate singular or plural); the syntax (is the word order the same as in English). Is there any way of recognizing verbs, or demonstrative and possessive pronouns from their forms? Are there any unusual features of grammar?

8.3 Guyanan Creole. Read the story recorded by Mrs. Celestina Jordan, which she based on an incident in her own childhood. What are the particular features of the story from (a) a linguistic, and (b) a literary standpoint?

Neil, Mr. Arthur, and the mango tree

One night, we an' we grandmother sit down, and she start to tell we about de trouble in keepin' bad company. She start like dis: Neil was a good lil boy, den he start to keep some troublesome company.

Everytime dese friends uses to go about, when it get dark, steal de people fruits off deh fruit trees. Deh would do hey one night, and dey anoder night, and so it uses to go on. Dis ting use to proper vex de people, an' deh all plan dat one night deh must catch dese lil scamps.

From *Our News*, a newspaper from Papua New Guinea, which is published in both Papuan and English.

PAPUA NEW GUINEANS IN THE NEWS

Mr. Raphael Doa Pamunda

MAN SAVES BABY

A Broadcasts Officer with Radio Mt. Hagen, Mr. Raphael Doa Pamunda, has saved the life of a 15-month old baby.

Mr. Pamunda was told by some young boys that they had seen a baby floating in the Warakum River.

Told of this incident, he raced to the scene, rescued the baby, who by that time had stopped breathing. He then applied artificial respiration to keep the child alive.

The baby was later rushed to the hospital. A doctor at the hospital said that Mr. Pamunda's quick action had saved the life of the baby.

WINNERS ANNOUNCED

The three, top prize-winners in the National Unity Play Competition have been announced by the D.I.E.S.' Literature Bureau.

The First Prize of $100 was awarded to Peter Wandau, of the University of Papua New Guinea for his play, 'The New Dawn' which shows university life and its part in breaking down language and other barriers in Papua New Guinea.

The Second prize of $50 was awarded to Eleanor Pemo of Lae, for her play, 'A Many-Sided Sacrifice'. 'Walk Every Step', written by Allan Jaria of De Boismenu College, won the third prize of $25.

Five other worthy entrants were awarded a prize of $5. They include: James Garasalek of Madang; Russell Soaba, U.P.N.G.; J.B. Bray of Marawaha; Ellen Lyons of Limi; and Bernadette Kouye of Port Moresby Teachers' College.

The National Unity Play Competition was conducted by the Literature Bureau of the Department of Information and Extension Services, and sponsored by the Political Education Committee.

Miss Margaret Loko

GIRL APPOINTED

A young Papuan girl will take up an appointment as Secretary of the Local Government Association of Papua New Guinea in September of this year.

Miss Margaret Loko, aged 21, of Port Moresby is one of three girls graduating from the University of Papua New Guinea next month with a Bachelor of Arts degree.

At the end of August, Miss Loko will attend a course on Local Government Training College near Rabaul.

She will attend a Four-month course at A.S.O.P.A. in February next year after taking up her new position in September.

Miss Loko said her new appointment as Secretary of the Local Government Association would require a lot of work with Local Government Councils throughout Papua New Guinea as well as the Government.

She said although she would be stationed in Port Moresby, her new job would mean a lot of travel. She added that she liked to travel and didn't like staying in one place.

Miss Loko has been studying at the University of Papua New Guinea since 1968.

PNG MAN ELECTED ARAWA COMMISSION DEPUTY COMMISSIONER

A Papua New Guinean man has been elected Deputy Commissioner of the Arawa Muncipal Commission in the Bougainville District.

He is Mr. Aloysius Nase, 22, from Nissan Island in the Sohano Sub-district of Bougainville.

Mr. Nase stood for the Arawa Municipal Commission because he believed that Papua New Guineans on Arawa needed a voice on the Commission. He said he would raise any complaints from the Arawa people at the Commission's meetings.

Mr. Nase obtained his Intermidiate Certificate at St. Joseph's High School in 1967 and in 1968 joined Radio Bougainville when it first commenced operation. He is now the Senior Broadcasts Officer with the Station.

Published by the Department of Information and Extension Services and printed by G. W. Reid, Government Printer.—3522/13.8.72.

PAPUA NIUGINIAN ISTAP LONG NIUS

Mr. Raphael Doa Pamunda

MAN SEVIM PIKININI

Wanpela Brotkast Ofisa long Radio Mt. Hagen, Mr. Raphael Doa Pamunda, i bin sevim laip bilong wanpela pikinini bikpela inap long 15 mun.

Mr. Pamunda sampela liklik boi i bin tokim em long taim ol lukim dispela pikinini trip i go daun long Warakum River.

Em harim dispela na ron i go daun long riva na holim dispela pikinini, dispela taim pikinini hia no inap long pulim win. Bihain em givim sampela win na pikinini hia kirap gen. Bihain ol kisim dispela pikinini i go long haus sik.

Wanpela dokta long haus sik i bin tok olsem wok bilong Mr. Pamunda mekim hariap tru long sevim laip bilong dispela pikinini.

GIVIM NEM LONG WIN

Tripela pipal winim pinis namba wan prais insait long resis rait ol kolim National Unity Play Competition em Literature Bureau bilong D.I.E.S. i givim aut nem bilong ol.

Namba wan $100 prais em givim i go long Peter Wandau, bilong Papua Niugini Universiti long pilai bilong em kolim, 'The New Dawn' long soim Universiti laip na hap bilong em katim daun ol tokples na arapela mak bilong Papua Niugini.

Namba tu $50 prais em givim i go long Eleanor Perno bilong Lae, long pilai bilong em kolim 'A Many-Sided Sacrifice'.

Namba tri $25 prais em givim i go long Allan Jaria bilong De Boismenu College, long raitim stori kolim 'Walk Every Step'.

Ol arapela faivpela prais bilong $5 em givim i go long dispela lain: James Garasalek bilong Madang; Russell Soaba, U.P.N.G.; J.B. Bray bilong Marawaha; Ellen Lyons bilong Lumi na Bernadette Kouye bilong Port Moresby Teachers' College.

National Unity Play Competition em Literature Bureau bilong Dipatmen ov Information na Extension Services makim long raitim i stap, na Political Edukeisin Komiti makim long ol gutpela raiting.

Miss Margaret Loke

MERI HOLIM WOK

Wanpela yangpela Papuan meri bambai holim wok olsem namba wan kuskus long Lokal Gavman Asosiesin bilong Papua Niugini insait long mun Septemba long dispela yia.

Miss Margaret Loko, krismas 21, bilong Port Moresby na wanpela long ol tripela meri bambai winim skul long Papua Niugini Universiti long narapela mun bihain na holim hap pepa kolim Bachelor of Arts Degree.

Taim mun Ogas i pinis, Miss Loko bai i go kisim wanpela kos bilong Lokal Gavman long Vunadidir Lokal Gavman Treining Skul i stap klostu long Rabaul.

Em tu bai i go kisim kos foapela mun long A.S.O.P.A. long mun Februeri long yia bihain na i kam bek holim wok bilong em long mun Septemba.

Miss Loko i tok long holim nupela wok bilong em olsem namba wan kuskus bilong ol Lokal Gavman Asosiesin em bai mekim moa wok i stap wantaim olgeta Lokal Gavman Kaunsil wok insait long olgeta hap bilong Papua Niugini.

Em i tok long ting olsem em bai i stap long Port Moresby, tasol nupela wok bilong em givim em planti wok raun i stap wantaim. Em i go bet na i tok olsem em bin laik wok raun long olgeta hap na no laik wok i stap long wanpela ples tasol.

ILEKTIM PNG MAN ARAWA KOMISIN DEPUTI KOMISINA

Wanpela Papua Niuginian man ol ilektim pinis long kamap Deputi Komisina long hap kolim Arawa Municpal Commission insait long Bougainville Distrik.

Man hia Mr. Aloysius Nase, krismas 22, i kam long Nissan Island insait long Sohano Sab-distrik long Bougainville.

Mr. Nase makim sanap long Arawa Municpal Commission long wanem em bilip olsem planti Papua Niuginian nau sindaun long Arawa ha laikim maus long Komisin. Em i tok em bai kamapim sampela toktok nabaut ol Arawa pipal mekim long taim bilong Komisin miting.

Mr. Nase i bin holim Intermidiate Setifiket bilong em long St. Joseph High Skul long yia 1967 na long 1968 kisim wok wantaim Radio Bougainville, taim stesin statim namba wan wok bilong em. Nau em wanpela long ol namba wan Brotkast Ofisa wok i stap long Stesin.

Page 16

Published by the Department of Information and Extension Services and printed by G. W. Reid, Government Printer.—5522/15.8.72.

De boys plan to go an raid ol' Mr. Arthur tree. He had a nice big tree full o' nice sweet spice Buxton mangoes. He uses to look out for dem every night.

De boys plan de raid. It was to be five o' dem. Deh kun decide who gun go up in de tree. Well, de res(t) say, "Neil, you never go up yet, so, le(t) two o' we watch out for see when he comin', and two can catch de mango when he drop, and you go up. All right?"

Poor Neil agree. De night come, and deh go as plan.

Mr. Arthur, too, out he lamp (limp) and sit down watch-manning he tree, as he always use to do. Neil climb up easy, while de odder four do as deh plan.

He start pickin' and trowin' down, and den everybody start putting up de mango in de bag. Nobody no remember to look to see if de man comin.

Jus' den, Mr. Arthur come down stairs easy, wid a big stick in he han(d) and he torch light behin(d) he back. Suddenly he shine de torch light 'pon dem and he shout out, "Stan(d) up right day! Ah got you now! Aye!" Since they hear dah, de res(t) start shout, "Oh Laud! Oh God! He comin'! Come down Neil! Jump down quick!" Neil say, "How? Oh God help me! Me gun fall dow(n)! Catch me! Wait!" Everybody start runnin' like wil(d). Neil lef(t) shoutin' "Wait dere! All you come an' help me now! Oh wait dere!" but deh did all gone.

Mr. Arthur vex like de devil. Jus' den he say, 'You! You gun sleep in de station tonight. Always comin' tiefin' we fruits.'

Poor Neil won't come down. He say, 'Come down! Come down right now, or else ah gun loose me bad dog on you!' (But Mr. Arthur ain't had no dog.) But poor Neil, frighten like de devil, come down.

He cryin' for break he heart. He beg for he life. He beg pardon. Mr. Arthur listen. He say 'All right. Ah gun carry you home to you parents an' le(t) dem see wha(t) you does be doin' in de night. But before ah go makin' sure dat ah put up me bag o' mangoes. Dis time he holdin' Neil han(d) an' Neil trying for fight.

After de struggle, he loose he han(d), and while he carrying he home Neil jus' run way.

He reach home breathless, all de time tinkin' how de res(t) go way an' lef(t) he alone in all de trouble.

He modder notice he look so frighten, and dat he did come home so late. She ask he, 'What is de matter wid you?' He won't talk. He won't talk. So, she say, 'If you ain't talk ah gun beat you'. He decide dat he gun tell she, an' he tell she de whole story.

She listen good, and den she ask he, 'Why you go wid dem? And nex(t) ting, why non o' de odders din decide for go up in de tree. Now, ah hope you see, dat you does pay for learn sense, and de nex(t) ting ah really want you to remember is dis, "Show me you company, and ah gun tell you who you is".' Neil vow never again to go wanderin' around such company.

8.4   There follows an extract from a valuable article entitled 'Dialect in School', arising out of the work of the team on the Schools Council Project *Concept 7 to 9* and written by Jim Wight, the Director, on their behalf (Wight, 1971). In it he speaks of the nature of the difficulties of Creole-speaking children in this country:

Performance in School

It is not easy to summarise the position of the Creole speaking child at school, but certain generalisations can be made:
1 He will soon speak at least two dialects.
2 The formal school dialect will contain certain Creole features, but it will be intelligible to non-Creole speakers. (Spoken Creoles can be entirely unintelligible to outsiders.)
3 In spite of this facility with the school dialect, Creole is the child's first language. At various points in his school career this Creole background places the child at a considerable disadvantage.
   Attitudes vary about the role of dialect in school. Attitudes are also changing. Tolerance is on the increase. Correctness (i.e., conformity to standard rules) is less important in the hierarchy of English teaching objectives. There is a growing awareness that there are other criteria for judging 'good English', and that at certain stages in the child's education these criteria outweigh the value of insisting on standard spelling, standard grammar etc.
   However, the instinctive reaction of most teachers to such features as a double negative is still 'it's wrong', rather than 'it is not standard, but very common in various regional and social dialects'. It is difficult to know exactly what effect it has on young children to hear their own language, the language of their parents, described as wrong. In the case of a child for whom school represents a fair amount of failure in other respects this extra hurdle will certainly hinder his general school performance and may have much more serious psychological implications. A child's own language is a very personal possession.

Production—the written language
The two most obvious areas of dialect interference are seen in the children's writing. It will affect the spelling and the syntax. Any child learning to read and write comes face to face with the fact that the standard written language and his own spoken language do not match each other very well. At the age of six the Jamaican Creole equivalent of the notorious 'The cat sat on the mat.' would be /dikyatsitpandimat/. It is written out without spaces between the words. This is because a five year old child cannot automatically and easily analyse and sequence the units of his spoken sentences in the manner required for writing. Mackay and Thompson (1968) report that the lexical items (words with high information content) are easily recognised and handled, but that there is some doubt in the child's mind about the status of the grammatical elements in the sentence. This is true for children whose

spoken language corresponds fairly closely in syntax and lexis to standard English. For a 5 year old Creole speaker the intellectual problems of analysis and matching are much greater. In addition to analysing his spoken language into the appropriate sequence of units for writing, the dialect speaker has to fit the sounds of his spoken words to the written symbols. Teachers report that West Indian children who make reasonable progress learning to recognise whole words sometimes fail badly at phonic word building. This is hardly surprising when even the spelling rules which convert received pronunciation speech into writing would not win prizes for simplicity or logical consistency. But at least with that rule system the teacher can appreciate the ambiguities and make allowances for them.

To return to the Creole sentence above, the three words 'cat', 'sat' and 'mat' each have different central sounds, /ya/, /i/ and /a/, which must all be represented by the letter 'a' in the written sentence. It takes considerable time and sensitivity for a teacher without special training to make allowance for ambiguities of that sort even assuming that her analysis does not stop at a judgement of 'wrong pronunciation'.

Reception—the spoken language
As mentioned above the dialect speaking child's approach to *written* English quickly reveals some of the more obvious problems. It is more difficult to assess the submerged difficulties that the children experience in their *oral* language transactions in the classroom. In the infant school the Creole speaking child is sometimes unintelligible. Differences of syntax and pronunciation will make a simple sentence hard for the teacher to understand. Unusual intonation and stress and a couple of unfamiliar lexical items will make the same sentence completely un-intelligible. The most difficult question to answer, though, is how much the child understands the teacher.

Speaking to a group of children, a teacher can see if they are all listening. She cannot necessarily tell if they are all fully understanding. When a child fails to respond in the expected way to a question or an instruction, she can only guess at the reason. It might be the result of poor concentration, a short memory span, or limited experience. It might be a question of the child's confidence or intelligence. All these reasons are likely to suggest themselves before the possibility of dialect interference is considered. Yet if the teacher, a skilful listener with vocabulary and experience far greater than the child's sometimes fails to understand the child's dialect, the odds are that that child in an infant school frequently fails to understand the teacher.

Until some delicate testing procedure is available to measure the extent to which dialect interference is a factor in comprehension failure in young children, it is only possible to guess at the dis-advantages of the Creole speaking child in the infant school. It should be mentioned, though, that Keislar and Stern (1968) investigated the hypothesis that Head Start children who receive instruction in a familiar dialect will learn more than a comparable group who receive the same instruction in Standard English. Their results gave no support at all to this hypothesis. In fact the groups instructed in Standard English achieved better results!

Whatever the actual situation is for the Jamaican Creole speaker in the infant class, it is certainly true that most suppositions made by linguists about the situation need testing before they can be confidently accepted. If however it is accepted that a Creole speaking background is likely to decrease the child's understanding in the infant school, there is some evidence that as the child grows older it becomes a less critical factor.

It is a truism that a child's ability to understand language exceeds his ability to produce it. This being so, the child's development of a more standard dialect for school use is likely to indicate an ability to understand dialects which are closer still to the standard.

The research (Wight and Norris, 1970) that preceded the Project's present development of teaching materials also suggested that where West Indian children do have difficulty in oral comprehension—Creole interference is not the principal cause. In this research phase a test was developed to examine the effect of Creole interference in situations where the teacher is talking to the whole class. The test was given to eight junior school classes in the 7-9 age range. It contained 50 items, 25 of which were designed to present special difficulty to Creole speakers. The other (control) items were designed to be of equal difficulty to both speakers of Creole and of Birmingham dialects. The special West Indian items focused on grammatical and phonological points of difference between Jamaican Creole and Standard English.

In Jamaican Creole, for example, the standard rules of subject verb agreement do not apply and there is a tendency not to mark noun plurals with the morpheme 's'. A sentence which begins 'When the horse comes back . . . . .' contains two grammatical clues for most English speakers that only one horse is likely to come back. It was assumed that for Jamaican Creole speakers these clues would be obscured. Therefore clauses like this were embedded in short stretches of narrative and the children asked to answer such questions as: 'How many horses were expected back?' The assumption was that West Indian children would find particular difficulty with items of this sort because of dialect interference. In fact the results obtained were far from those expected. By and large the West Indian children (both those born in England and those recently arrived from the Caribbean) scored significantly lower on *all* the items. There was little evidence that the special West Indian items were creating relatively more difficulty than the control items. There was an exception to this. Children recently arrived from the Caribbean did have more difficulty with those items based on Creole pronunciation.

This test result suggested that Creole interference was not the principal cause of the children's comprehension failure. A small scale experiment carried out the year before also supported this view. In this experiment a number of 12 year old West Indians who had been in

165

England a relatively short while played a word association game. The teacher said a word and the children responded by writing down the first word that came into their minds. Many of the words were potentially ambiguous to the children because of differences in Creole pronunciation. By examining the children's responses it was possible to see which word the children had 'heard'. For example, a Creole speaker will pronounce the number 3—/tree/. If the stimulus word therefore was 'tree', the associated response 'leaves' or 'wood', might be expected, but a response of 'four' or 'number', etc., would indicate Creole interference. Only 6% of the children's answers to potentially ambiguous stimulus words showed evidence of dialect interference. A number of the children who played this word association game spoke quite broad Creole themselves, yet they were able to adjust to the pronunciation of the English teacher so well that with impressive consistency they could interpret the teacher's words without the help of any context. This was a small scale experiment, but it suggests very sophisticated skills on the part of these children as they adjusted to a system of pronunciation quite different from their own.

The tentative conclusion to be drawn from all this is that although dialect will continue to have a marked influence on the child's language *production*, he will, provided he has reasonable exposure to the dialect of the teacher and the school, develop skills of language *reception* to cope with the contrasts between Creole and Standard English. This is not to say that there are not difficulties of comprehension for these older children, but it is likely that for them the principal sources of difficulty lie elsewhere. If there is dialect interference it operates like a filter on the communication channel when there are other non-dialect reasons which already make the communication difficult—such as the speed, or the intellectual complexity of the teacher's language, the novelty of the subject matter, etc.

Chapters 9 and 10

9.2.1   Here follows a further extract from the conversation started by
Edmund and Lois. Analyse its functions in terms of the categories
given in 10.2, or devise other categories if these are inadequate.

E: when can we talk
L: when is Mr Wilkins coming
A: now what are we going to play at
E: this
A: let's play at zoos first shall
E: yes
L: yes we've got to clear it up first
A: I see/well what do we do first
L: we have to clear it up first (*zoo consists of 'tray' in which animals
      and cages are scattered*)
A: I see well let's start putting it right shall we
L: yes/take everything out/won't we
A: yes
E: I don't want to
A: you don't want to don't you/do you want to help Lois
L: yes/he/some should go there
A: where're you going to put this
L: no we haven't got it all out yet
A: must get it all out first
L: yes/all the paper out of the way/we don't want paper in do we
E: yes those are the tickets
L: oh. . ./don't want that—in the house/in the house
E: we do/that's for the lions
L: I know it is
E: we need both of them
A: now what are we going to do first
L: put the cages in
A: I see
E: that's the hippo's/upside down/
L: upside down/well I was going to put it the right way up (*does so*)/
      I'll have to put it another way cause they can't get in through that
      door/no we'll open this so they can get in won't we/now we'll have
      to put this here won't we
E: can we talk yet

167

A: yes you can talk if you want now
L: put him in (*elephant*)
A: you tell him to go in
L: go in
E: I will/go in/no/he won't go in
A: what are we going to do about that
E: he doesn't want to go in does he
A: he doesn't want to go in/so what are we going to do
E: he's got to drink some water first
A: ask him if he wants to go in
E: (*elephant's voice*) I don't want to go in
A: ask him if he wants to go in
E: do you want to go in/yes/all right I'll go in
L: where's that baby one/where's that baby one/where's that baby
    one
E: (*elephant's voice*) here I am (*too elephantine to be understood by
    L*)
L: where's that baby one
E: here I am (*clearer*)/do you want to go in/no
L: oh dear
A: what does his mummy say to him
E: Rod you naughty boy you naughty girl Rod come in
A: and Lois what does the little baby say
L: you've got to come in the mummy said
E: I'm sticking my nose in I've got to get in here because (*gives baby
    words*)
L: now they've both got a drink of water now haven't they/Edmund
E: I've got baby to drink it
L: ... those are drinking then aren't they/aren't they/those are
    drinking then
E: (*terrific shriek*)
A: oh, what's that/shriek
L: I've got it upside down
E: It's Mr Elephant (*further incoherent elephant noises*)/bash bang
    (*elephant falls off bar above gate*)
A: what sort of a noise was that he was making
E: he was making gre--- (*shriek again*)
L: I'm just going to the toilet cause I know where it is
E: (*elephant noise*) bash/he's falling everywhere (*elephant 'falls'
    again*)/Help me/bash/he's stuck on there/(*on bar*)

A: oh what a shame/how's he going to get down
E: he can easily squirt water and then he'll fall down like this plonk on his nose

10.1.1 Halliday. Here is an extract from M.A.K. Halliday's 'Relevant Models of Language' (Halliday, 1973) which pointed the way to an examination of language in terms of function rather than of form. An explanation with examples of these models is given in Wilkinson (1971a, pp. 142-149).

Perhaps the simplest of the child's models of language, and one of the first to be evolved, is what we may call the INSTRUMENTAL model. The child becomes aware that language is used as a means of getting things done. About a generation ago, zoologists were finding out about the highly developed powers of chimpanzees; and one of the observations described was of the animal that constructed a long stick out of three short ones and used it to dislodge a bunch of bananas from the roof of its cage. The human child, faced with the same problem, constructs a sentence. He says "I want a banana"; and the effect is the more impressive because it does not depend on the immediate presence of the bananas. Language is brought in to serve the function of "I want", the satisfaction of material needs. Success in this use of language does not in any way depend on the production of well-formed adult sentences; a carefully contextualised yell may have substantially the same effect, and although this may not be language there is no very clear dividing line between, say, a noise made on a commanding tone and a full-dress imperative clause.

The old *See Spot run. Run, Spot, run!* type of first reader bore no relation whatsoever to this instrumental function of language. This by itself does not condemn it, since language has many other functions besides that of manipulating and controlling the environment. But it bore little apparent relation to any use of language, at least to any with which the young child is familiar. It is not recognisable as language in terms of the child's own intentions, of the meanings that he has reason to express and to understand. Children have a very broad concept of the meaningfulness of language, in addition to their immense tolerance of inexplicable tasks; but they are not accustomed to being faced with language which, in their own functional terms, has no meaning at all, and the old-style reader was not seen by them as language. It made no connexion with language in use.

Language as an instrument of control has another side to it, since the child is well aware that language is also a means whereby others exercise control over him. Closely related to the instrumental model, therefore, is the REGULATORY model of language. This refers to the use of language to regulate the behaviour of others. Bernstein and his colleagues have studied different types of regulatory behaviour by parents in relation to the process of socialisation of the child, and their work provides important clues concerning what the child may be expected to derive from this experience in constructing his own model of language. To adapt one of Bernstein's examples, as described by Turner, the mother who finds that her small child has carried out of the supermarket, unnoticed by herself or by the cashier, some object that was not paid for, may exploit the power of language in various ways, each of which will leave a slightly different trace or after-image of this role of language in the mind of the child. For example, she may say *you mustn't take things that don't belong to you* (control through conditional prohibition based on a categorisation of objects in terms of a particular social institution, that of ownership); *that was very naughty* (control through categorisation of behaviour in terms of opposition approved/disapproved); *if you do that again I'll smack you* (control through threat of reprisal linked to repetition of behaviour); *you'll make Mummy very unhappy if you do that* (control through emotional blackmail); *that's not allowed* (control through categorisation of behaviour as governed by rule), and so on. A single incident of this type by itself has little significance; but such general types of regulatory behaviour, through repetition and reinforcement, determine the child's specific awareness of language as a means of behavioural control.

The child applies this awareness, in his own attempts to control his peers and siblings; and this in turn provides the basis for an essential component in his range of linguistic skills, the language of rules and instructions. Whereas at first he can make only simple unstructured demands, he learns as time goes on to give ordered sequences of instructions, and then progresses to the further stage where he can convert sets of instructions into rules, including conditional rules, as in explaining the principles of a game. Thus his regulatory model of language continues to be elaborated, and his experience of the potentialities of language in this use further increases the value of the model.

Closely related to the regulatory function of language is its function in social interaction, and the third of the models that we may postulate as forming part of the child's image of language is the INTER-ACTIONAL model. This refers to the use of language in the interaction between the self and others. Even the closest of the child's personal relationships, that with his mother, is partly and, in time, largely mediated through language; his interaction with other people, adults and children, is very obviously maintained linguistically. (Those who come nearest to achieving a personal relationship that is not linguistically mediated, apparently, are twins.)

Aside, however, from his experience of language in the maintenance of permanent relationships, the neighbourhood and the activities of the peer group provide the context for complex and rapidly changing interactional patterns which make extensive and subtle demands on the individual's linguistic resources. Language is used to define and consolidate the group, to include and to exclude, showing who is " one of us" and who is not; to impose status, and to contest status that is imposed; and humour, ridicule, deception, persuasion, all the forensic and theatrical arts of language are brought into play. Moreover, the young child, still primarily a learner, can do what very few adults can do in such situations; he can be internalising language while listening and talking. He can be, effectively, both a participant and an observer at the same time, so that his own critical involvement in this complex interaction does not prevent him from profiting linguistically from it.

Again there is a natural link here with another use of language, from which the child derives what we may call the PERSONAL model. This refers to his awareness of language as a form of his own individuality. In the process whereby the child becomes aware of himself, and in particular in the higher stages of that process, the development of his personality, language plays an essential role. We are not talking here merely of "expressive" language—language used for the direct expression of feelings and attitudes—but also of the personal element in the inter-actional function of language, since the shaping of the self through interaction with others is very much a language-mediated process. The child is enabled to offer to someone else that which is unique to himself, to make public his own individuality; and this in turn reinforces and creates this individuality. With the normal child, his awareness of himself is closely bound up with speech: both with hearing himself speak, and with having at his disposal the range of behavioural options that constitute language. Within the concept of the self as an actor, having discretion, or freedom of choice, the "self as a speaker" is an important component.

Thus for the child language is very much a part of himself, and the "personal" model is his intuitive awareness of this, and of the way in which his individuality is identified and realised through language. The other side of the coin, in this process, is the child's growing under-standing of his environment, since the environment is, first of all, the "non-self", that which is separated out in the course of establishing where he himself begins and ends. So, fifthly, the child has a HEURISTIC model of language, derived from his knowledge of how language has enabled him to explore his environment.

The heuristic model refers to language as a means of investigating reality, a way of learning about things. This scarcely needs comment, since every child makes it quite obvious that this is what language is for by his habit of constantly asking questions. When he is questioning, he is seeking not merely facts but explanations of facts, the generalisa-tions about reality that language makes it possible to explore. Again, Bernstein has shown the importance of the question-and-answer routine in the total setting of parent-child communication and the significance of the latter, in turn, in relation to the child's success in formal education: his research has demonstrated a significant correlation be-tween the mother's linguistic attention to the child and the teacher's assessment of the child's success in the first year of school.

The young child is very well aware of how to use language to learn, and may be quite conscious of this aspect of language before he reaches school; many children already control a metalanguage for the heuristic function of language, in that they know what a "question" is, what an "answer" is, what "knowing" and "understanding" mean, and they can talk about these things without difficulty. Mackay and Thompson have shown the importance of helping the child who is learning to read and write to build up a language for talking about language; and it is the heuristic function which provides one of the foundations for this, since the child can readily conceptualise and verbalise the basic categories of the heuristic model. To put this more concretely, the normal five-year-old either already uses words such as *question, answer* in their correct meanings or, if he does not, is capable of learning to do so.

The other foundation for the child's "language about language" is to be found in the imaginative function. This also relates the child to his environment, but in a rather different way. Here, the child is using language to create his own environment; not to learn about how things are but to make them as he feels inclined. From his ability to create, through language, a world of his own making he derives the IMAGINATIVE model of language; and this provides some further elements of the metalanguage, with words like *story, make up* and *pretend*.

Language in its imaginative function is not necessarily "about" anything at all: the child's linguistically created environment does not have to be a make-believe copy of the world of experience, occupied by people and things and events. It may be a world of pure sound, made up of rhythmic sequences of rhyming or chiming syllables; or an edifice of words in which semantics has no part, like a house built of playing cards in which face values are irrelevant. Poems, rhymes, riddles and much of the child's own linguistic play reinforce this model of language, and here too the meaning of what is said is not primarily a matter of content. In stories and dramatic games, the imaginative function is, to a large extent, based on content; but the ability to express such content is still, for the child, only one of the interesting facets of language, one which for many purposes is no more than an optional extra.

So we come finally to the REPRESENTATIONAL model. Language is, in addition to all its other guises, a means of communicating about something, of expressing propositions. The child is aware that he can convey a message in language, a message which has specific reference to the processes, persons, objects, abstractions, qualities, states and relations of the real world around him.

This is the only model of language that many adults have; and a very inadequate model it is, from the point of view of the child. There is no need to go so far as to suggest that the transmission of content is, for the child, the least important function of language; we have no way of evaluating the various functions relatively to one another. It is certainly not, however, one of the earliest to come into prominence; and it does not become a dominant function until a much later stage in the development towards maturity. Perhaps it never becomes in any real sense the dominant function; but it does, in later years, tend to become the dominant *model*. It is very easy for the adult, when he attempts to formulate his ideas about the nature of language, to be simply unaware of most of what language means to the child; this is not because he no longer uses language in the same variety of different functions (one or two may have atrophied, but not all), but because only one of these functions, in general, is the subject of conscious attention, so that the corresponding model is the only one to be externalised. But this presents what is, for the child, a quite unrealistic picture of language, since it accounts for only a small fragment of his total awareness of what language is about.

The representational model at least does not conflict with the child's experience. It relates to one significant part of it; rather a small part, at first, but nevertheless real. In this it contrasts sharply with another view of language which we have not mentioned because it plays no part in the child's experience at all, but which might be called the "ritual" model of language. This is the image of language internalised by those for whom language is a means of showing how well one was brought up; it downgrades language to the level of table-manners. The ritual element in the use of language is probably derived from the inter-actional, since language in its ritual function also serves to define and delimit a social group; but it has none of the positive aspects of linguistic interaction, those which impinge on the child, and is thus very partial and one-sided. The view of language as manners is a needless complication, in the present context, since this function of language has no counterpart in the child's experience.

Our conception of language, if it is to be adequate for meeting the needs of the child, will need to be exhaustive. It must incorporate all the child's own "models", to take account of the varied demands on language that he himself makes. The child's understanding of what language it is derived from his own experience of language in situations of use. It thus embodies all of the images we have described: the instrumental, the regulatory, the interactional, the personal, the heuris-tic, the imaginative and the representational. Each of these is his inter-pretation of a function of language with which he is familiar. Doughty has shown, in a very suggestive paper, how different concepts of the role of the English teacher tend to incorporate and to emphasise different functions, or groups of functions, from among those here enumerated.

*10.1.2 Britton's article 'What's the Use?—A schematic account of language functions' is given here in full. Study it and attempt to apply the categories to pieces of children's writing, such as those that follow the article (Britton, 1971).

173

Language and education

1 *A preliminary note*

We shall be concerned in this article with the functions of extended discourse—a text or a piece of extended speech (not excluding dialogue). Thus, the notion of an overall function, a function that dominates in a hierarchy of functions, must be kept in mind.

We shall be concerned with 'typical function': necessarily so if we are to face up to the distressing facts that a speaker may have hidden and devious intentions in making himself heard; that he may fail to do what he intended; that the effect of an utterance may differ for each member of an audience: and that an utterance may set up a chain of consequences with no determinable cut-off point.

Our salvation lies in the notion of 'context' as Lyons has interpreted it: 'I consider that the idea of context as "universe of discourse" (in Urban's sense) should be incorporated in any linguistic theory of meaning. Under this head I include the conventions and pre-suppositions maintained by "the mutual acknowledgement of communicating subjects" in the particular type of linguistic behaviour (telling a story, philosophizing, buying and selling, praying, writing a novel, etc). . . (Lyons, 1963, pp. 83-84).'

Thus 'the conventions and presuppositions maintained by the mutual acknowledgement of communicating subjects' provide a mature speaker or writer with a repertoire of known choices of function within our culture, and enable a mature listener or reader to recognize which choice has been made.

The rules of the game operate within 'the mutual acknowledgement of communicating subjects' and are therefore open to change. If advertisers, for example, insist on writing what seem to be fragments of autobiography for the purpose of selling tours, additional rules come to be written in.

2 *The process of representation*

Some of the things we say suggest that we may use words to support more general ways of classifying or representing experience: more general and perhaps more elementary ways. Thus (as has often been noticed) we speak of 'sinking into despair' and 'rising to the height of our ambitions'; we 'fall into disfavour' and 'rise to an occasion', and we call education 'a ladder'. It seems likely that some general spatial sense of height and depth constitutes a non-verbal mode of classifying, and that this underlies the habits of speech by which the things we aspire to or strive for are located 'up above', while the things we shun or are at the mercy of are located 'down below'. (When we speak of 'the height of folly' or 'the height of the ridiculous', we are probably mocking some instance by giving it, so to speak, a prize—a booby prize.)

Certainly language, as a way of representing the world, is inextricably interwoven with other forms of representation. My example was trivial, but the statement is crucial, and takes us on to an even more important hypothesis, that what distinguishes man from the other animals is not language *per se*, but the whole process of representation.

174

It is the process of representation that makes a man's view of the world (if we interpret behaviour aright) so vastly different from that of the other animals who live in it with him. Indeed, to speak of an animal's 'view of the world' at all is probably misleading; whereas man's every response to the environment is likely to be mediated by his total view of the world as he knows it. By symbolising, by representing to himself the world as he experiences it, man creates, if Cassirer is right, a retrospect which by projection gives him also a prospect. (Cassirer, 1946, p. 38). In the human world, the here-and-now is set in a rich context, a world constructed of experiences derived from else-where and other times. In such a world, what goes away may be expected to come back, 'out of sight' does not mean 'out of mind', change need not be kaleidoscopic, and very little that happens to us will be wholly unforeseen.

I have laboured the point because I want to suggest that it is typically human to be insistently preoccupied with this world representation, this retrospect and prospect a man constructs for himself. It is of immense importance to him, I believe. It is his true theatre of opera-tions since all he does is done in the light of it; his hopes for the future depend upon its efficacy; and above all his sense of who he is and what it is worth for him to be alive in the world derive from it. We might even say that he is more preoccupied with it than he is with the moment by moment interaction with environment that constitutes his immediate experience. A man's consciousness, in fact, is like the little dog with the brass band: it is for ever running ahead, or dropping back, or trotting alongside, while the procession of actual events moves steadily on.

Our world representation may owe its vividness to sense images and the symbols (however we think of them) that mark emotional categories: for its *organisation* it relies very largely upon language. As we talk about events—present, past or imagined—we shape them in the light of, and incorporate them into, the body of our experience, the total. We may of course fail in our attempt to adjust the corpus and digest the new event: life does sometimes make irreconcilable demands upon all of us. To preserve the order, harmony, unity of our represen-ted world we may ignore the recalcitrant event (or aspect of events); or we may, over a period of time, continue the effort to come to terms with it. Those who too readily ignore disturbing aspects of experience are destined to operate in the actual world by means of a represented world that grows less and less like it: and so the fool has his paradise.

3 The expressive function

If human consciousness is like the little dog with the brass band we may expect to find its volatile nature revealed in a man's expressive speech. Being more or less intimate, unrehearsed, such speech is free to follow the shifting focus of attention, clothing a speaker's pre-occupations the more faithfully because it is committed to no other task, meets no demands but his own, takes for granted a listener's readiness to be interested both in the speaker and his message.

Expressive speech is language close to the speaker: what engages his attention is freely verbalised, and as he presents his view of things, his loaded commentary upon the world, so he also presents himself. Thus, it is above all in expressive speech that we get to know one another, each offering his unique identity and (at our best) offering and accepting both what is common and what differentiates us.

Secondly, it is in expressive speech that we are likely to rehearse the growing points of our formulation and analysis of experience. Thus we may suppose that all the important products and projects that have affected human society are likely to have been given their first draft in talk between the originator and someone who was sufficiently 'in the picture' to hear and consider utterances not yet ready for a wider hearing. Such a listener would ideally concern himself first with the speaker and his thinking, those mental processes that lie behind the utterance; though, having 'understood', he might take account also of the forms of the utterance itself and assist in its modification to suit a wider audience.

But of course our use of expressive speech is not limited to the original and far-reaching. It is our principal means of exchanging opinions, attitudes, beliefs in face-to-face situations. As such, I would judge it to be a far more important instrument for influencing each other and affecting public opinion and social action than any sermon, political speech, pamphlet, manifesto or other public utterance.

'Expressive' is one of the three principal language functions in the scheme I want to outline. It is a scheme that was worked out in the course of classifying some two thousand pieces of written work, in all school subjects, produced by boys and girls of eleven to eighteen, though its application is not confined to the written language. In order to explain the remaining terms, I need to refer back to the general theory with which I began.

4 The role of participant and spectator

Once we suppose that man operates in the actual world by means of his representation of it, we can see for him an alternative mode of behaviour: he may operate *upon the representation itself* without seeking any direct effect in the actual world. We may in fact see in this formulation a way of describing a great deal of his spontaneous image-making. (Susanne Langer calls man 'a proliferator of images' and postulates a new need not recognized in the other animals, a 'need of symbolization') (Langer, 1960, p. 41). These two kinds of behaviour seem to me essentially and interestingly different. (For a fuller discussion see Chapter II in my *Language and Learning*.) 'Operating in the actual world' I want to call 'being in the role of participant': 'operating directly upon the represented world' (improvising upon past experience, for example, or supplying gaps in our picture by drawing upon other people's experiences—but both taken up out of concern for our world picture and not as a means to some end in the actual here-and-now)—this I want to call 'being in the role of spectator'. Contrast Othello telling the story of his life to Desdemona and her father (where all three are in the role of spectator) with a beggar telling a hardluck story to enhance his appeal, or a historian reading a novel, or any other narrative, in order to check on a point of historical fact (each of them, in pursuing his own current ends through the agency of the narrative being in the role of participant).

To be in the role of spectator is to be concerned with events not now taking place (past events or imagined events), and to be concerned with them *per se* (as an interruption to or a holiday from the march of actual events) and *not as a means to some ongoing transaction with the actual*.

Suppose I recount an interesting experience to a friend—for his entertainment and my own pleasure in doing so. I shall continue to breathe, stand up, sit down, drink maybe, or eat, attend occasionally to what is going on around me—offer him another drink, move nearer the fire if I am cold, answer a child's question, and so on. But mentally I am 'living in the past'—these other things are seen as unattended background to, or interruptions of, what I am principally concerned to do; which is to rehearse in mind an experience that is not now going on, but has been experienced in the past.

What I feel as background or interruption to my spectator role activity is likely to be similarly felt by my listener. In other words, in sharing this past experience with him I induce him also to take up the spectator role. But it is an experience I had, he did not. It follows that I may similarly take up the role of spectator of experiences *I* have never had—and that, I suggest, is what I do when I read a novel or watch a film, or when I enter into possible future experiences in my day-dreaming.

When we use language to get something done, we are in the role of participants—participants in a very general sense in the world's affairs: and, as we have suggested, this must be taken to include the use of language to recount or recreate real or imagined experience in order to inform, or teach, or make plans, or solicit help, or achieve any other practical outcome.

We must note finally that taking up the spectator role does not indicate any lack of involvement in the experiences being recounted: we do indeed 'participate' in the story or the fiction or the dream, but since the events that involve us are distinct from ongoing events, and not subordinated to ongoing events as means to end, this participation does not put us in the role of participant.

4 *The three main categories*

The two roles of participant and spectator are thus seen to represent two different relationships between what is being *said* (or written or thought) and what is being *done*, and to cover between them all uses of language. We see our three main function categories, Transactional, Expressive and Poetic, related to the two roles as follows:

Participant | Spectator
role | role

TRANSACTIONAL——EXPRESSIVE——POETIC

When the demands made of a participant (in the world's affairs) are at a maximum, we have called the function 'transactional', a term that will need no explaining. Where the use of language in spectator role achieves its fullest satisfactions, we have called the function 'poetic', a term meant to include any example of the verbal arts. The expressive function straddles the participant/spectator distinction, but the dividing line at this mid-point is a shadowy one, and expressive language, as we have seen, is loosely structured, free to fluctuate. Thus, to modify an earlier example, if I recount the story of my recent holiday for your entertainment (and to enjoy it myself in retrospect), the talk is likely to be expressive, in the spectator role. If as you listen you become interested in the place I am describing as a possible holiday trip for yourself, you may ask for information about it—switching to participant role, but probably staying in the expressive. If, however, you pursue this line of enquiry and begin seriously to plan your holiday, your questions, directing my answers, may have the effect of shifting us both into transactional speech. A less likely alternative: if you were to become so interested in my account *as narrative*, and if under your encouragement I warmed to my task of constructing a story (and had the talent to do so), my language might move from the expressive to the poetic function. Finally (lest it appear that the expressive function operates only as a stage *en route* to something else) if as you listen to my talk we warm *to each other*, we may begin to exchange experiences, opinions, evaluations, and—now in spectator role, now in participant— intensify the reciprocal processes of exploring the other and revealing the self that constitute the expressive function of conversational utterance.

5 *The poetic function*

D.W. Harding long ago laid the foundations of the theory that associates literature with the role of spectator (Harding, 1937). He saw gossip and the novel as two instances of 'imaginary spectatorship in a social setting', and suggested that in each a *detached evaluative response* to the possibilities of experience was being offered by the speaker (writer) and invited of the listener (reader). 'The result', he said, 'is a vast extension of the range of possible human experience that can be offered socially for contemplation and assessment.' Though as participants we evaluate a situation in order to operate within it, as spectators we are able to relate events more amply to a broader spectrum of values. 'Detached and distanced evaluation is sometimes sharper for avoiding the blurrings and bufferings that participant action brings, and the spectator often sees the event in a broader context than the participant can tolerate. To obliterate the effects on a man of the occasions on which he was only an onlooker would be profoundly to change his outlook and values.' (Harding, 1962, p. 136).

To put this point very simply: freed of a participant's need to *act* (to interact socially, to keep his end up, to turn events to his own advantage etc.), a spectator is able to attend more fully and more exclusively to the evaluative processes. I want now to add a new point within the same framework: freed of the necessity for action, a spectator is able to attend more fully to the utterance *as utterance*—that is to say, to its forms of language and to formal features of whatever the language portrays: the pattern of events in a narrative; the configuration of an idea or a theory; and, above all, the pattern of feelings evoked—the rise and fall of emotional tension, the succession of love, hate, anger, fear, relief, pity that may attend his response to the experiences portrayed. I say 'above all' because I believe Harding's view of the detached evaluative response may be enhanced by recognizing that the effect of feeling upon a participant has this marked difference from its effect upon a spectator. As we participate in events, feeling seems to operate primarily as a spur to action: we might even say that it discharges itself in action. As spectators, we hold it to savour it; and as we read on (or listen, or speak, or write), to savour not simply an emotion but the formal design created by a complex of emotions dynamically related.

If gossip and the novel are linked as examplars of language in the spectator role, they are differentiated in the degree to which they realise the opportunities for formal organisation. In our terms, most gossip will be expressive in function (as will also the loosely autobiographical written narratives of the English lesson): the novel, the play, the poem, on the other hand, take on the poetic function in so far as they achieve the necessary degree of formal organisation, formal unity. (What is the necessary degree will be an arbitrary decision related to the purpose of making an analysis.)

For the poetic utterance is a construct or artifact, a verbal object. To exaggerate the matter, as many poets and critics have done, its function is not *to say*, but *to be*: or—more commodiously—where other utterances have *meaning*, a poetic utterance has *import*. This is a matter we shall return to in a moment.

6 *The transactional function*

Transactional language has two main sub-divisions which we have labelled, familiarly enough, *informative* and *conative*. The informative covers both the giving and the seeking of information; the full range of what is meant by 'information' takes us into considerable complications in the way of sub-categories. The conative is quite straightforward in theory since we have chosen to define it narrowly, but applying the distinctions in practice presents difficulties. For language to qualify as conative in function, the speaker's intention to change his listener's behaviour, opinions or attitudes must be deliberate and recognizable—

recognizable, that is, to an observer even where it is so disguised as to deceive a victim to whom it is addressed.

7 *Transactional and poetic contrasted*

Before describing further sub-categories of the transactional, let us attempt to clarify some of the major issues, first by briefly contrasting the two poles of the system, transactional and poetic language.

Transactional	*Poetic*
(Participant role)	(Spectator role)
The utterance is an immediate means to an end outside itself.	The utterance is an immediate end in itself, and not a means. i.e. it is a verbal artifact, a construct.
The form it takes, the way it is organised, is dictated primarily by the desire to achieve that end efficiently.	The arrangement *is* the construct i.e. the way items are formally disposed is an inseparable part of the meaning of the utterance.
Attention to the forms of the language is incidental to understanding, and will often be minimal.	Attention to the forms of the language is an essential part of a listener's (reader's) response.
The speaker(writer) is concerned in his utterances to enmesh with his listener's relevant knowledge, experience, interests: and the listener is at liberty to contextualize what he finds relevant, selectively. This 'piecemeal contextualisation' we take to be a part of the conventions governing transactional language.	The speaker (writer) is concerned to create relations internal to the utterance, and achieve a unity, a construct that is discrete from actuality. Thus he resists piecemeal contextualisation; i.e. the conventions holding between speaker and listener in poetic language call for 'global contextualisation'.

8 *Contextualisation of the poetic*

The difference in mode of contextualisation (the manner in which we relate what is in the utterance to what we know, think, feel already) is a crucial one. As we read a poetic text we must of course draw at all points upon our own experience in order to interpret what is on the page: but, if we are responding according to the conventions governing poetic language, our principle selection and organisation of this material will be one of subordination to every clue the text can offer us. This process, then, might be thought of as the converse of 'piecemeal contextualisation'—in fact the converse of contextualisation itself. When we have completed the structuring of the raw material of our own experience in obedience to the demands of the text—having as it were recreated the construct as a unity—we may then go on to relate its total import to our own experience as a whole, our general views and beliefs on the issues involved.

It is in this way that the artist with a message get his message across. A work that invites piecemeal contextualisation must forgo the formal coherence and unity of the poetic construct: its message may be forceful, but it is not poetically conveyed: we should classify it is 'transactional'. On the other hand, the first thing to record about the poetic work is to classify it as 'poetic': however, we may then go on and allot it to a second category in accordance with the function that seems appropriate to its 'global contextualisation'. We might for example call *1984* or *Catch 22* 'Poetic (Conative)'; C.P. Snow's *The New Men* or Patrick White's *The Tree of Man*, 'Poetic (Informative)'; and perhaps Lowry's *Under the Volcano* and Joyce's *Ulysses*, 'Poetic (Expressive)'. That the scheme should make room for such judgements is more important than that we should agree in making them—mercifully. And for the vast majority of works of literature all we shall need to say, or want to say, will probably be said in classifying them as 'Poetic'.

As far as satire is concerned, our claim that the poetic function should rank as primary is perhaps somewhat encouraged by the consideration that most of the satires that continue to be read concern themselves with causes which, if not lost, are at least won.

9 *Sub-categories of the informative*

Of the many possible ways of subdividing informative uses of language, we have chosen one based on James Moffett's analysis of the relation between a speaker and his topic: between the 'I' and the 'it', where 'I', 'you' and 'it' represent the three components of a communication situation. (Moffett, 1968). He calls his analysis 'an abstractive scale', and sees it as operating in close interconnexion with a 'rhetorical scale' representing the range of relations between the 'I' and the 'you'. He marks off four positions on his abstractive scale, moving from the least to the most abstract, from the 'codification of our world that most nearly reflects the structure of that world to codification that more and more resembles the structure of the mind'. (Moffett, 1968, p. 9). Here, more or less in the form that he gives them, are his four categories:

1 Recording: the drama of what is happening.
   Chronologic of perceptual selectivity.
   (e.g. an on the spot recording of what is happening before the guillotine.)
2 Reporting: the narrative of what happened.
   Chronologic of memory selectivity.
   (e.g. an eye-witness account of what happened one day during the French Revolution.)
3 Generalizing: the exposition of what happens.
   (e.g. a historical generalisation about the Reign of Terror.)
4 Theorizing: the argumentation of what will, may, happen.
   Tautologic of transformation.
   (e.g. a political scientist's theory about revolutions.)
                    (Moffett, 1968, pp. 34, 35 and 47.)
Having acknowledged a substantial debt (which will become obvious),

I shall leave Moffett's account in bare outline and go into greater detail in explaining the modified form of scale we have used to subdivide our informative category.

But first to make a more general point: Moffett in fact applies his scale to all forms of discourse: we have used it where it seemed focal, where it systematized observed differences between utterances that seemed important. The relation between a speaker and his topic is likely to be crucial in the informative category, which is after all the category Jakobson called 'the referential function' and which he defined as 'focus upon the topic'. (See Sebeok, 1960, p. 357). The scale might be applied to expressive discourse, but would not add a great deal of information, or to conative discourse, but somewhat irrelevantly. To apply it to poetic discourse would, I suspect, be to introduce an alien concept (and our notion of global contextualisation will suggest reasons).

Basing our requirements on the data to be classified—the two thousand scripts collected from secondary schools—we finally introduced three transitional categories, making seven out of Moffett's four.

(i) *Record.* The speaker records what is going on *here and now*, and/ or describes what is to be observed here and now. (Compare what is often called 'running commentary'.) The principle of organisation is chronological or 'spatial' (qualitative, descriptive).

We have made the assumption that the prerequisite classifying processes are no more demanding if one says, 'The policeman's coat is blue with silver buttons' than if one says, 'The policeman is shouting and waving his baton': i.e. that *describing* is not *per se* a generalising activity and thus related to the analogic in a way *narrating* is not.

(ii) *Report.* The speaker reports what went on or what was to be observed on a particular occasion at a particular place. The principle of organisation is, again, chronological/spatial. Note that the speaker, since he takes up a retrospective stance, has a basis of selection not available to the speaker of *record*.

Some historical statements are in this category since they deal with directly observable events: e.g. 'In May 1836 an exploring expedition led by the surveyor-general attacked a party of aborigines killing seven and wounding four.' But more commonly, historical statements are generalisations based upon scattered observations and observations over a period of time: e.g. 'The record of relations between the settlers and the natives was an unhappy one.' Such statements, in themselves, are *analogic* (Category (v)). However, isolated sentences of either type are likely to be embedded in a text that contains both types: classification will in any case be in accordance with what seems to be dominant, and in this particular case a balance of analogic statements with related statements of report is likely to be characteristic of the best analogic discourse.

(iii) *Generalised narrative or descriptive information.* The speaker reports what goes on (or used to go on) habitually, or what might be, or have been, habitually observed over a series of occasions in a series of

1▲ 2▼

Liz Bennett

3▼

Euan Duff

4▲ 5▼

6▼

places. E.g. What we do on Sundays; what coffee-houses were like; how we get our water supply. Classes of events or of 'appearances' are organised on a chronological/spatial principle. This category thus marks the first step towards generalisation, away from the particularity of report.

We include in this sub-category a great deal of everyday informational discourse, discourse in which the speaker generalises from a number of observable events or procedures or concrete situations (e.g. recipes, practical hints, descriptions of simple processes or procedures).

(iv) *Analogic, low level of generalisation.* An arrangement of loosely related and low-level general statements: a concatenation or agglomeration of such statements, for example about the industries of Scotland or the effects of the Thirty Years War. The principle of organisation, is, however, classificatory rather than chronological/spatial.

(v) *Analogic.* This, rather than (iii) or (iv), is Moffett's 'generalizing' category. Here generalisations are made and are related hierarchically or logically: i.e. the principle of organisation is again classificatory, but more rigorously so than in (iv).

A great deal of scientific and historical discourse will come into this category, but it will include any attempt to relate statements on the basis of their respective levels of generality, from whatever areas of experience they may be drawn. E.g. 'The differences are large and variable. Taking an objective view of my parents as the adults I know best, an obvious difference is that I am at school learning, whereas they have left school and work. This means that they bring home the money and I do not. I am dependent on them and responsible to them.'

(vi) *Speculative (Analogic/tautologic).* This is another transitional category that seemed to be required since a great deal of open-ended speculation arises when a speaker makes, as it were, horizontal moves in his thinking—framing general hypotheses on the basis of general propositions—and yet does not reach conclusions which would provide a genuinely theoretical analysis.

(vii) *Tautologic (Moffett's 'theorizing').* Here the systematic combining of abstract propositions leads to new conclusions, which form a further extension of the system or theory. The basis of organisation is, in a strict sense, *theoretical.*

Though its claims to belong to this category can hardly be sustained on the evidence of one sentence, we judged the school-boy's piece from which this was taken to qualify for inclusion: 'The social life of man is characterised not by virtue of his being a tool-using animal but by virtue of his being a language-generating animal.'

At this point I imagine a reader might be tempted by a common common-sense to ask with me a low-level question: What then becomes of these high-level abstractions? Do they reverberate for ever in a perpetual tautology? And I suppose our answer should be along these lines: that we give them intellectual assent in so far as (1) we accept as valid the steps in thinking by which they were arrived at and (2) they support or strengthen important ideas or beliefs we already hold; and perhaps (3) they modify some lesser beliefs or replace them with ones that fit better into the total edifice: then presumably at some points in the whole network there will be tests applied which show whether the system works in practice, whether it provides reliable guidelines to choice at the level of behaviour.

What is important is to realize, as Moffett points out, that the more abstract processes derive from *and remain dependent on* those at lower levels. Thus, the series of categories from (i) to (vii) has clear developmental implications: to say this, however, is to broach an important aspect of our study which this article cannot attempt to deal with.

10 *Sub-categories of the conative*

We distinguish two sub-categories of the conative, *regulative* and *persuasive*. The regulative represents a direct exercise of influence, and it aims more often at affecting action or behaviour than at changing attitudes, opinions or beliefs. It covers on the one hand simple requests such as 'Pass the mustard', and on the other, rules and instructions issued to those obliged to obey them, and recommendations that carry the weight of authority or the force of a speaker's wishes.

It should be noted that recipe books, and a great many other varieties of technological discourse, may use a conative form, but since their function is informative they are classified in the informative categories.

In ordinarily polite society a request to pass the mustard is not expected to be refused: the regulative utterance is enough. In authority situations those giving the instructions speak in the expectation that they will be obeyed. Persuasive language, the second sub-division of the conative, is employed where no such expectation of compliance operates: usually becuase it is inappropriate, but sometimes in cases where the expectation has met disappointment, or the speaker has chosen not to invoke it although he might have done. Here the speaker's will is, as it were, diverted into an effort to *work upon* the listener in support of the course of action he recommends, or (more typically perhaps) the opinion, attitude, belief he is putting forward. Thus it is one strategy of persuasive language to foresee and counter possible objections, bringing the weight of logical argument to bear; it is another strategy to work upon a listener's feelings, employing perhaps the wiles of classical rhetoric, whether recognized as such or not.

11 *What's the use?*

So there it is—the outline of a scheme in progress (an appendix gives the category numbering). If it seems to us rather tenuous at times we take heart from the thought that we shall understand it much better when we have completed a study of the two thousand scripts, and have applied it also to a four-year follow-up study of the school-work of about a hundred eleven-year-olds and a hundred fourteen-year-olds.

We believe it may offer one approach to the consideration of 'language across the curriculum'—an undertaking that must call into question some very general matters concerning teachers' objectives, as well as some very particular ones regarding the diverse linguistic demands made on children as they move from one lesson to another in the day's programme.

Of the general matters, it is the interrelationships of the main categories that interest us most—as well as the *interrelatedness* of the various linguistic demands and achievements. We would hope, for instance, that expressive language may be increasingly seen to play a key role in all learning (even the most subject-oriented) as well as in learning to use language; and that the educational value of spectator role activities may come to be better understood and more convincingly argued. We see such activities indeed as reflecting a concern for 'the compleat man': for it is the corpus of an individual's experience that makes him the person he is; that generates the pluses and minuses of his fluctuating verdict on the world, his fluctuating acceptance of the human condition, his fluctuating faith in himself. And spectator role activities, across the whole range from expressive to poetic utterance, represent a concern for this corpus.

Appendix

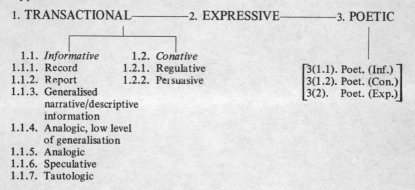

1. TRANSACTIONAL———————2. EXPRESSIVE———————3. POETIC

1.1. *Informative*	1.2. *Conative*	
1.1.1. Record	1.2.1. Regulative	⎡3(1.1). Poet. (Inf.)⎤
1.1.2. Report	1.2.2. Persuasive	⎢3(1.2). Poet. (Con.)⎥
1.1.3. Generalised narrative/descriptive information		⎣3(2).　Poet. (Exp.)⎦
1.1.4. Analogic, low level of generalisation		
1.1.5. Analogic		
1.1.6. Speculative		
1.1.7. Tautologic		

The following pieces of children's writing are offered as examples but cannot be a substitute for the reader collecting pieces for himself in terms of the categories discussed above.

I have got a party dress for when I go out on special occasions. I have got A best green dress a old dress a best pinafore dress with a best Jumper a pear of slacks a pear of shorts and a tea shirt and lots of other things (Aged 9)

When you are young you are nearly always fiddling with loose teeth. But when you are grown up you are always writing letters and doing bills and going shopping in the pouring rain. When you are very very old

you can lie in bed all day but I suppose its rather nice leaving school
and passing exams and being a teacher or nurse or doctor or train driver.
But life I suppose is all the same. When you are older you burn your
fingers when cooking. (Aged 10)

Hot smelling, sweaty beads of water covered my body. 'No, its not
true', I tell myself, not convinced. 'You'll see', I say, as a mother softly
to her child. 'You'll see, it will be all gone in the morning'. 'Sleep' a
quavering voice speaks, 'sleep'. But I will not sleep. The nightmare still
there. Still near. Rational explanations of why and wherefore were not
for now. My mind one-tracked. Immediate instincts 'call Mum',
suppressed by some adult graces even now. (Aged 15)

The function of punishment was seldom questioned. It seemed self-
evident that someone who had commited an offence ought in justice to
be punished. Why he had done it was not taken into account; whether
prison would stop him doing it again was not considered. Nor was the
punishment really made to fit the criminals: first offenders were often
incarcerated with hardened lags. It is true that sometimes the punishment fitted the crime in rather a ghoulish way—scolds wore bridles, and
drunks were made to walk around wearing nothing but barrels.
(Aged 17)

Chapter 11

11.3.1 Vygotsky's comments on Piaget's original views on the growth of thought and speech were not seen by Piaget until after Vygotsky's death. He fully agreed with them, and they have become a point of reference in discussions of the topic. The extract below is from the chapter entitled 'Thought and Word' from Vygotsky's *Thought and Language* (1962).

Inner speech is speech for oneself; external speech is for others. It would indeed be surprising if such a basic difference in function did not affect the structure of the two kinds of speech. Absence of vocalization per se is only a consequence of the specific nature of inner speech, which is neither an antededent of external speech nor its reproduction in memory but is, in a sense, the opposite of external speech. The latter is the turning of thought into words, its materialization and objectification. With inner speech, the process is reversed: Speech turns into inward thought. Consequently, their structures must differ.

The area of inner speech is one of the most difficult to investigate. It remained almost inaccessible to experiments until ways were found to apply the genetic method of experimentation. Piaget was the first to pay attention to the child's egocentric speech and to see its theoretical significance, but he remained blind to the most important trait of egocentric speech—its genetic connection with inner speech—and this warped his interpretation of its function and structure. We made that relationship the central problem of our study and thus were able to investigate the nature of inner speech with unusual completeness. A number of considerations and observations led us to conclude that egocentric speech is a stage of development preceding inner speech: Both fulfill intellectual functions; their structures are similar; egocentric speech disappears at school age, when inner speech begins to develop. From all this we infer that one changes into the other.

If this transformation does take place, then egocentric speech provides the key to the study of inner speech. One advantage of approaching inner speech through egocentric speech is its accessibility to experimentation and observation. It is still vocalized, audible speech, i.e., external in its mode of expression, but at the same time inner speech in function and structure. To study an internal process it is necessary to externalize it experimentally, by connecting it with some outer activity; only then is objective functional analysis possible. Egocentric speech is, in fact, a natural experiment of this type.

This method has another great advantage. Since egocentric speech can be studied at the time when some of its characteristics are waning and new ones forming, we are able to judge which traits are essential to inner speech and which are only temporary, and thus to determine the goal of this movement from egocentric to inner speech—i.e., the nature of inner speech.

Before we can go on to the results obtained by this method, we shall briefly discuss the nature of egocentric speech, stressing the differences between our theory and Piaget's. Piaget contends that the child's egocentric speech is a direct expression of the egocentrism of his thought, which in turn is a compromise between the primary autism of his thinking and its gradual socialization. As the child grows older, autism recedes and socialization progresses, leading to the waning of egocentrism in his thinking and speech.

In Piaget's conception, the child in his egocentric speech does not adapt himself to the thinking of adults. His thought remains entirely egocentric; this makes his talk incomprehensible to others. Egocentric speech has no function in the child's realistic thinking or activity—it merely accompanies them. And since it is an expression of egocentric thought, it disappears together with the child's egocentrism. From its climax at the beginning of the child's development, egocentric speech drops to zero on the threshold of school age. Its history is one of involution rather than evolution. It has no future.

In our conception, egocentric speech is a phenomenon of the transition from interpsychic to intrapsychic functioning, i.e., from the social, collective activity of the child to his more individualized activity —a pattern of development common to all the higher psychological functions. Speech for oneself originates through differentiation from speech for others. Since the main course of the child's development is one of gradual individualization, this tendency is reflected in the function and structure of his speech.

Our experimental results indicate that the function of egocentric speech is similar to that of inner speech: It does not merely accompany the child's activity; it serves mental orientation, conscious understanding; it helps in overcoming difficulties; it is speech for oneself, intimately and usefully connected with the child's thinking. Its fate is very different from that described by Piaget. Egocentric speech develops along a rising, not a declining, curve; it goes through an evolution, not an involution. In the end, it becomes inner speech.

Our hypothesis has several advantages over Piaget's: It explains the function and development of egocentric speech and, in particular, its sudden increase when the child faces difficulties which demand consciousness and reflection—a fact uncovered by our experiments and which Piaget's theory cannot explain. But the greatest advantage of our theory is that it supplies a satisfying answer to a paradoxical situation described by Piaget himself. To Piaget, the quantitative drop in egocentric speech as the child grows older means the withering of that form of speech. If that were so, its structural peculiarities might also be expected to decline; it is hard to believe that the process would affect only its quantity, and not its inner structure. The child's thought becomes infinitely less egocentric between the ages of three and seven. If the characteristics of egocentric speech that made it incomprehensible to others are indeed rooted in egocentrism, they should become less apparent as that form of speech becomes less frequent; egocentric speech should approach social speech and become more and more intelligible. Yet what are the facts? Is the talk of a three-year-old harder to follow than that of a seven-year-old? Our investigation established that the traits of egocentric speech which make for inscrutability are at their lowest point at three and at their peak at seven. They develop in a reverse direction to the frequency of egocentric speech. While the latter keeps falling and reaches zero at school age, the structural characteristics become more and more pronounced.

This throws a new light on the quantitative decrease in egocentric speech, which is the cornerstone of Piaget's thesis.

What does this decrease mean? The structural peculiarities of speech for oneself and its differentiation from external speech increase with age. What is it then that diminishes? Only one of its aspects: vocalization. Does this mean that egocentric speech as a whole is dying out? We believe that it does not, for how then could we explain the growth of the functional and structural traits of egocentric speech? On the other hand, their growth is perfectly compatible with the decrease of vocalization—indeed, clarifies its meaning. Its rapid dwindling and the equally rapid growth of the other characteristics are contradictory in appearance only.

To explain this, let us start from an undeniable, experimentally established fact. The structural and functional qualities of egocentric speech become more marked as the child develops. At three, the difference between egocentric and social speech equals zero; at seven, we have speech that in structure and function is totally unlike social speech. A differentiation of the two speech functions has taken place. This is a fact—and facts are notoriously hard to refute.

Once we accept this, everything else falls into place. If the developing structural and functional peculiarities of egocentric speech progressively isolate it from external speech, then its vocal aspect must fade away; and this is exactly what happens between three and seven years. With the progressive isolation of speech for oneself, its vocalization becomes unnecessary and meaningless and, because of its growing structural peculiarities, also impossible. Speech for oneself cannot find expression in external speech. The more independent and autonomous egocentric speech becomes, the poorer it grows in its external manifestations. In the end it separates itself entirely from speech for others, ceases to be vocalized, and thus appears to die out.

But this is only an illusion. To interpret the sinking coefficient of egocentric speech as a sign that this kind of speech is dying out is like saying that the child stops counting when he ceases to use his fingers and starts adding in his head. In reality, behind the symptoms of dissolution lies a progressive development, the birth of a new speech form.

The decreasing vocalization of egocentric speech denotes a developing abstraction from sound, the child's new faculty to "think words" instead of pronouncing them. This is the positive meaning of the sinking coefficient of egocentric speech. The downward curve indicates development toward inner speech.

We can see that all the known facts about the functional, structural, and genetic characteristics of egocentric speech point to one thing: It develops in the direction of inner speech. Its developmental history can be understood only as a gradual unfolding of the traits of inner speech.

We believe that this corroborates our hypothesis about the origin and nature of egocentric speech. To turn our hypothesis into a certainty, we must devise an experiment capable of showing which of the two interpretations is correct. What are the data for this critical experiment?

Let us restate the theories between which we must decide. Piaget believes that egocentric speech stems from the insufficient socialization of speech and that its only development is decrease and eventual death. Its culmination lies in the past. Inner speech is something new brought in from the outside along with socialization. We believe that egocentric speech stems from the insufficient individualization of primary social speech. Its culmination lies in the future. It develops into inner speech.

To obtain evidence for one or the other view, we must place the child alternately in experimental situations encouraging social speech and in situations discouraging it, and see how these changes affect egocentric speech. We consider this an *experimentum crucis* for the following reasons.

If the child's egocentric talk results from the egocentrism of his thinking and its insufficient socialization, then any weakening of the social elements in the experimental setup, any factor contributing to the child's isolation from the group, must lead to a sudden increase in egocentric speech. But if the latter results from an insufficient differentiation of speech for oneself from speech for others, then the same changes must cause it to decrease.

We took as the starting point of our experiment three of Piaget's own observations: (1) Egocentric speech occurs only in the presence of other children engaged in the same activity, and not when the child is alone; i.e., it is a collective monologue. (2) The child is under the illusion that his egocentric talk, directed to nobody, is understood by those who surround him. (3) Egocentric speech has the character of external speech: It is not inaudible or whispered. These are certainly not chance peculiarities. From the child's own point of view, egocentric speech is not yet separated from social speech. It occurs under the subjective and objective conditions of social speech and may be considered a correlate of the insufficient isolation of the child's individual consciousness from the social whole.

In our first series of experiments [46, 47], we tried to destroy the illusion of being understood. After measuring the child's coefficient of egocentric speech in a situation similar to that of Piaget's experiments, we put him into a new situation: either with deaf-mute children or with children speaking a foreign language. In all other respects the setup remained the same. The coefficient of egocentric speech dropped to zero in the majority of cases, and in the rest to one-eighth of the previous figure, on the average. This proves that the illusion of being understood is not a mere epiphenomenon of egocentric speech but is functionally connected with it. Our results must seem paradoxical from the point of view of Piaget's theory: The weaker the child's contact is with the group—the less the social situation forces him to adjust his thoughts to others and to use social speech—the more freely should the egocentrism of his thinking and speech manifest itself. But from the point of view of our hypothesis, the meaning of these findings is clear: Egocentric speech, springing from the lack of differentiation of speech for oneself from speech for others, disappears when the feeling of being understood, essential for social speech, is absent.

In the second series of experiments, the variable factor was the possibility of collective monologue. Having measured the child's coefficient of egocentric speech in a situation permitting collective monologue, we put him into a situation excluding it—in a group of children who were strangers to him, or by himself at a separate table in a corner of the room; or he worked quite alone, even the experimenter leaving the room. The results of this series agreed with the first results. The exclusion of the group monologue caused a drop in the coefficient of egocentric speech, though not such a striking one as in the first case— seldom to zero and, on the average, to one-sixth of the original figure. The different methods of precluding collective monologue were not equally effective in reducing the coefficient of egocentric speech. The trend, however, was obvious in all the variations of the experiment. The exclusion of the collective factor, instead of giving full freedom to egocentric speech, depressed it. Our hypothesis was once more confirmed.

In the third series of experiments, the variable factor was the vocal quality of egocentric speech. Just outside the laboratory where the experiment was in progress, an orchestra played so loudly, or so much noise was made, that it drowned out not only the voices of others but the child's own; in a variant of the experiment, the child was expressly forbidden to talk loudly and allowed to talk only in whispers. Once again the coefficient of egocentric speech went down, the relation to the original figure being 5:1. Again the different methods were not equally effective, but the basic trend was invariably present.

The purpose of all three series of experiments was to eliminate those characteristics of egocentric speech which bring it close to social speech. We found that this always led to the dwindling of egocentric speech. It is logical, then, to assume that egocentric speech is a form developing out of social speech and not yet separated from it in its manifestation, though already distinct in function and structure.

The disagreement between us and Piaget on this point will be made quite clear by the following example: I am sitting at my desk talking to a person who is behind me and whom I cannot see; he leaves the room without my noticing it, and I continue to talk, under the illusion that he listens and understands. Outwardly, I am talking with myself and for myself, but psychologically my speech is social. From the point of view of Piaget's theory, the opposite happens in the case of the child: His egocentric talk is for and with himself; it only has the appearance of social speech, just as my speech gave the false impression of being egocentric. From our point of view, the whole situation is much more complicated than that: Subjectively, the child's egocentric speech already has its own peculiar function—to that extent, it is independent from social speech; yet its independence is not complete because it is not felt as inner speech and is not distinguished by the child from speech for others. Objectively, also, it is different from social speech but again not entirely, because it functions only within social situations. Both subjectively and objectively, egocentric speech represents a transition from speech for others to speech for oneself. It already has the function of inner speech but remains similar to social speech in its expression.

Chapter 12

For an introduction to the topic of language and thought, see Wilkinson (1971a, Ch. IV).

The following extract, from an essay entitled 'Science and Linguistics' (Whorf, 1966, pp. 212-17), states what is known as the Whorfian hypothesis. In it Whorf argues that it is the grammar of a language as well as its vocabulary which determines our awareness of reality.

When linguists became able to examine critically and scientifically a large number of languages of widely different patterns, their base of reference was expanded; they experienced an interruption of phenomena hitherto held universal, and a whole new order of significances came into their ken. It was found that the background linguistic system (in other words, the grammar) of each language is not merely a re-producing instrument for voicing ideas but rather is itself the shaper of ideas, the program and guide for the individual's mental activity, for his analysis of impressions, for his synthesis of his mental stock in trade. Formulation of ideas is not an independent process, strictly rational in the old sense, but is part of a particular grammar, and differs, from slightly to greatly, between different grammars. We dissect nature along lines laid down by our native languages. The categories and types that we isolate from the world of pheonmena we do not find there because they stare every observer in the face; on the contrary, the world is presented in a kaleidoscopic flux of impressions which has to be organized by our minds—and this means largely by the linguistic systems in our minds. We cut nature up, organize it into concepts, and ascribe significances as we do, largely because we are parties to an agreement to organize it in this way—an agreement that holds throughout our speech community and is codified in the patterns of our language. The agreement is, of course, an implicit and unstated one, BUT ITS TERMS ARE ABSOLUTELY OBLIGATORY; we cannot talk at all except by sub-scribing to the organization and classification of data which the agreement decrees.

This fact is very significant for modern science, for it means that no individual is free to describe nature with absolute impartiality but is constrained to certain modes of interpretation even while he thinks himself most free. The person most nearly free in such respects would be a linguist familiar with very many widely different linguistic systems. As yet no linguist is in any such position. We are thus introduced to a new principle of relativity, which holds that all observers are not led by the same physical evidence to the same picture of the universe, unless their linguistic backgrounds are similar, or can in some way be calibrated.

Language and education

This rather startling conclusion is not so apparent if we compare only our modern European languages, with perhaps Latin and Greek thrown in for good measure. Among these tongues there is a unanimity of major pattern which at first seems to bear out natural logic. But this unanimity exists only because these tongues are all Indo-European dialects cut to the same basic plan, being historically transmitted from

OBJECTIVE FIELD	SPEAKER (SENDER)	HEARER (RECEIVER)	HANDLING OF TOPIC, RUNNING OF THIRD PERSON
SITUATION 1a.			ENGLISH... "HE IS RUNNING" HOPI... "WARI" (RUNNING. STATEMENT OF FACT)
SITUATION 1b. OBJECTIVE FIELD BLANK DEVOID OF RUNNING			ENGLISH... "HE RAN" HOPI... "WARI" (RUNNING, STATEMENT OF FACT)
SITUATION 2			ENGLISH..."HE IS RUNNING" HOPI... "WARI" (RUNNING, STATEMENT OF FACT)
SITUATION 3 OBJECTIVE FIELD BLANK			ENGLISH..."HE RAN" HOPI... "ERA WARI" (RUNNING. STATEMENT OF FACT FROM MEMORY)
SITUATION 4 OBJECTIVE FIELD BLANK			ENGLISH..."HE WILL RUN" HOPI... "WARIKNI" (RUNNING, STATEMENT OF EXPECTATION)
SITUATION 5 OBJECTIVE FIELD BLANK			ENGLISH..."HE RUNS" (E.G. ON THE TRACK TEAM) HOPI... "WARIKNGWE" (RUNNING, STATEMENT OF LAW)

Figure 11 Contrast between a "temporal" language (English) and a "timeless" language (Hopi). What are to English differences of time are to Hopi differences in the kind of validity.

what was long ago one speech community; because the modern dialects have long shared in building up a common culture; and because much of this culture, on the more intellectual side, is derived from the linguistic backgrounds of Latin and Greek. Thus this group of languages satisfies the special case of the clause beginning "unless" in the statement of the linguistic relativity principle at the end of the preceding paragraph. From this condition follows the unanimity of description of the world in the community of modern scientists. But it must be

194

emphasized that "all modern Indo-European-speaking observers" is not the same thing as "all observers". That modern Chinese or Turkish scientists describe the world in the same terms as Western scientists means, of course, only that they have taken over bodily the entire Western system of rationalizations, not that they have corroborated that system from their native posts of observation.

When Semitic, Chinese, Tibetan, or African languages are contrasted with our own, the divergence in analysis of the world becomes more apparent; and, when we bring in the native languages of the Americas, where speech communities for many millenniums have gone their ways independently of each other and of the Old World, the fact that languages dissect nature in many different ways becomes patent. The relativity of all conceptual systems, ours included, and their dependence upon language stand revealed. That American Indians speaking only their native tongues are never called upon to act as scientific observers is in no wise to the point. To exclude the evidence which their languages offer as to what the human mind can do is like expecting botanists to study nothing but food plants and hothouse roses and then tell us what the plant world is like!

Let us consider a few examples. In English we divide most of our words into two classes, which have different grammatical and logical properties. Class 1 we call nouns, e.g., 'house, man'; class 2, verbs, e.g., 'hit, run.' Many words of one class can act secondarily as of the other class, e.g., 'a hit, a run,' or 'to man (the boat),' but, on the primary level, the division between the classes is absolute. Our language thus gives us a bipolar division of nature. But nature herself is not thus polarized. If it be said that 'strike, turn, run,' are verbs because they denote temporary or short-lasting events, i.e., actions, why then is 'fist' a noun? It also is a temporary event. Why are 'lightning, spark, wave, eddy, pulsation, flame, storm, phase, cycle, spasm, noise, emotion' nouns? They are temporary events. If 'man' and 'house' are nouns because they are long-lasting and stable events, i.e., things, what then are 'keep, adhere, extend, project, continue, persist, grow, dwell,' and so on doing among the verbs? If it be objected that 'possess, adhere' are verbs because they are stable relationships rather than stable percepts, why they should 'equilibrium, pressure, current, peace, group, nation, society, tribe, sister,' or any kinship be among the nouns? It will be found that an "event" to us means "what our language classes as a verb" or something analogized therefrom. And it will be found that it is not possible to define 'event, thing, object, relationship,' and so on, from nature, but that to define them always involves a circuitous return to the grammatical categories of the definer's language.

In the Hopi language, 'lightning, wave, flame, meteor, puff of smoke, pulsation' are verbs—events of necessarily brief duration cannot be anything but verbs. 'Cloud' and 'storm' are at about the lower limit of duration for nouns. Hopi, you see, actually has a classification of events (or linguistic isolates) by duration type, something strange to our modes of thought. On the other hand, in Nootka, a language of

Vancouver Island, all words seem to us to be verbs, but really there are no classes 1 and 2; we have, as it were, a monistic view of nature that gives us only one class of word for all kinds of events. 'A house occurs' or 'it houses' is the way of saying 'house,' exactly like 'a flame occurs' or 'it burns.' These terms seem to us like verbs because they are inflected for durational and temporal nuances, so that the suffixes of the word for house event make it mean long-lasting house, temporary house, future house, house that used to be, what started out to be a house, and so on.

Hopi has one noun that covers every thing or being that flies, with the exception of birds, which class is denoted by another noun. The former noun may be said to denote the class $(FC-B)$—flying class minus bird. The Hopi actually call insect, airplane, and aviator all by the same word, and feel no difficulty about it. The situation, of course, decides any possible confusion among very disparate members of a broad linguistic class, such as this class $(FC-B)$. This class seems to us too large and inclusive, but so would our class 'snow' to an Eskimo. We have the same word for falling snow, snow on the ground, snow packed hard like ice, slushy snow, wind-driven flying snow—whatever the situation may be. To an Eskimo, this all-inclusive word would be almost unthinkable; he would say that falling snow, slushy snow, and so on, are sensuously and operationally different, different things to contend with; he uses different words for them and for other kinds of snow. The Aztecs go even farther than we in the opposite direction, with 'cold,' 'ice,' and 'snow' all represented by the same basic word with different terminations; 'ice' is the noun form; 'cold,' the adjectival form; and for 'snow,' "ice mist."

What surprises most is to find that various grand generalizations of the Western world, such as time, velocity, and matter, are not essential to the construction of a consistent picture of the universe. The psychic experiences that we class under these headings are, of course, not destroyed; rather, categories derived from other kinds of experiences take over the rulership of the cosmology and seem to function just as well. Hopi may be called a timeless language. It recognizes psychological time, which is much like Bergson's "duration," but this "time" is quite unlike the mathematical time, T, used by our physicists. Among the peculiar properties of Hopi time are that it varies with each observer, does not permit of simultaneity, and has zero dimensions; i.e., it cannot be given a number greater than one. The Hopi do not say, "I stayed five days," but "I left on the fifth day." A word referring to this kind of time, like the word day, can have no plural. The puzzle picture (Fig. 11, page 194) will give mental exercise to anyone who would like to figure out how the Hopi verb gets along without tenses. Actually, the only practical use of our tenses, in one-verb sentences, is to distinguish among five typical situations, which are symbolized in the picture. The timeless Hopi verb does not distinguish between the present, past, and future of the event itself but must always indicate what type of validity the SPEAKER intends the statement to have: (a) report of an event (situations 1, 2, 3 in the picture); (b) expectation of an event (situation 4); (c) generalization or law about events (situation 5). Situation 1, where the speaker and listener are in contact with the same objective field, is divided by our language into the two conditions, 1*a* and 1*b*, which it calls present and past, respectively. This division is unnecessary for a language which assures one that the statement is a report.

Further reading: The most readable critique of the Whorfian hypothesis comes in Farb's *Word Play* (1974) Chapters 8 and 9. See Brown (1968). 'The research on culture and equivalence' is reported in Greenfield, Reich, Olver *et al.* (1966); part of this paper is reprinted in Adams (1972).

Chapters 13 and 14

13   Non-verbal communication

It is useful to study photographs of classroom teaching (photos 8–10, between pp. 214 and 215) in terms of the headings used in Chapter 13. See also suggestions for further work on Chapter 2.

A way of understanding for oneself the complicated nature of the various means of non-verbal communication operating at any one time is to observe and attempt to write profiles of two contrasting lessons, or selected parts of them—perhaps on the lines of those in this chapter.

*Further reading: There are few studies of non-verbal communication in the classroom. King (1973) has tried to apply Goffman's theories on the presentation of self. There is a useful research review by Rosenshine (1970) called 'Enthusiastic Teaching'.

14   Classroom language

The work suggested on classroom language requires recording and transcription of part of a lesson or lessons. A technically first-class recording is not easy to obtain, partly because of the acoustic properties of many classrooms, and partly because of the large number of voices involved. It is sometimes better, therefore, to carry out a piece of 'microteaching', to take part of a lesson with a group of six or eight. Even so, a good deal can be done with a no more than adequate recording of a classroom lesson providing the teacher is in on the discussion to explain what is going on.

*14.1.1   One of the schemes of analysis referred to in this section is known as 'interaction analysis'. N. Flanders (1970) developed this 'system for observing and coding the verbal interchange between a teacher and his pupils'. The research requires trained observers in classrooms to write down the code number of a category every three seconds. It is not suggested that this detailed procedure should be followed, unless the reader wishes to go deeply into the matter, but a good deal is to be learned by attempting to apply the categories to a portion of a recording. Flanders found that in general teachers took up a far greater amount of talking time than did the pupils put together.

Table 2—1
Flanders' interaction analysis categories* (FIAC)
from *Analysing Teaching Behaviour* (1970), Addison-Wesley

Teacher Talk	Response	1. *Accepts feeling.* Accepts and clarifies an attitude or the feeling tone of a pupil in a nonthreatening manner. Feelings may be positive or negative. Predicting and recalling feelings are included. 2. *Praises or encourages.* Praises or encourages pupil action or behaviour. Jokes that release tension, but not at the expense of another individual; nodding head, or saying "Um hm?" or "go on" are included. 3. *Accepts or uses ideas of pupils.* Clarifying, building, or developing ideas suggested by a pupil. Teacher extensions of pupil ideas are included but as the teacher brings more of his own ideas into play, shift to category five.
		4. *Asks questions.* Asking a question about content or procedure, based on teacher ideas, with the intent that a pupil will answer.
	Initiation	5. *Lecturing.* Giving facts or opinions about content or procedures; expressing *his own* ideas, giving *his own* explanation, or citing an authority other than a pupil. 6. *Giving directions.* Directions, commands, or orders to which a pupil is expected to comply. 7. *Criticizing or justifying authority.* Statements intended to change pupil behaviour from nonacceptable to acceptable pattern; bawling someone out; stating why the teacher is doing what he is doing; extreme self-reference.
Pupil Talk	Response	8. *Pupil-talk—response.* Talk by pupils in response to teacher. Teacher initiates the contact or solicits pupil statement or structures the situation. Freedom to express own ideas is limited.
	Initiation	9. *Pupil-talk—initiation.* Talk by pupils which they initiate. Expressing own ideas; initiating a new topic; freedom to develop opinions and a line of thought, like asking thoughtful questions; going beyond the existing structure.
Silence		10. *Silence or confusion.* Pauses, short periods of silence and periods of confusion in which communication cannot be understood by the observer.

*There is *no* scale implied by these numbers. Each number is classificatory; it designates a particular kind of communication event. To write these numbers down during observation is to enumerate not to judge a position on a scale.

*In *The Language, the Learner and the School* (1969), Barnes uses a somewhat different system of analysis. He considers the nature of:

teacher's questions; pupil's participation; the language of instruction; the language of relationships. This system of analysis throws up things different from that of Flanders.

(a) Teacher's questions

Analyse *all* questions asked by the teacher into these categories:

1 factual ('what?' questions)
   (i) meaning
   (ii) information
2 reasoning ('how?' and 'why?' questions)
   (i) 'closed' reasoning—recalled sequences
   (ii) 'closed' reasoning—not recalled
   (iii) 'open' reasoning
   (iv) observation
3 'open' questions not calling for reasoning
4 Social
   (i) control ('won't you . . . ?' questions)
   (ii) appeal ('aren't we . . . ?' questions)
   (iii) other

(b) Pupil's participation

1 Was all speech initiated by the teacher? Note any exchanges initiated by pupils.
   (i) If these were initiated by questions, were they 'what?', 'how?', or 'why?' questions? Were they directed towards the material studied or towards performing the given tasks?
   (ii) If they were unsolicited statements or comments, how did the teacher deal with them?
2 Were pupils required to express personal responses
   (i) of perception?
   (ii) of feeling and attitude?
3 How large a part did pupils take in the lesson? Were any silent throughout? How large a proportion took a continuous part in the discussion?
4 What did pupils' contributions show of their success in following the lesson?
5 How did the teacher deal with inappropriate contributions?

(c) The language of instruction

1 Did the teacher use a linguistic register specific to his subject? Find examples of vocabulary and structure characteristic of the register.
2 Did any pupils attempt to use this register? Was it expected of them?
3 What did the teacher do to mediate between the language and experience of his pupils and the language and concepts of the subject?
4 Did the teacher use forms of language which, though not specific to his subject, might be outside the range of eleven year olds? Find examples, if any.

(d) Social relationships
    1 How did the relationship between the teacher and pupils show itself in language?
    2 Were there differences between the language of instruction and the language of relationships? Was the language of relationships intimate or formal? Did it vary during the lesson?
(e) Language and other media
    1 Was language used for any tasks that might have been done better by other means (e.g. pictures, practical tasks, demonstrations)?
    2 Were pupils expected to verbalize any non-verbal tasks they were engaged in?

14.2   An elementary approach is to ask the questions explained and demonstrated in this section:
    What determines the course of the lesson?
    In what way does the learning take place?
    What is the role of the type of language used?

*Further reading: Sinclair *et al.* (1975). This report of work at Birmingham also gives a very useful survey of other systems. The approach of the report itself is helpfully summarized in Coulthard (1974). See also Bellack (1963, 1966), Cazden *et al.* (1972).

Chapter 15

15.1   For a general account of register in relation to situation, see
Wilkinson (1971a, Chapter 2) or Wilkinson, Stratta, Dudley (1974
Chapter 4).

15.2   Consider the following passages in the light of the three-fold
classification of curriculum (child-centred, knowledge-centred, and
teacher-centred) that they imply. How far do the metaphors and other
figures of speech contribute to this impression?

a. You can remove this young tree from the highway and shield it from
the crushing force of social contention. Tend and water it ere it dies.
One day its fruit will reward your care. From the outset raise a wall
round your child's soul; another may sketch the plan, you alone
should carry it into execution.

Plants are fashioned by cultivation, man by education. If a man were
born tall and strong his size and strength would be of no good to
him till he had learnt to use them; they would even harm him by
preventing others from coming to his aid; left to himself he would
die of want before he knew his needs. . . All that we lack at birth, all
that we need when we come to man's estate is the gift of education.

b. The adult portion of the community, organised in the forms of the
Family, the State, the Church, and various miscellaneous associations,
desires to promote the welfare of the rising generation. This it seeks
to do by the employment of certain deliberate modes of influence,
as an addition to the inevitable influences of culture and environment
that operate upon *all* human life. Those specific influences are called
Education, and those who exercise them (whether professionally or
incidently) are called Teachers, and those who are subjected to this
educational process are called scholars . . . . .The fount or source of
Education is not the teacher. However much he may pride himself
upon the name of 'master' he has not the supreme control at the outset; he is the servant of the community . . . . the *subject* of
Education is the rising generation. The young, the immature, are
subjected to this process by the adult community.

c. The purpose of the Public Elementary School is to form and
strengthen the character and to develop the intelligence of the
children entrusted to it, and to make the best use of the school years
available, in assisting both girls and boys, according to their different
needs, to fit themselves, practically as well as intellectually, for the
work of life.

With this purpose in view it will be the aim of the School to train the children carefully in habits of observation and clear reasoning so that they may gain an intelligent acquaintance with some of the facts and laws of nature; to arouse in them a living interest in the ideals and achievements of mankind, and to bring them to some familiarity with the literature and history of their own country; to give them some power over language as an instrument of thought and expression, and, while making them conscious of the limitations of their knowledge, to develop in them such a taste for good reading and thoughtful study as will enable them to increase that knowledge in after years by their own efforts.

The School must at the same time encourage to the utmost the children's natural activities of hand and eye by suitable forms of practical work and manual instruction; and afford them every opportunity for the healthy development of their bodies, not only by training them in appropriate physical exercises and encouraging them in organised games, but also by instructing them in the working of some of the simpler laws of health.

It will be an important though subsidiary object of the School to discover individual children who show promise of exceptional capacity, and to develop their special gifts (so far as this can be done without sacrificing the interests of the majority of the children), so that they may be qualified to pass at the proper age into Secondary Schools, and be able to derive the maximum of benefit from the education there offered them.

And, though their opportunities are but brief, the teachers can yet do much to lay the foundations of conduct. They can endeavour, by example and influence, aided by the sense of discipline which should pervade the School to implant in the children habits of industry, self-control, and courageous perseverance in the face of difficulties; they can teach them to reverence what is noble, to be ready for self-sacrifice, and to strive their utmost after purity and truth; they can foster a strong sense of duty and instil in them that consideration and respect for others which must be the foundation of unselfishness and the true basis of all good manners; while the corporate life of the School, especially in the playground, should develop that instinct for fair-play and for loyalty to one another which is the germ of a wider sense of honour in later life.

d. At the heart of the educational process lies the child. No advances in policy, no acquisitions of new equipment have their desired effect unless they are in harmony with the nature of the child, unless they are fundamentally acceptable to him. We know a little about what happens to the child who is deprived of the stimuli of pictures, books and spoken words; we know much less about what happens to a child who is exposed to stimuli which are perceptually, intellectually or emotionally inappropriate to his age, his state of development or the sort of individual he is. We are still far from knowing how best to identify in an individual child the first flicker of a new intellectual or emotional awareness, the first readiness to embrace new sets of concepts or to enter into new relations.

Knowledge of the manner in which children develop, therefore, is of prime importance, both in avoiding educationally harmful practices and in introducing effective ones. In the last 50 years much work has been done on the physical, emotional and intellectual growth of children. There is a vast array of facts, and a number of general principles have been established. This chapter is confined to those facts which have greatest educational significance and those principles which have a direct bearing on educational practice and planning.

*There is very little written on the subject of metaphorical language in educational writing, though Max Black's, *Models and Metaphors* (1962) is a notable book on the relationship of metaphor to thought in science. See also Israel Scheffler *The Language of Education* (1962). Wilkinson (1968) in a brief review comments unfavourably on the metaphors in the Dainton Report.

15.3   A variety of projects is possible here: a study of the metaphors or general language of different subjects; a study of the language of examination papers or text books. It is also rewarding to collect samples of the work of one particular child in a variety of subjects, as in the text, and to consider the nature of the language demands being made. Samples of work by a particular child before or after a significant break, like the change from primary or middle or to secondary school, could be interesting. The attempt of children to rewrite what they have heard or said (as with the kinetic energy passages) may indicate the nature of some of their learning difficulties, linguistic or otherwise.

*The Schools Council and London University Institute of Education Project, 'Writing across the Curriculum 11-13 years', directed by Nancy Martin, with Peter Medway, Harold Smith, and Pat D'Arcy, is examining the topic using as a basis the expressive/poetic/transactional language model (see 10.1.2 and the article by J.L. Britton in Part 2, further work on Chapter 10). On the general topic see Thornton (1975).

Note: The passages quoted above are Rousseau (1957 ed., pp. 5-6), Findlay (1923, pp. 2-3), *Handbook of Suggestions for Teachers* (1927, pp. 8-9) and *Plowden Report* (1967, p. 7).

Chapter 16

16.1 - 16.2 The picture of the mother and child (photograph 7, facing p. 214) gives us some of the feeling of a 'bonding' relationship. What kinds of communication are going on? What means of communicating are used?

Michael Rutter's book, *Maternal Deprivation Reassessed* (1972), which is drawn on in 16.2 gives an excellent account of the present state of thinking. See, for instance, Chapter 2, 'Qualities of Mothering Needed for Normal Development'. *The major work on attachment is Bowlby (1971).

16.4 Here follows the full transcript of the dialogue of Benjamin's 10 o'clock feed, which repays careful study. Notice the features of the language his mother uses. What functions are they serving (see 10.2)? In what ways might they be related to Benjamin's eventual learning of language?

If the opportunity presents itself, it is valuable to make one's own recording of language used to a baby before it can speak and to compare it with this one.

(*R × 1 etc. indicates a repetition and the number of times*)
(*The baby awakens and is carried into the lounge for feeding*)
M: there were you when the lights went out/hey/golly/yes/stay down there for one second (*bib is put on*) what have we got for Benjie Bear tonight/there we are (*baby begins to feed and seems to notice, as usual, the black beam set in the white ceiling over his head*)/that's my friend, beamy/oh, have you been scratching your face again/oh, dear me.
(*Conversation between Mother and Father*)
    golly/it used to take hours when you were a little boy/that's two ounces gone already/yes it is (*sing-song*) I don't know about a little bird/he's more like a rhinoceros (*baby gurgles as he feeds*) what kind of noise is that/that's a funny noise (*sing-song*) Benjie/ that's four ounces already/you must stop to take a breath my darling/I should think so too/I should think you would pant and blow (*baby makes a loud burp*) my word/what a burpies/you may well look ashamed/that was a real Henry the Eighth/you don't want any more do you (*R × 1*)

(*Conversation between Mother and Father*)

you didn't know, Benjie/you were asleep (*baby gurgles and be-comes sleepy*) come on/wake up/you'll be early for your next feed/come on/you're going all over the place (*baby chokes a little*)/that wasn't a nice one/was it (*R × 1*) did that give you a fright (*R × 1*)/that was your worst chokey/yes it was/that was a horrible chokey

you want to burp him (*to father*)/hey, Benjie Bear, what are you doing down there (*song*)/who's got dirty fingernails/I have/I have (*sing-song*)

F: come on little fellah

M: but, daddy, we want to go to sleep/Benjie and I/wake you up for a cuddle/won't that be nice (*R × 1*)

F: hello/don't go to sleep/it's time for burpies/come on/get it up (*R × 1*) (*father burps*) just like that/what a face/this is my intelligent look/yes it is/are you going smileys/ooh/have you got a smiley for us

M: (*baby burps*) ooh/that was a nice one/what a good one/you feel better for that/don't you/yes you do (*R × 3*)/are you going to sleep/Benjie is a little boy … (*song in full*)

(*Conversation between Mother and Father*)

are you waking up/have you have a nice little snooze (*R × 1*)/are you ready for a kick now (*R × 1*)/yes you are (*R × 1*) (*The baby is carried into the bedroom and placed on changing-pad*) one leg/ and the other leg/hello/it's kickeys time/have you woken up/are we going to have smileys tonight/(*baby gurgles and smiles*) oh/ what lovely smileys/daddy missed that/where are you going tonight (*baby kicking vigorously*)/where are you going/we'll have to buy you a bicycle/(*baby gurgles*) what a lovely noise (*sing-song*)/are you so happy/are you going to tell us a story/sing us a song/all about your grandmary/hello/can you see me in the mirror/isn't that funny (*R × 3*)/I don't like that baby/mmmmm/ is that a funny noise/your daddy keeps missing your smiles/he does (*R × 1*)/gosh/you are excited tonight/yes you are (*sing-song R × 1*)/(*baby sneezes*) god bless you/are you on your run again/ all the way to Pottery Cay/are you off to see your girl-friend/ (*mother sings 'Kalinka'*) la, la, la, la… . (*baby is still kicking vigorously, but now his clean nappy is put on*) Don't you like this bit/mummy/I can't move with this big nappy on/you'll get a cold bum-bum/if I don't put this on/one leg in (*sing-song*)/(*baby yawns*) what a tired baby/what do you want to tell me/the story about three bears/Mother Bear/Father Bear/and/Benjie Bear (*song*)/there we are/comb your hair/have you seen your little bath duck/there we are/what a smart fellow/here I am, daddy/ ready for my kiss/daddy's listening to everything I'm saying/give me a kiss, daddy/daddy (*song*) hurry up and give me a kiss/oh dear/sickey dickey/what a lot of kisses/night night (*baby put in cot*)

Chapters 17, 18, and 19

*Chomsky's review (Chomsky, 1971) of B.F. Skinner's *Verbal Behaviour* (1957) is a *locus classicus*. Skinner presents the behaviourist position, arguing that man acquires language by operant conditioning. Unfortunately it is not possible to quote Skinner selectively: his whole argument needs to be followed through. However, Chomsky's review, part of which follows, does not depend for its comprehensibility on a knowledge of Skinner, but is a statement of his own position. Skinner never replied to Chomsky; he is reported to have said that he once glanced at the review, and, immediately realizing that Chomsky had misunderstood his whole argument, he did not bother to take the matter further. Be that as it may, no cogent answer to Chomsky has yet appeared from a behaviourist source.

Criticism of reinforcement theory

It is a common observation that a young child of immigrant parents may learn a second language in the streets, from other children, with amazing rapidity, and that his speech may be completely fluent and correct to the last allophone, while the subtleties that become second nature to the child may elude his parents despite high motivation and continued practice. A child may pick up a large part of his vocabulary and 'feel' for sentence structure from television, from reading, from listening to adults, etc. Even a very young child who has not yet acquired a minimal repertoire from which to form new utterances may imitate a word quite well on an early try, with no attempt on the part of his parents to teach it to him. It is also perfectly obvious that, at a later stage, a child will be able to construct and understand utterances which are quite new, and are, at the same time, acceptable sentences in his language. Every time an adult reads a newspaper, he undoubtedly comes upon countless new sentences which are not at all similar, in a simple, physical sense, to any that he has heard before, and which he will recognize as sentences and understand; he will also be able to detect slight distortions or misprints. Talk of 'stimulus generalization' in such a case simply perpetuates the mystery under a new title. These abilities indicate that there must be fundamental processes at work quite independently of 'feedback' from the environment. I have been able to find no support whatsoever for the doctrine of Skinner and others that slow and careful shaping of verbal behaviour through differential reinforcement is an absolute necessity. If reinforcement theory really requires the assumption that there be such meticulous care, it seems best to regard this simply as a *reductio ad absurdum* argument against this approach. It is also not easy to find any basis (or, for that matter, to attach very much content) to the claim that reinforcing contingencies set up by the verbal community are the single factor responsible for maintaining the strength of verbal behaviour. The sources of the 'strength' of this behaviour are almost a total mystery at present. Reinforcement undoubtedly plays a significant role, but so do a variety of motivational factors about which nothing serious is known in the case of human beings.

As far as acquisition of language is concerned, it seems clear that reinforcement. casual observation, and natural inquisitiveness (coupled with a strong tendency to imitate) are important factors, as is the remarkable capacity of the child to generalize, hypothesize, and 'process information' in a variety of very special and apparently highly complex ways which we cannot yet describe or begin to understand, and which may be largely innate, or may develop through some sort of learning or through maturation of the nervous system. The manner in which such factors operate and interact in language acquisition is completely unknown. It is clear that what is necessary in such a case is research, not dogmatic and perfectly arbitrary claims based on analogies to that small part of the experimental literature in which one happens to be interested.

The pointlessness of these claims becomes clear when we consider the well-known difficulties in determining to what extent inborn structure, maturation, and learning are responsible for the particular form of a skilled or complex performance. To take just one example, the gaping response of a nestling thrust is at first released by jarring of the nest, and, at a later stage, by a moving object of specific size, shape, and position relative to the nestling. At this later stage the response is directed towards the part of the stimulus object corresponding to the parent's head, and characterized by a complex configuration of stimuli that can be precisely described. Knowing just this, it would be possible to construct a speculative, learning-theoretic account of how this sequence of behaviour patterns might have developed through a process of differential reinforcement, and it would no doubt be possible to train rats to do something similar. However, there appears to be good evidence that these responses to fairly complex 'sign stimuli' are genetically determined and mature without learning. Clearly, the possibility cannot be discounted. Consider now the comparable case of a child imitating new words. At an early stage we may find rather gross correspondences. At a later stage, we find that repetition is, of course, far from exact (i.e. it is not mimicry, a fact which itself is interesting) but that it reproduces the highly complex configuration of sound features that constitute the phonological structure of the language in question. Again, we can propose a speculative account of how this result might have been obtained through elaborate arrangement of reinforcing contingencies. Here too, however, it is possible that ability to select out of the complex auditory input those features that are phonologically relevant may develop largely independently of reinforcement, through genetically determined maturation. To the extent that this is true, an account of the development and causation of behaviour that fails to consider the structure of the organism will provide no understanding of the real processes involved.

It is often argued that experience, rather than innate capacity to handle information in certain specific ways, must be the factor of overwhelming dominance in determining the specific character of language acquisition since a child speaks the language of the group in which he lives. But this is a superficial argument. As long as we are speculating, we may consider the possibility that the brain has evolved to the point where, given an input of observed Chinese sentences, it produces (by an 'induction' of apparently fantastic complexity and suddenness) the 'rules' of Chinese grammar, and given an input of observed English sentences, it produces (by, perhaps, exactly the same process of induction) the rules of English grammar; or that given an observed application of a term to certain instances it automatically predicts the extension to a class of complexly related instances. If clearly recognized as such, this speculation is neither unreasonable nor fantastic; nor, for that matter, is it beyond the bounds of possible study. There is, of course, no known neural structure capable of performing this task in the specific ways that observation of the resulting behaviour might lead us to postulate; but for that matter, the structures capable of accounting for even the simplest kinds of learning have similarly defied detection.

Summarizing this brief discussion, it seems that there is neither empirical evidence nor any known argument to support any specific claim about the relative importance of 'feedback' from the environment and the 'independent contribution of the organism' in the process of language acquisition.

19.2 The best single explanation of Chomsky's work is given by John Lyons *Chomsky* (1970).

Chapters 20 and 21

20.1 - 20.2   The most interesting work on young children's language acquisition has been done as studies of individual children. The rapid language development at certain stages makes recording of a child's language at stages of a month or so a rewarding and practicable study.

21.1   Chomsky's distinction between 'competence' and 'performance' has caused a good deal of discussion. He speaks of 'competence' as an ideal, the way we 'know' how to make or understand a 'well formed sentence', possessing a generative grammar—that is, the rules for making both phrase structures and transformations. See Chomsky (1965).

Linguistic theory is concerned primarily with an ideal speaker-listener, in a completely homogeneous speech-community, who knows its language perfectly and is unaffected by such grammatically irrelevant conditions as memory limitations, distractions, shifts of attention and interest, and errors (random or characteristic) in applying his knowledge of the language in actual performance. This seems to me to have been the position of the founders of modern general linguistics, and no cogent reason for modifying it has been offered. To study actual linguistic performance, we must consider the interaction of a variety of factors, of which the underlying competence of the speaker-hearer is only one. In this respect, study of language is no different from empirical investigation of other complex phenomena.

We thus make a fundamental distinction between *competence* (the speaker-hearer's knowledge of his language) and *performance* (the actual use of language in concrete situations). Only under the idealization set forth in the preceding paragraph is performance a direct reflection of competence. In actual fact, it obviously could not directly reflect competence. A record of natural speech will show numerous false starts, deviations from rules, changes of plan in mid-course, and so on. The problem for the linguist, as well as for the child learning the language, is to determine from the data of performance the underlying system of rules that has been mastered by the speaker-hearer and that he puts to use in actual performance. Hence, in the technical sense, linguistic theory is mentalistic, since it is concerned with discovering a mental reality underlying actual behaviour. Observed use of language or hypothesized dispositions to respond, habits, and so on, may provide evidence as to the nature of this mental reality, but surely cannot constitute the actual subject matter of linguistics, if this is to be a serious discipline. The distinction I am noting here is related to the *langue-parole* distinction of Saussure; but it is necessary to reject his concept of *langue* as merely a systematic inventory of items and to return rather to the Humboldtian conception of underlying competence as a system of generative processes. For discussion, see Chomsky (1964).

A grammar of a language purports to be a description of the ideal speaker-hearer's intrinsic competence. If the grammar is, furthermore, perfectly explicit—in other words, if it does not rely on the intelligence of the understanding reader but rather provides an explicit analysis of his contribution—we may (somewhat redundantly) call it a *generative grammar*.

A fully adequate grammar must assign to each of an infinite range of sentences a structural description indicating how this sentence is understood by the ideal speaker-hearer. This is the traditional problem of descriptive linguistics, and traditional grammars give a wealth of information concerning structural descriptions of sentences. However, valuable as they obviously are, traditional grammars are deficient in that they leave unexpressed many of the basic regularities of the language with which they are concerned. This fact is particularly clear on the level of syntax, where no traditional or structuralist grammar goes beyond classification of particular examples to the stage of formulation of generative rules on any significant scale. An analysis of the best existing grammars will quickly reveal that this is a defect of principle, not just a matter of empirical detail or logical preciseness. Nevertheless, it seems obvious that the attempt to explore this largely uncharted territory can most profitably begin with a study of the kind of structural information presented by traditional grammars and the kind of linguistic processes that have been exhibited, however informally, in these grammars.

Returning to the main theme, by a generative grammar I mean simply a system of rules that in some explicit and well-defined way assigns structural descriptions to sentences. Obviously, every speaker of a language has mastered and internalized a generative grammar that expresses his knowledge of his language. This is not to say that he is aware of the rules of the grammar or even that he can become aware of them, or that his statements about his intuitive knowledge of the language are necessarily accurate. Any interesting generative grammar will be dealing, for the most part, with mental processes that are far beyond the level of actual or even potential consciousness; furthermore, it is quite apparent that a speaker's reports and viewpoints about his behaviour and his competence may be in error. Thus a generative grammar attempts to specify what the speaker actually knows, not what he may report about his knowledge. Similarly, a theory of visual perception would attempt to account for what a person actually sees and the mechanisms that determine this rather than his statements about what he sees and why, though these statements may provide useful, in fact, compelling evidence for such a theory.

To avoid what has been a continuing misunderstanding, it is perhaps worth while to reiterate that a generative grammar is not a model for a speaker or a hearer. It attempts to characterize in the most neutral possible terms the knowledge of the language that provides the basis for actual use of language by a speaker-hearer. When we speak of a grammar as generating a sentence with a certain structural description, we mean simply that the grammar assigns this structural description to the sentence. When we say that a sentence has a certain derivation with respect to a particular generative grammar, we say nothing about how the speaker or hearer might proceed, in some practical or efficient way, to construct such a derivation. These questions belong to the theory of language use—the theory of performance. No doubt, a reasonable model of language use will incorporate, as a basic component, the generative grammar that expresses the speaker-hearer's knowledge of the language; but this generative grammar does not, in itself, prescribe the character or functioning of a perceptual model or a model of speech production.

*Hymes (1972) criticizes Chomsky's notion of 'competence' and 'performance', arguing that what really matters is linguistic ability as represented in a variety of situations where we need to know at least the registers and relationships.

Communicative competence

For the perspective associated with transformational generative grammar, the world of linguistic theory has two parts: linguistic *competence* and linguistic *performance*. Linguistic competence is understood as concerned with the tacit knowledge of language structure, that is, knowledge that is commonly not conscious or available for spontaneous report, but necessarily implicit in what the (ideal) speaker-listener can say. The primary task of theory is to provide for an explicit account of such knowledge, especially in relation to the innate structure on which it must depend. It is in terms of such knowledge that one can produce and understand an infinite set of sentences, and that language can be spoke of as 'creative', as *energeia*. Linguistic performance is most explicitly understood as concerned with the processes often termed encoding and decoding.

Such a theory of competence posits ideal objects in abstraction from sociocultural features that might enter into their description. Acquisition of competence is also seen as essentially independent of sociocultural features, requiring only suitable speech in the environment of the child to develop. The theory of performance is the one sector that might have a specific sociocultural content; but while equated with a theory of language use, it is essentially concerned with psychological by-products of the analysis of grammar, not, say, with social interaction. As to a constitutive role for sociocultural features in the acquisition or conduct of performance, the attitude would seem quite negative. Little or nothing is said, and if something were said, one would expect it to be depreciatory. Some aspects of performance are, it is true, seen as

Barneby's Picture Library
Henry Grant

7▲ 8▼

Henry Grant

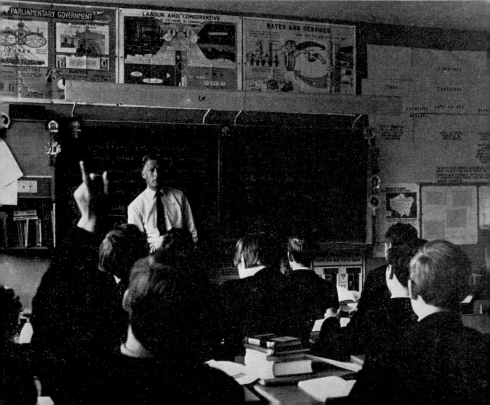

having a constructive role (e.g., the cycling rules that help assign stress properly to sentences), but if the passage quoted at the outset is recalled, however, and if the illustrations of performance phenomena in the chapter from which the passage comes are reviewed, it will be seen that the note struck is persistently one of limitation, if not disability. When the notion of performance is introduced as 'the actual use of language in concrete situations', it is immediately stated that only under the idealization quoted could performance directly reflect competence, and that in actual fact it obviously could not. 'A record of natural speech will show numerous false starts, deviations from rules, changes of plan in mid-course, and so on.' One speaks of primary linguistic data as 'fairly degenerate in quality' (Chomsky, 1965, p. 31), or even of linguistic performance as 'adulteration' of ideal competence (Katz, 1967, p. 144). While 'performance' is something of a residual category for the theory, clearly its most salient connotation is that of imperfect manifestation of underlying system.

I do not think the failure to provide an explicit place for socio-cultural features to be accidental. The restriction of competence to the notions of a homogeneous community, perfect knowledge, and inde-pendence of sociocultural factors does not seem just a simplifying assumption, the sort that any scientific theory must make. If that were so, then some remark to that effect might be made; the need to include a sociocultural dimension might be mentioned; the nature of such inclusion even be suggested. Nor does the predominant association of performance with imperfection seem accidental. Certainly, any stretch of speech is an imperfect indication of the knowledge that underlies it. For users that share the knowledge, the arrangement might be thought of as efficient. And if one uses one's intuitions as to speech, as well as to grammar, one can see that what to grammar is imperfect, or un-accounted for, may be the artful accomplishment of a social act (Garfinkel, in press), or the patterned, spontaneous evidence of problem solving and conceptual thought (John, 1967, p. 5). These things might be acknowledged, even if not taken up.

It takes the absence of a place for sociocultural factors, and the linking of performance to imperfection, to disclose an ideological aspect to the theoretical standpoint. It is, if I may say so, rather a Garden of Eden view. Human life seems divided between grammatical competence, an ideal innately-derived sort of power, and performance, an exigency rather like the eating of the apple, thrusting the perfect speaker-hearer out into a fallen world. Of this world, where meanings may be won by the sweat of the brow, and communication achieved in labor (cf. Bonhoffer, 1965, p. 365), little is said. The controlling image is of an abstract, isolated individual, almost an unmotivated cognitive mechanism, not, except incidentally, a person in a social world.

Given these considerations, I think there is not sufficient reason to maintain a terminology at variance with more general usage of 'com-petence' and 'performance' in the sciences of man, as is the case with the present equations of competence, knowledge, systemic possibility, on the one hand, and of performance, behaviour, implementational constraints, appropriateness, on the other. It seems necessary to distinguish these things and to reconsider their relationship, if their investigation is to be insightful and adequate.

I should take *competence* as the most general term for the capabilities of a person. (This choice is in the spirit, if at present against the letter, of the concern in linguistic theory for underlying capability.) Competence is dependent on both (tacit) *knowledge* and (ability for) *use. Knowledge* is distinct, then, both from competence (as its part) and from systemic possibility (to which its relation is an empirical matter.) Notice that Cazden (1967), by utilizing what is in effect systemic possibility as a definition of competence is forced to separate it from what persons can do. The 'competence' underlying a person's behavior is identified as one kind of 'performance' (performance A, actual behavior being performance B). The logic may be inherent in the linguistic theory from which Cazden starts, once one tries to adapt its notion of competence to recognized facts of personal knowledge. The strangely misleading result shows that the original notion cannot be left unchanged.

Chapter 22

*Compare the following range of spoken and written English. How far is it possible to say that the language used is the result of the situation presented and the expectations of the teacher (or the child's interpretation of them)? All are by children of 8 years.

Neil: spoken

Im a judo I go to judo and I do/move orange belt with one green stripe and/I go with my two friends Malcolm and John and they er theyre/the same as me yes/and/theyre er/lots of boys there who go and/there are/ a few/people who are black belts and/and I mm/and a few little one/ little boys who/who-er/whove just only started may/can do a lot of things now and I have been working with them for a bit and showing them the right falls and everything/and/there/is one boy that er he is going is is a brown belt one brown stripe and he goes/he/I cant remember now

Neil: written

every Sunday I go to Judo with my two friends and there names are Malcon and John and I have a Orange belt with one green strip and

Kevin: spoken

What are you going to tell us about
About/when I'm going to Silverstone
Yes well go on then
Mm when Im going to Silverstone /Im going to see motor cars going round the track about a hundred miles an hour/and mm my mum has made me mm/a pair of trousers and she make them in/one day and a half/and shes only just pressed them today

Kevin: written

I am going to Silverstone. I am going to watch motor cars going round a bend and my mum has made me a pair of trousers and she has pressed them today.

Struan: spoken

well when we went to Scotland em/we went to Bendherloch and er/we out out em/to Trulee bay/you see my grannie lives there and er/she lives very near the beach/and/so er/you see there was this speed boat on the beach/and this man who owned them let us go out in them/so we went out to this little island/and mm/we took a picnic lunch and it was fantastic we stayed in this little castle/oh boy we went down to see the dungeons/we/went up and saw a few swords and armour/oh it was fantastic that was/ooh/and then we went we came back/we went out to another one/and it was terribly it was exactly the same/but we went on

the other side of the island you see because it was too far to walk/so we
had to take the/speed boat and then then we came back/and then we went
home

Struan: written

When we went to Bendherlock in Scotland. We went to Trulee beach
and my Grandma's and we saw two speed boat's and the man that was
beside them said that we could go on them and we went out to an I
land and we had a picnic.

Chapter 23

*23.1 The following extract from an article by W. Labov, 'The logic
of non-standard English' (1972), indicates that non-standard language
can be an effective instrument for thinking with, and that sometimes
the standard language is marked by redundancies. Of course, no
generalization about middle-class and working-class language can be
made on the basis of two passages. It could be that the non-standard
speaker here just happened to be more logical. Labov is making a contribution to a debate largely initiated by Basil Bernstein, in which
Bernstein was taken to be saying that certain working-class speakers
have a 'restricted code' which limits their thinking powers. In fact
Bernstein is making a comment on the context bound nature of certain
language uses, which could occur independent of class, and which are
certainly associated with certain ways of talking to children in their
earlier years. (For a recent statement see Bernstein, 1971.)

For a succinct and eminently sane view of the 'linguistic deficit'
versus 'linguistic difference' controversy, see Criper and Davies (1974).

Verbosity

There are undoubtedly many verbal skills which children from ghetto
areas must learn in order to do well in the school situation, and some of
these are indeed characteristic of middle-class verbal behavior. Precision
in spelling, practice in handling abstract symbols, the ability to state
explicitly the meaning of words, and a richer knowledge of the Latinate
vocabulary, may all be useful acquisitions. But is it true that *all* of the
middle-class verbal habits are functional and desirable in the school
situation? Before we impose middle-class verbal style upon children
from other cultural groups, we should find out how much of this is
useful for the main work of analyzing and generalizing, and how much
is merely stylistic—or even dysfunctional. In high school and college
middle-class children spontaneously complicate their syntax to the
point that instructors despair of getting them to make their language
simpler and clearer. In every learned journal one can find examples of
jargon and empty elaboration—and complaints about it. Is the
'elaborated code' of Bernstein really so 'flexible, detailed and subtle' as
some psychologists believe (Jensen, 1968, p. 119)? Isn't it also turgid,
redundant, and empty? It is not simply an elaborated *style*, rather than
a superior code or system?

Our work in the speech community makes it painfully obvious that
in many ways working-class speakers are more effective narrators,
reasoners and debators than many middle-class speakers who
temporize, qualify, and lose their argument in a mass of irrelevant
detail. Many academic writers try to rid themselves of that part of

219

middle-class style that is empty pretension, and keep that part that is needed for precision. But the average middle-class speaker that we encounter makes no such effort; he is enmeshed in verbiage, the victim of sociolinguistic factors beyond his control.

I will not attempt to support this argument here with systematic quantitative evidence, although it is possible to develop measures which show how far middle-class speakers can wander from the point. I would like to contrast two speakers dealing with roughly the same topic—matters of belief. The first is Larry H., a 15-year-old core member of the Jets, being interviewed by John Lewis. Larry is one of the loudest and roughest members of the Jets, one who gives the least recognition to the conventional rules of politeness. For most readers of this paper, first contact with Larry would produce some fairly negative reactions on both sides: it is probable that you would not *like* him any more than his teachers do. Larry causes trouble in and out of school; he was put back from the eleventh grade to the ninth, and has been threatened with further action by the school authorities.

JL: What happens to you after you die? Do you know?
LH: Yeah, I know.
JL: What?
LH: After they put you in the ground, your body turns into—ah—bones, an' shit.
JL: What happens to your spirit?
LH: Your spirit—soon as you die, your spirit leaves you.
JL: And where does the spirit go?
LH: Well, it all depends . . .
JL: On what?
LH: You know, like some people say if you're good an' shit, your spirit goin' t'heaven . . . 'n if you bad, your spirit goin' to hell. Well, bullshit! Your spirit goin' to hell anyway, good or bad.
JL: Why?
LH: Why? I'll tell you why. 'Cause you see, doesn' nobody really know that it's a God, y'know, 'cause I mean I have seen black gods, pink gods, white gods, all color gods, and don't nobody know it's really a God. An' when they be sayin' if you good, you goin' t'heaven, tha's bullshit, 'cause you ain't goin' to no heaven, 'cause it ain't no heaven for you to go to.

Larry is a paradigmatic speaker of nonstandard Negro English (NNE) as opposed to standard English (SE). His grammar shows a high concentration of such characteristic NNE forms as negative inversion [*don't nobody know* . . .], negative concord [*you ain't goin' to no heaven* . . .], invariant *be* [*when they be sayin'* . . .], dummy *it* for SE *there* [*it ain't no heaven* . . .], optional copula deletion [*if you're good . . . if you bad* . . .], and full forms of auxiliaries [*I have seen* . . .]. The only SE influence on this passage is the one case of *doesn't* instead of the invariant *don't* of NNE. Larry also provides a paradigmatic example of the rhetorical style of NNE: he can sum up a complex argument in a few words, and the full force of his opinions comes through without qualification or reservation. He is eminently quotable, and his interviews give us many concise statements of the NNE point of view. One can almost say that Larry *speaks* the NNE culture (see Labov, Cohen, Robins and Lewis, 1968, vol. 2, pp. 38, 71-3, 291-2).

It is the logical form of this passage which is of particular interest here. Larry presents a complex set of interdependent propositions which can be explicated by setting out the SE equivalents in linear order. The basic argument is to deny the twin propositions

(A) If you are good, (B) then your spirit will go to heaven.
(-A) If you are bad, (C) then your spirit will go to hell.

Larry denies (B), and asserts that *if* (A) *or* (-A), *then* (C). His argument may be outlined as follows:

(1) Everyone has a different idea of what God is like.
(2) Therefore nobody really knows that God exists.
(3) If there is a heaven, it was made by God.
(4) If God doesn't exist, he couldn't have made heaven.
(5) Therefore heaven does not exist.
(6) You can't go somewhere that doesn't exist.
(-B) Therefore you can't go to heaven.
(C) Therefore you are going to hell.

The argument is presented in the order: (C), because (2) because (1), therefore (2), therefore (-B) because (5) and (6). Part of the argument is implicit: the connection (2) therefore (-B) leaves unstated the connecting links (3) and (4), and in this interval Larry strengthens the propositions from the form (2) *Nobody knows if there is* . . . to (5) *There is no* . . . Otherwise, the case is presented explicitly as well as economically. The complex argument is summed up in Larry's last setnence, which shows formally the dependence of (-B) on (5) and (6):

An' when they be sayin' if you good, you goin' t'heaven, [*The proposition, if* A, *then* B]
Tha's bullshit,
[*is absurd*]
'cause you ain't goin' to no heaven
[*because* -B]
'cause it ain't no heaven for you to go to.
[*because* (5) *and* (6)] .

This hypothetical argument is not carried on at a high level of seriousness. It is a game played with ideas as counters, in which opponents use a wide variety of verbal devices to win. There is no personal commitment to any of these propositions, and no reluctance to strengthen one's argument by bending the rules of logic as in the (2-5) sequence. But if the opponent invokes the rule of logic, they hold. In John Lewis' interviews, he often makes this move, and the force of his argument is acknowledged and countered within the rules of logic. In this case, he pointed out the fallacy that the argument (2-3-4-5-6) leads to (-C) as well as (-B), so it cannot be used to support Larry's assertion (C):

JL: Well, if there's no heaven, how could there be a hell?
LH: I mean—ye—eah. Well, let me tell you, it ain't no hell, 'cause this is hell right here, y'know!
JL: This is hell?
LH: Yeah, this is hell right here!

Larry's answer is quick, ingenious and decisive. The application of the (3-4-5) argument to hell is denied, since hell is here, and therefore conclusion (C) stands. These are not ready-made or preconceived opinions, but new propositions devised to win the logical argument in the game being played. The reader will note the speed and precision of Larry's mental operations. He does not wander, or insert meaningless verbiage. The only repetition is (2), placed before and after (1) in his original statement. It is often said that the nonstandard vernacular is not suited for dealing with abstract or hypothetical questions, but in fact speakers from the NNE community take great delight in exercising their wit and logic on the most improbable and problematical matters. Despite the fact that Larry H. does not believe in God, and has just denied all knowledge of him. John Lewis advances the following hypothetical question:

JL: . . . But, just say that there is a God, what color is he? White or black?
LH: Well, if it is a God . . . I wouldn' know what color. I couldn' say,—couldn' nobody say what color he is or really *would* be.
JL: But now, jus' suppose there was a God—
LH: Unless'n they say . . .
JL: No, I was jus' sayin' jus' suppose there is a God, would he be white or black?
LH: . . . He'd be white, man.
JL: Why?
LH: Why? I'll tell you why. 'Cause the average whitey out here got everything, you dig? And the nigger ain't got shit, y'know? Y'understan'? So—um—for—in order for *that* to happen, you know it ain't no black God that's doin' that bullshit.

No one can hear Larry's answer to this question without being convinced that they are in the presence of a skilled speaker with great 'verbal presence of mind', who can use the English language expertly for many purposes. Larry's answer to John Lewis is again a complex argument. The formulation is not SE, but it is clear and effective even for those not familiar with the vernacular. The nearest SE equivalent might be: 'So you know that God isn't black, because if he was, he wouldn't have arranged things like that.'

The reader will have noted that this analysis is being carried out in standard English, and the inevitable challenge is: why not write in NNE, then, or in your own nonstandard dialect? The fundamental reason is, of course, one of the firmly fixed social conventions. All communities agree that SE is the 'proper' medium for formal writing and public communication. Furthermore, it seems likely that SE has an advantage over NNE in explicit analysis of surface forms, which is what we are doing here. We will return to this opposition between explicitness and logical statement in the section on grammaticality. First, however, it will be helpful to examine SE in its primary natural setting as the medium for informal spoken communication of middle-class speakers.

Let us now return to the second speaker, an upper-middle-class, college educated Negro man being interviewed by Clarence Robins in our survey of adults in Central Harlem.

CR: Do you know of anything that someone can do, to have some-one who has passed on visit him in a dream?

CM: Well, I even heard my parents say that there is such as thing as something in dreams some things like that, and sometimes dreams do come true. I have personally never had a dream come true. I've never dreamt that somebody was dying and they actually died. (Mhm) or that I was going to have ten dollars the next day and somehow I got ten dollars in my pocket. (Mhm). I don't particularly believe in that, I don't think it's true. I do feel, though, that there is such a thing as—ah—witchcraft. I do feel that in certain cultures there is such a thing as witchcraft, or some sort of *science* of witchcraft; I don't think that it's just a matter of believing hard enough that there is such a thing as witchcraft. I do believe that there is such a thing that a person can put himself in a state of *mind* (Mhm), or that er—something could be given them to intoxicate them in a certain—to a certain frame of mind—that—that could actually be considered witch-craft.

Charles M. is obviously a 'good speaker' who strikes the listener as well-educated, intelligent and sincere. He is a likeable and attractive person—the kind of person that middle-class listeners rate very high on a scale of 'job stability' and equally high as a potential friend. His language is more moderate and tempered than Larry's; he makes every effort to qualify his opinions, and seems anxious to avoid any misstatements or over-statements. From these qualities emerges the primary character-istic of this passage—its *verbosity*. Words multiply, some modifying and qualifying, others repeating or padding the main argument. The first half of this extract is a response to the initial question on dreams, basically:

1 Some people say that dreams sometimes come true.
2 I have never had a dream come true.
3 Therefore I don't believe (1).

Some characteristic filler phrases appear here: *such a thing as, some things like that, particularly.* Two examples of dreams given after (2) are afterthoughts that might have been given after (1). Proposition (3) is stated twice for no obvious reason. Nevertheless, this much of Charles M's response is well-directed to the point of the question. He then volunteers a statement of his beliefs about witchcraft which shows the difficulty of middle-class speakers who (a) want to express a belief in something but (b) want to show themselves as judicious, rational and free from superstitions. The basic proposition can be stated simply in five words: 'But I believe in witchcraft'. However, the idea is enlarged to exactly 100 words, and it is difficult to see what else is being said. In the following quotations, padding which can be removed without change in meaning is shown in brackets.

1 'I [do] feel, though, that there is [such a thing as] witchcraft.' *Feel* seems to be a euphemism for 'believe'.
2 '[I do feel that] in certain cultures [there is such a thing as witchcraft].' This repetition seems designed only to introduce the word *culture*, which lets us know that the speaker knows about anthropology. Does *certain cultures* mean 'not in ours' or 'not in all'?
3 '[or some sort of *science* of witchcraft.]' This addition seems to have no clear meaning at all. What is a 'science' of witchcraft as opposed to just plain witchcraft? The main function is to introduce the word 'science', though it seems to have no connection to what follows.
4 'I don't think that it's just [a matter of] believing hard enough that [there is such a thing as] witchcraft.' The speaker argues that witchcraft is not merely a belief; there is more to it.
5 'I [do] believe that [there is such a thing that] a person can put himself in a state of *mind* . . . that [could actually be considered] witchcraft.' Is witchcraft as a state of mind different from the state of belief denied in (4)?
6 'or that something could be given to intoxicate them [to a certain frame of mind] . . .' The third learned word, *intoxicate*, is introduced by this addition. The vacuity of this passage becomes more evident if we remove repetitions, fashionable words and stylistic decorations:

But I believe in witchcraft.
I don't think witchcraft is just a belief.
A person can put himself or be put in a state of mind that is witchcraft.

Without the extra verbiage and the OK words like *science, culture* and *intoxicate*, Charles M. appears as something less than a first-rate thinker. The initial impression of him as a good speaker is simply our long-conditioned reaction to middle-class verbosity: we know that people who use these stylistic devices are educated people, and we are inclined to credit them with saying something intelligent. Our reactions are accurate in one sense: Charles M. is more educated than Larry. But is he more rational, more logical, or more intelligent? Is he any better at thinking out a problem to its solution? Does he deal more easily with abstractions? There is no reason to think so. Charles M. succeeds in letting us know that he is educated, but in the end we do not know what he is trying to say, and neither does he.

23.2 Here is the full transcription of the conversation with Ben (except that the adult contributions are somewhat curtailed). This will repay careful study in terms of the linguistic function categories of Chapter 10. Notice as well syntax, accidence, vocabulary, the functions of recall, prediction, hypothesis, reasoning, role play, and empathy.

Conversation with Ben (11 years)

A: now/tell me about yourself/I mean how old are you, where d'you live, and so on

B: eleven/I live Stratfield

A: I see yes/and what sort of a house do you live in

B: its some/bricks house/in a bricks house

A: in a bricks house is it/yes I see/good/what sort of rooms has it got

B: mm/I we got/we got/some up the front/we got two up the front/ mm/its one not very old and one best one (*incoherent*) we . . . got a colour telly

A: oh yes what sort of programmes do you like watching on the colour telly

B: Tarzan/and football/

A: I see/now tell me about Tarzan

B: he always/go (*begins gestures of breast beating*) I can't do it

A: you can't do it/I see/what else does he do

B: he swims/in the river/and mm/and he/got a knife/by his (*gesticulates to thigh*)

A: on his leg

B: on his leg/and when he's got (*incoherent*). . . .

A: can you remember/what you did/last weekend

B: oh yes/I er/on Saturday/on Saturday/I went to Launton and (*jock?*) off my friend/and she called Madeline/(*yes*) and/she went in to the station for the/the/train

A: she went where

B: up the platform and she get on and I really left and we left/and we came home/and/we/when I came home/I was asleep and my dad/we stopped/for my sister she not a very good/traveller/she feel ill/and/and/and/then/and then/she was all right we . . . . (*incoherent*) tow-er (*told her*)/tow-er/tell me when you want to

stop/she said please stop now please dad/and she went out/
mummy and dad/then and my sister and dad went out for a walk
I wake up/and look and back I fall asleep

A: do you remember going on holiday/tell me about it
B: I went a new/I can't remember what it called/I/we did like it/
(*incoherent*) we have/and then we go up on the boat/car boat/
ferry (yes) and go over Isle of Wight we stay there two days
... ah we went out (*incoherent*) one day it was rain/to
twelve o'clock/and some day it rain all day we didn't/we couldn't
go out then with my dad/my mum/my dad had the sleep first/
and then my mum played cards/then dad/mum go to sleep/then/
mmm/dad played cards with us
A: what would you like to do tomorrow
B: go up breck/my cousin play football
A: what happens when he plays football
B: he/sometimes have a kick/in the leg/
A: has he been badly hurt
B: no he's all right/he can work/my brother/that's my Tony he
sometimes/he have a bad foot an his (*unclear*) he kick it/and I
cried/that's my first time I watch/football/he said/my friend said
he will be all right/. . . .
A: supposing the fire alarm sounded/what do you think would
happen
B: we go out this/out that/playground/and call the fire brigade
A: who would call the fire brigade
B: the/headmaster/think
A: supposing both gates into the playground were locked/what
would they do
B: they got a/axe/and open it
A: if he hadn't got his axe
B: dunno/they/ask for the key . . . .
(*picture of a boy cleaning his bicycle*)
A: look at this picture/what's the boy doing
B: he doing his/polishing his bike
A: why
B: it was dirty
A: what will he do when he's done
B: I think he will ride it
A: what's he feeling
B: he's feeling I can't remember what's that called

A: a piece of the frame

B: yes/the frame

A: what do you think that he's thinking

B: I dunno

A: have a guess

B: he's thinking/he's smiling

A: what do you think that means

B: he will do something

A: yes what sort of thing

B: I dunno

A: well have a guess

B: ride his bike

A: I'm sure you're right

      (*picture of a baker and housewife*)

A: look at this picture what are they doing

B: she touching the bread

A: what is she doing with her other hand

B: she's pointing to that

A: at what

B: fruit cake

A: what is she saying to the baker

B: can I have/a fruit cake please/

A: and what will the baker say

B: yes

A: and what would she say then

B: she/how much is it/

A: and what would he say/have a guess

B: thirty three pence

A: I'll tell you something about that boy/cleaning his bike made him late for school/the teacher will say to him why are you late/what will he say

B: sorry miss/I was late/I had to do something for my mum

A: and what would she say

B: that's all right

A: but supposing she had seen him cleaning his bike

B: he would say/I was cleaning/my bike/

A: supposing she said/why didn't you clean it last night/what would he say

B: sorry miss/I didn't thought

Bibliography

Adams, P. (ed.), 1972, *Language and Thinking*, Penguin.

Aitchison, J., 1972, *General Linguistics*, English Universities Press.

Argyle, M., 1967, *The Psychology of Interpersonal Behaviour*, Penguin.

—1972, 'Non-verbal communication in human social interaction', in Hinde, 1972.

Argyle, M., Salter V., Burgess, P., Nicholson, N.C., and Williams, M., 1970, 'The communication of inferior and superior attitudes by verbal and non-verbal signals', *Brit. J. Soc. Clin. Psychol. 9*, pp. 222-31.

Barker, L.L., and Kibler, R.J., 1971, *Speech Communication Behaviour*, Prentice Hall, Inc.

Barnes, D., Britton, J., and Rosen, H., 1969, *Language, the Learner and the School*, Penguin.

Bellack, A.A. (ed.), 1963, *Theory and Research in Teaching*, N.Y. Teachers College Press.

Bellack, A.A., Kliebard, H.M., Hyman, R.T. and Smith, F.L., 1966, *The Language of the Classroom*, N.Y. Teachers College Press.

Bernstein, B., 1971, *Class Codes and Control*, Vol. I, Routledge and Kegan Paul.

Black, M., 1962, *Models and Metaphors*, Cornell.

Bonhoffer, D., 1965, 'What is meant by "telling the truth"?', *Ethics*, pp. 363-72.

Bowlby, J., 1971, *Attachment*, Penguin.

Britton, J.L., 1970, *Language and Learning*, Penguin.

—1971, 'What's the Use', in Wilkinson (ed.), 1971b.

Brown, R., 1968, *Words and things*, The Free Press, Glencoe.

—1970, 'The first sentences of child and chimpanzee', *Selected Psycholinguistical Papers*, Macmillan, N.Y.

—1973, *A first language: the early stages*, Allen and Unwin.

Brown, R., and Bellugi, U., 1964, 'Three processes in the child's acquisition of syntax', in Lennenberg (ed.), 1964, pp. 131-61.

228

Bibliography

Brown, R., and Fraser, C., 1963, 'The acquisition of syntax', in Cofer, L.N., and Musgrave, B.S. (eds.), 1963.

Bruner, J., 1964, 'The Course of Cognitive Growth', in *American Psychologist 19*, pp. 1-15.

Bruner, J.S., Olver, R. and Greenfield, P.M., 1966, *Studies in Cognitive Growth*, Wiley.

Bühler, K., 1933, 'Die Axiomatik der Sprachwissenschaft', *Kant-Studien* 38, 19-90, Berlin.

Cassirer, E., 1946, *Language and Myth*, translated Suzanne K. Langer, Dover Publications, N.Y.

Cazden, C., 1965, 'Environmental assistance to the child's acquisition of grammar', unpublished doctoral thesis, referred to in McNeill, 1970, p. 109.

—1967, 'On individual differences in language competence and performance', *J. Spec. Educ.* I. pp. 135-50.

Cazden, C.B., John, V.P., and Hymes, D., 1972, *Functions of Language in the Classroom*, Teachers College Press, Columbia.

Chazan, M., 1971, *Just Before School*, Blackwell.

Cheverst, W.J., 1972, 'The role of metaphor in educational thought' in *Journal of Curriculum Studies* 4, No. 1., May, pp. 71-82.

Cheyne, W.M., 1970, 'Stereotyped reactions to speakers with Scottish and English regional accents', *British J. Soc. Clin. Psychol.* 9, pp. 77-9.

Chomsky, C., 1969, *The Acquisition of Syntax in Children from 5 to 10*, M.I.T.

Chomsky, N., 1957, *Syntactic Structures*, Mouton, The Hague.

—1964, *Current Issues in Linguistic Theory*, Mouton, The Hague.

—1965, *Aspects of the Theory of Syntax*, M.I.T.

—1971, *Selected Readings*, ed. Allen, J.P.B., and Van Buren, P., O.U.P.

Cofer, C.N., and Musgrave, B.S. (eds.), 1963, *Verbal Behaviour and Learning*, McGraw-Hill.

Cook, M., 1971, *Interpersonal Perception*, Penguin.

Coulthard, M., 1969, 'A discussion of restricted and elaborated codes' in Wilkinson (ed.), 1969.

—1974, 'Approaches to the Analysis of Classroom Interaction' in Wade (ed.), 1974.

Criper, C., and Davies, A., 1974, *Research on Spoken Language in the Primary School* (A Report to the Scottish Education Department), Dept. of Linguistics, University of Edinburgh.

DeVito, J., 1970, *The Psychology of Speech and Language: An Introduction to Psycholinguistics*, Random House, N.Y.

Dixon, J. *et al.*, n.d., *Criteria of Success in English Teaching*, NATE publications, National Association for the Teaching of English, 5 Imperial Road, Huddersfield.

Elkins, W.R., 1974, *A New English Primer: An introduction to linguistic concepts and systems*, Macmillan.

Emerson, L.L., 1931, 'The effect of bodily orientation upon the young child's memory for position of objects', *Child Development*, 2, pp. 125-42.

Ervin-Tripp, S., 1964, 'Interaction of Language, Topic and Listener' in *American Anthropologist*, 66, pp. 86-102.

Farb, P., 1974, *Word Play. What happens when people talk*, Jonathan Cape.

Fay, P.J., and Middleton, W.C., 1940, 'Judgement of intelligence from the voice as transmitted over a public address system', *Sociometry* 3, pp. 186-91.

Feldman, C.F., and Rodgon, M., 1970, 'The effects of various types of adult responses in the syntactic acquisition of two to three-year-olds', unpublished paper, University of Chicago Dept. of Psychology. Referred to in McNeill, 1970, p. 109.

Findlay, J.J., 1923, *Principles of Class Teaching*, Macmillan (first ed. 1902).

Flanders, N.A., 1970, *Analysing Teaching Behaviour*, Addison-Wesley, Reading, Mass.

Fodor, J.A., and Katz, J.J. (eds.), 1964, *The Structure of Language, Readings in the Philosophy of Language*, Prentice Hall.

Fowler, R., 1974, *Understanding Language: An Introduction to Linguistics*, Routledge and Kegan Paul.

Gardner, R.A., and Gardner, B.T., 1969, 'Teaching Sign Language to a Chimpanzee' included in Adams, 1972.

Gardner, R.A., and Gardner, B.T., 1971, *Behaviour in Non-human Primates*, vol. 4, ed. Schrier, A., and Stollnitz, F., N.Y. Academic Press.

Garfinkel, H., 1972, 'Remarks on ethomethodology' in Gumperz and Hymes (eds.), 1972.

Giles, H., 1970, 'Evaluative reactions to accents', *Educational Review* 22. 2.

Goffman, E., 1969, *The Presentation of Self in Everyday Life*, Allen Lane. Also Penguin, 1971.

Bibliography

Goldman-Eisler, F., 1958, 'Speech production and the predictability of words in context', *Qu. J. Exp. Psychol.* X, pp. 96-106.
—1961, 'A comparative study of two hesitation phenomena', *Language and Speech*, 4, pp. 18-26.
—1968, *Psycholinguistics*, Academic Press.

Goodlad, J.J., 1968, 'Curriculum: A Janus Look' in *Journal of Curriculum Studies*, I. 1. November.

Greenberg, J.H. (ed.), 1961, *Universals of Language*, M.I.T. Press.

Greenfield, P., Reich, L., and Olver, R., 1966, 'On culture and equivalence' in Adams (ed.), 1972.

Gumperz, J.J. and Hymes, D., (eds.), 1972, *Directions in Sociolinguistics*, Holt, Reinhart and Winston.

Halliday, M.A.K., 1971, 'Language in a social perspective', in Wilkinson (ed.), 1971b.
—1973, 'Relevant models of language' in *Explorations in the Functions of Language*, Edward Arnold, pp. 11-17. Also in Wilkinson (ed.), 1969.

Harding, D.W., 1937, 'The role of the onlooker' in *Scrutiny* VI (3), pp. 247-58.
—1962, 'Psychological Processes in the Reading of Fiction' in *British Journal of Aesthetics*, 11 (2), pp. 133-47.

Harlow, H.F., 1969, 'Love in Infant Monkeys', *Scientific American*, June.

Hayes, K.G., and Hayes, C., 1955, in *The Non-human Primates and Human Evolution*, ed. Wayne, G.J.D., Detroit U.P.

Hinde, R.A. (ed.), 1972, *Non-Verbal Communication*, C.U.P.

HMSO, 1927, *Handbook of Suggestions for Teachers*.

Hockett, C.F., and Altmann, S.A., 1968, 'A note on design features' in Sebeok, 1968.

Honikman, B., 1964, 'Articulatory settings' in Abercrombie, D., Fry, D.B., MacCarthy, P.A.D., Scott, N.C., and Trim, J.L., (eds.), *In Honour of Daniel Jones*, Longman.

Hymes, D., 1972, 'On communicative competence', excerpts in Pride, J.B., and Holmes, J., (eds.), 1972, *Sociolinguistics: Selected Readings*, Penguin, pp. 269-93.

Jackson, P.W., 1966, 'The Student's World' in *The Elementary School Journal*, 66, pp. 345-57, University of Chicago.

Jakobson, R., 1960, 'Concluding Statement: linguistics and poetics' in Sebeok, 1960.

Jensen, A., 1968, 'How much can we boost IQ and scholastic achievement?', *Harvard Educational Review*, 39. 1.

John, V., 1967, 'Communicative competence of low income children', *Report of Language Development Study Group*, Ford Foundation.

Jourard, S.M., 1966, 'An exploratory study of body accessibility' *Brit. J. Soc. Clin. Psychol.* 5, pp. 221-31.

Katz, J.J., 1967, 'Recent issues in semantic theory', *Foundations of Language*, 3, pp. 124-94.

Keislar, E., and Stern, C., 1968, 'Effects of Dialects and Instructional Procedures on Children's Oral Language Production and Conception Acquisition' in *Urban Education* 3 (3), pp. 169-76.

King, E.W., 1973, 'The Presentation of Self in the Classroom' in Meighan (ed.), 1973.

LaBarre, W., 1964, 'Paralinguistics, kinesics, and cultural anthropology', in Sebeok *et al.*, 1964.

Labov, W., 1964, 'Stages in the acquisition of standard English' in Shuy, R.W., (ed.), *Social Dialects and Language Learning*, National Council of Teachers of English (USA), Champaign, Illinois.

—1972, 'The logic of non-standard English' in *Language in Education*, pp. 198-212, Routledge and Kegan Paul for the Open University.

Also in *Language and Poverty*, 1970, ed. Williams, F., Markham.

Labov, W., Cohen, P., Robins, C., and Lewis, J., 1968, *A Study of the Non-Standard English of Negro and Puerto Rican Speakers in New York City*, Final Report, Co-operative Research Project 3288, Office of Education, Washington D.C. Vols. 1 and 2.

Langer, S.K., 1960, *Philosophy in a New Key*, Harvard University Press.

Laver, J., 1968, 'Voice quality and Indexical Information', reprinted in Laver and Hutcheson, 1972.

Laver, J., and Hutcheson, S., 1972, *Communication in Face to Face Interaction*, Penguin.

Laycock, S., 1910, *Collected Writings*, ed. Clegg, W.E., Oldham.

Lennenberg, E.H., 1964, 'The capacity for language acquisition' in Fodor and Katz (eds.), 1964.

Lennenberg, E.H. (ed.), 1964, *New Directions in the Study of Language*, M.I.T. Press.

Lepschy, G.C., 1970, *A Survey of Structural Linguistics*, Faber.

Luria, A.R., 1961, *The Role of Speech in the Regulation of Normal and Abnormal Behaviour*, Liveright, N.Y.

Luria, A.R., and Yudovich, F. la, 1971, *Speech and the Development of Mental Processes in the Child*, Penguin.

Bibliography

Lyons, J., 1963, *Structural Semantics*, Blackwell.
—1970, *Chomsky*, Fontana.

Mackay, D., and Thompson, B., 1968, *The Initial Teaching of Reading and Writing*, Programme in Linguistics and English Teaching, paper 3, Longmans.

McKnight, P.C., 1971, 'Microteaching in Teacher Training: A Review of Research' in Morrison and McIntyre, 1972.

McNeill, D., 1966, 'The creation of language', *Discovery* 27, no. 7 (July), pp. 34-8.
—1970, *The Acquisition of Language*, Harper and Row.

Malinowski, B., 1953, 'The problem of meaning in primitive languages', in Ogden, C.K., and Richards. I.A., *The Meaning of Meaning*, pp. 296-336, Harcourt Brace Jovanitch.

Mandler, G., 1962, 'From Association to Structure', *Psychological Review*, 69, pp. 415-27.

Mansikka, V.T., 1929, *Litauische Zaubersprüche, Folklore Fellows communications*, 87.

Marty, A., 1908, *Untersuchungen zur Grundlegung der allgemeinen Grammatik und Sprachphilosophie*, Vol. 1., Berlin.

Meighan, R., (ed.), 1973, *Sociology and Teaching*, Educational Review, University of Birmingham.

Miller, G.A., 1962, 'Some Psychological Studies of Grammar', *American Psychologist*, 17, pp. 748-62.

Moffet, J., 1968, *Teaching the Universe of Discourse*, Houghton, Mifflin and Co.

Morrison, A., and McIntyre, D., (eds.), 1972, *The Social Psychology of Teaching: Selected Readings*, Penguin.

Otswall, P.F., 1964, 'How the patient communicates about disease with the doctor', in Sebeok *et al.*, 1974.

Parry, J., 1967, *The Psychology of Human Communication*, U.L.P.

'Plowden Report', 1966, *Children and Their Primary Schools*, Vol. 1., HMSO.

Premack, A.J., and Premack, D., 1972, 'Teaching Language to an Ape', in *Scientific American*, October, pp. 92-99.

Pride, J.B. and Holmes, J. (eds.), 1972, *Sociolinguistics: Selected Readings*, Penguin.

Robins, R.H., 1964, *General Linguistics: An Introductory Survey*, Longmans.

Robinson, W.P., 1972, *Language and Social Behaviour*, Penguin.

Rosenshine, B., 1970, 'Enthusiastic Teaching: A Research Review' in Morrison and McIntyre (eds.), 1972.

Rousseau, J.J., 1957, *Emile*, transl. B. Foxley, Everyman ed., Dent, (first published 1762).

Rutter, M., 1972, *Maternal Deprivation Reassessed*, Penguin.

Rybnikov, P.N., 1910, *Pesni*, Vol. 3.

Sapir, E. (ed.), 1949, *Language*, Harcourt Brace Jovanitch.

Scheffler, I., 1962, *The Language of Education*, Thomas, Illinois.

Sebeok, T.A., (ed.), 1960, *Style in Language*, M.I.T.

—(ed.), 1968, *Animal Communication*. pp. 61-72, Indiana U.P.

Sebeok, T.A., Hayes, A.S., and Bateson, M.C., (eds.), 1964, *Approaches to Semiotics*, The Hague, Mouton.

Sergeant, H., (ed.), 1968, *Poetry from Africa*, Pergamon Press Ltd.

Sexton, A., 1965, *Bedlam and Part Way Back*, Houghton Mifflin Co.

Sinclair, J. McH., and Coulthard, R.M., 1975, *Towards an Analysis of Discourse*, O.U.P.

Skinner, B.F., 1957, *Verbal Behaviour*, Appleton, Century, Crofts.

Slobin, D.I., 1966, 'The acquisition of Russian as a native language' in Smith and Miller (eds.), 1966.

—1971, *Psycholinguistics*, Scott, Foresman and Co., Glenview, Illinois, and London.

Smith, F., and Miller, G.A., (eds.), 1966, *The Genesis of Language*, M.I.T.

Smith, W.O.H., and Hore, S., 1970, 'Some non-verbal aspects of communication between mother and child', *Child Development*, 41, pp. 889-95.

Stratta, L., Dixon, J., and Wilkinson, A.M., 1973, *Patterns of Language*, Heinemann.

Strettan, T.S., 1960, *Outlines of General Science*, Hulton.

Strongman, K., and Woozley, J., 1967, 'Stereotyped reactions to regional accents', *Brit. J. Soc. Psychol.* 6, pp. 164-67.

Thornton, G., 1975, *Language, Experience, and School*, E.J. Arnold.

Thorpe, W.H., 1972, 'The comparison of vocal communication in Animals and Man', in Hinde, 1972.

Tough, J., 1969, 'The Language of Young Children', in Chazan (ed.), 1969.

—1973, *Focus on Meaning*, Allen and Unwin.

—1974, 'Children's Use of Language' in Wade (ed.), 1974.

Tulkin, S.R., and Kagan, J., 1972, 'Mother Child Interaction in the First Years of Life', *Child Development*, 43, pp. 31-41.

Bibliography

Ullmann, S., 1961, 'Semantic Universals' in Greenberg, 1961.

von Frisch, K., 1967, *The Dance Language and Orientation of Bees*, The Belknap Press of Harvard U.P.

Vygotsky, L.S., 1962, *Thought and Language*, M.I.T. Press.

Wade, B., (ed.), 1974, *The Context of Language*, Educational Review, Vol. 26, No. 3., University of Birmingham.

Weir, R., 1962, *Language in the Crib*, Mouton, The Hague.

Wells, P.H., and Wenner, A.M., 1973, 'Do Honey Bees have a Language?', *Nature*, 241, Jan. 19, 1973.

Whorf, B.L., 1966, *Language, Thought and Reality*, ed. J.B. Carroll, M.I.T.

Wight, J., 1971, 'Dialect in School', *Educational Review* Vol. 24. No. 1., pp. 47-59.

Wight, J. and Norris, R.A., 1970, *Teaching English to West Indian Children*, Schools Council Working Paper, No. 29, Evans/Methuen Educational.

Wilkinson, A.M., 1965, *Spoken English*, with contributions by A. Davies and D. Atkinson, University of Birmingham School of Education.

Wilkinson, A.M., 1968, 'The Flow of Candidates' in *English in Education*, 2. 3.

Wilkinson, A.M., (ed.), 1969, *The State of Language*, Educational Review Vol. 22, No. 1., University of Birmingham.

Wilkinson, A.M., 1971a, *The Foundations of Language*, O.U.P.

Wilkinson, A.M. (ed.), 1971b, *The Context of Language*, Educational Review Vol. 23., No. 3., University of Birmingham.

Wilkinson, A.M., Stratta, L., and Dudley, P., 1974, *The Quality of Listening*, published by Macmillan for the Schools Council.

Acknowledgements

I should like to acknowledge with many thanks the assistance given by colleagues and friends. The following have helped me on particular linguistic or technical points, or by providing recordings of, or access to, classroom lessons: Mary Abraham, Annick Bantock, William Fraser, Maria Hadjipavlou, Andrew Meredith, John Raeburn, Lill Thompson, Irene Wells, Peter Uzzell. John Worsley of the University of Sheffield has advised me on immigrant language, and section 8.4. draws on a paper of his; Joseph Lefoto'o of the Solomon Islands has similarly advised me on pidgin; Celestina Jordan of Guyana kindly gave permission for her original Creole story, 'Neil, Mr. Arthur, and the mango tree', to be reproduced.

The book is in great measure based on the spoken and written language of a number of young children and school students too numerous to name here, but to whom I am very grateful. Particular thanks are, however, due to Benjamin Wrigley and his parents, for permission to quote the recording of Benjamin's 10 o'clock feed (pp. 206-8) and to Edmund Russell and Lois Deatheridge and their parents for the zoo game recording (pp. 167-68).

The skilled interpretation and typing of my secretary, Betty Browne, and in her absence, Pauline Lewis, call for particular mention—these being the only people in the south-west who can read my handwriting, and thus without whom the book would never have emerged in print. To both my very sincere thanks.

Acknowledgements are due to the following firms and individuals for permission to use copyright material:

Academic Press, N.Y.: table by R.A. Gardner and B.T. Gardner from *Behaviour in Non-human Primates*, 4, p. 174, ed. A. Schrier and F. Stollnitz.

Addison-Wesley, Reading, Mass.: table reprinted from *Analysing Teaching Behaviour*, 1970, by N. Flanders.

The Belknap Press of Harvard U.P.: figures 28, 29, 46, and 121 from

Acknowledgements

The Dance Language and Orientation of Bees by K. von Frisch. Copyright 1967 by the President and Fellows of Harvard College.

Educational Review: material reprinted from 'Dialect in School, by J. Wight; 'What's the Use' by J.L. Britton in *The Context of Language*, ed. A. Wilkinson; 'Relevant Models of Language' by M.A.K. Halliday in *The State of Language*, pp. 28-34, ed. A. Wilkinson.

Harcourt Brace Jovanovitch, Inc.: material reprinted from *Language*, pp. 3-12, ed. E. Sapir, 1949. Copyright 1921 Harcourt Brace Jovanovitch Inc. Copyright 1949 by Jean V. Sapir.

Indiana University Press: 'A Note on Design Features' by C.F. Hockett and S.A. Altmann; reprinted from *Animal Communication* ed. T.A. Sebeok 1968.

Roman Jakobson: material reprinted from 'Concluding Statement: Linguistics and Poetics' in *Style in Language* ed. T.A. Sebeok. M.I.T. Press 1960.

Macmillan, London and Basingstoke: material from *The Quality of Listening* 1973 by A. Wilkinson, L. Stratta, and P. Dudley.

M.I.T. Press, Cambridge, Mass.: material reprinted from *Aspects of the Theory of Syntax*, section 1.5, pp. 27-30, by Noam Chomsky © M.I.T. Press 1965; from *Thought and Language*, pp. 131-38, by L.S. Vygotsky © M.I.T. Press 1962; from *Language, Thought, and Reality*, pp. 212-17, by B. Whorf © M.I.T. Press 1966.

Markham Publishing Co., Chicago: material reprinted from 'The logic of non-standard English' in *Language and Poverty* by W. Labov, ed. F. Williams.

Oxford University Press: material reprinted from *Selected Readings*, by Noam Chomsky, ed. Allen, J.P.B., and van Buren, P. Copyright © Oxford University Press 1971.

Penguin Press: table reprinted from *Language, the Learner and the School*, by D. Barnes, *et al.* © Douglas Barnes, James Britton, Harold Rosen and the London Association for the Teaching of English 1969, 1971.

Pergamon Press: stanzas reprinted from 'Once upon a Time' by Gabriel Okara in *Poetry from Africa* ed. H. Sergeant.

Pennsylvania University Press: material reprinted from *On Communicative Competence,* by D.H. Hymes.

Scientific American: drawing after A.J. Premack and D. Premack in *Teaching Language to an Ape* 1972. Copyright © by Scientific American Inc. All rights reserved.

A.M.W., Exeter, December 1974

237

Index

Adams, P., 197
Aitchison, J., 151
Argyle, M., 12, 24, 146

Barker, L.L., and Kibler, R.J., 141
Barnes, D., 75, 93, 199-201
Bellack, A.A., 75, 201
Bernstein, B., 219
Black, M., 204
Blake, W., 49, 62, 96
Blishen, E., 124
Bowlby, J., 98, 206
Britton, J.L., 54-5, 92, 141, 173-85
    204
Brown, R., 33, 148-49, 197
Bruner, J., 58, 64

Cazden, C., 101, 201, 216
Cheverst, W.J., 87
Cheyne, W.M., 22
Chomsky, C., 121-22
Chomsky, N., 112-16, 123, 125,
    156-58, 209-11, 212-14, 215
Cook, M., 146
Criper, C., and Davies, A., 219
Coulthard, M., 201

Dainton Report, 204
D'Arcy, P., 204
DeVito, J., 141
Dixon, J., 90

Elkins, W.R., 151
Ervin-Tripp, S., 63
Eskimoes, 65

Farb, P., 197
Fay, P.J., and Middleton, W.C., 25
Feldman, C.F., and Rodgon, M., 101
Findlay, J.J., 205
Flanders, N., 75, 198-99
Fowler, R., 151

Gardner, R.A., and Gardner, B.T., 30,
    149
Giles, H., 21-2
Goffman, E., 11, 146, 198
Goldman-Eisler, F., 22, 23
Goodlad, J.J., 41
Greenberg, J.H., 41
Greenfield, P., Reich, L., and Olver, R.,
    64, 197

Halliday, M.A.K., 54, 169-73
Harlow, H.F., 98
Hayes, K.G., and Hayes, C., 29
Hinde, R.A., 146, 150
Hockett, C.F., 32
    and Altmann, S.A., 148
Honikman, B., 24
Hopi Indians, 65
Hymes, D., 123-24, 214-16

Jackson, P.W., 68
Jakobson, R., 141
Johnson, S., 15
Jordan, C., 159
Jourard, S.M., 12

Keats, J., 26
King, E.W., 198

LaBarre, W., 11
Labov, W., 21, 219
Laver, J., 24
    and Hutcheson, S., 146, 147
Laycock, S., 95
Lennenberg, E.H., 115
Lepschy, G.C., 151
Luria, A.R., 59
    and Yudovich, F., 60
Lyons, J., 211

Martin, N., 204
McKnight, P.C., 86
Medway, P., 204

Okara, G., 79-80
Otswall, P.F., 13

Parry, J., 141
Piaget, J., 60-1, 187
Plowden Report, 205
Premack, A.J., and Premack, D., 31

Robertson, J., 97
Robins, R.H., 151
Robinson, W.P., 147
Rosenshine, B., 198
Rousseau, J.J., 87, 205
Rutter, M., 96, 206

Sapir, E., 148, 151-55
Sarah, 31-2, 33
Scheffler, I., 204
Sebeok, T.A., 141
Sexton, A., 95
Shakespeare, W., 9
Sinclair, J. McH., 75, 201
Skinner, B.F., 109-110, 209
Slobin, D.I., 63
Smith, H., 204
Smith, R.L., 141

Stratta, L., 84
Strettan, J.S., 91
Strongman, K., and Woozley, J. 21, 147

Thorpe, W.H., 150
Thornton, G., 204
Tough, J., 55-6, 84, 132
Tulkin, S.R., and Kagan, J., 99

Ullman, S., 42

Vicki, 29, 33
von Frisch, K., 27-9, 148
Vygotsky, L.S., 60-61, 126, 187-92

Washoe, 29-31, 33, 148-49
Wells, P.H., and Wenner, A.M. 148
Whorf, B.L., 63, 65, 193−197
Wight, J., 163
Wilkinson, A., 21, 140, 169, 193, 202
   204
   Stratta, L., and Dudley, P., 84, 202
Wolofs, 64
Wordsworth, W., 98
Wrigley, S., 100